Lecture Notes in Computer Science 3599

Commenced Publication in 1973
Founding and Former Series Editors:
Gerhard Goos, Juris Hartmanis, and Jan van Leeuwen

Uwe Aßmann   Mehmet Aksit
Arend Rensink (Eds.)

Model Driven Architecture

European MDA Workshops: Foundations
and Applications, MDAFA 2003 and MDAFA 2004
Twente, The Netherlands, June 26-27, 2003 and
Linköping, Sweden, June 10-11, 2004
Revised Selected Papers

 Springer

Volume Editors

Uwe Aßmann
Technische Universität Dresden
Fakultät Informatik
Institut für Software- und Multimediatechnik
01062 Dresden, Germany
E-mail: uwe.assmann@inf.tu-dresden.de

Mehmet Aksit
Arend Rensink
University of Twente
Department of Computer Science
P.O. Box 217, 7500 AE Enschede, The Netherlands
E-mail: {rensink,aksit}@ewi.utwente.nl

Library of Congress Control Number: 2005930489

CR Subject Classification (1998): C.2, D.2, D.3, F.3, C.3, H.4

ISSN   0302-9743
ISBN-10   3-540-28240-8 Springer Berlin Heidelberg New York
ISBN-13   978-3-540-28240-2 Springer Berlin Heidelberg New York

Springer is a part of Springer Science+Business Media

springeronline.com

© Springer-Verlag Berlin Heidelberg 2005
Printed in Germany

Typesetting: Camera-ready by author, data conversion by Scientific Publishing Services, Chennai, India
Printed on acid-free paper   SPIN: 11538097   06/3142   5 4 3 2 1 0

Preface

Model-Driven Architecture (MDA) is an initiative proposed by the Object Management Group (OMG) for platform-generic software development. MDA separates the specification of system functionality from the implementation on a specific platform. It is aimed at making software assets more resilient to changes caused by emerging technologies. While stressing the importance of modeling, the MDA initiative covers a wide spectrum of research areas. Further efforts are required to bring them into a coherent approach based on open standards and supported by matured tools and techniques.

This volume contains the selected papers of two workshops on "Model-Driven Architecture – Foundations and Applications" (MDAFA): MDAFA 2003 held at the University of Twente, Twente, The Netherlands, June 26–27, 2003, and MDAFA 2004 held at Linköping University, Linköping, Sweden, June 10–11, 2004. The goal of the workshops was to understand the foundations of MDA, to share experience in applying MDA techniques and tools, and to outline future research directions. The workshops organizers encouraged authors of accepted papers to re-submit their papers to a post-workshop reviewing process; 15 of these papers were accepted to appear in this volume on MDA.

Our special thanks go to the program committee, which was willing to review the papers a second time, and to our assistants Henrik Larsson and Bodil Mattson-Kihlström, who took a great share of the workshop organization. We would also like to thank the supporters of the workshop, in particular the OMG, for taking part in the enthusiasm about scientific workshops on MDA. One of the invited speakers of MDAFA 2004, Dr. Liping Zhao from the Victoria University of Manchester, contributed her paper "Designing Application Domain Models with Roles" to the volume, which sheds new light on the relationship of MDA and role modeling. Thanks a lot.

In autumn 2004, the workshop joined forces with other European workshops on MDA, creating the new European Conference on Model-Driven Architecture – Foundations and Applications (ECMDA-FA, http://www.ecmda-fa.org). It will take place for the first time on Nov. 7–10, 2005 in Nuremberg, Germany, and is planned as a yearly conference, collecting papers on the foundations and applications of MDA. See you in Nuremberg!

June 2005   Uwe Aßmann, Arend Rensink, Mehmet Aksit

Organization

Referees

Mehmet Aksit, University of Twente, The Netherlands
Jesper Andersson, University of Växjö, Sweden
Uwe Aßmann, Technische Universität Dresden, Germany
Klaas van den Berg, University of Twente, The Netherlands
Jorn Bettin, SoftMetaWare, The Netherlands
Jean Bézivin, University of Nantes, France
Jan Bosch, University of Groningen, The Netherlands
Francois Bry, Munich University, Germany
Paul Clements, Software Engineering Institute, USA
Krzysztof Czarnecki, University of Waterloo, Canada
Pär Emanuelson, Ericsson, Sweden
Gregor Engels, University of Paderborn, Germany
Peter Fritzson, University of Linköping, Sweden
Wolfgang Hesse, University of Marburg, Germany
James Hunt, Aicas, Germany
Reiner Hähnle, Chalmers University of Technology, Sweden
Jean-Marc Jezequel, IRISA, France
Anneke Kleppe, Klasse Objecten, The Netherlands
Antonio Kung, Trialog, Paris, France
Tom Mens, University of Mons-Hainaut, Belgium
Arend Rensink, University of Twente, The Netherlands
Kristian Sandahl, University of Linköping, Sweden
Bedir Tekinerdogan, University of Twente, The Netherlands
Gerd Wagner, Technical University Eindhoven, The Netherlands
Andrew Watson, Vice President and Technical Director at OMG, USA
Kasper Østerbye, Copenhagen, Denmark
Steffen Zschaler, Technische Universität Dresden, Germany

Sponsoring Institutions

- Object Management Group (OMG, http://www.omg.org)
- REWERSE Network of Excellence of the European 6th framework programme (Reasoning on the Web, http://www.rewerse.net), in particular working group I3 "Composition and Typing for Reasoning Languages on the Web"
- HIDOORS EU project (High Integrity Distributed Object-Oriented Real-Time Systems, http://www.hidoors.org)

– RISE project (Research on Integrational Software Engineering,
http://www.ida.liu.se/~rise), financed by Swedish Stiftelsen för Strategisk
Forskning (SSF)
– SWEBPROD project (Semantic Web for Production,
http://www.ida.liu.se/~rise/SwebProd), financed by Vinnova Sweden.

Table of Contents

Designing Application Domain Models with Roles

Liping Zhao

School of Informatics, University of Manchester,
M60 1QD, Manchester, United Kingdom
liping.zhao@manchester.ac.uk

Abstract. This article is motivated by two related observations. First, roles, responsibilities and collaborators are central to object interactions, and viewing of objects from these three dimensions can yield a more dynamic and flexible design than that from the class dimension. Yet the orthodox object modeling approaches, such as UML, still adopt the class view of objects. Second, models have become increasingly important in constructing application systems. For example, OMG's Model Driven Architecture (MDA) uses models as building blocks to support application development. Based on the assumption that object-oriented approaches will still dominate the development of the MDA models, this article posits that the new models be oriented towards the roles, not towards the classes; it shows why roles are importance to MDA model design.

1 Why Pure Classes Not Enough

Object-oriented design has been dominated by class design. For example, Meyers [27] recommended 50 ways to improve programs and designs, but 34 of them are concerned with the design of classes and the rest 16 is about memory management and compiler optimization. Consequently, object-oriented modeling also focuses on class modeling [34]. The Unified Modeling Language (UML) [10] provides 12 diagrams and 8 of them are centered on class diagrams. The rest 4 diagrams, apart from the Use Case Diagram, are about model management.

The class concept is indeed central to object technology. A class is not only a description of the objects, but also an implementation technique for data abstraction, encapsulation and information hiding [23, 24]. The importance of classes to object technology is clear and undeniable, as Meyer maintained ([26], p.165): "Objects remain important to describe the execution of an O-O system. But the basic notion, from which everything in object technology derives, is class..." Henderson-Seller ([14], p34) also remarked: "In fact, 'object-oriented' is really a misnomer because what we really should be talking about is 'class-oriented,' since the essence of the object-oriented technique is actually the class."

Despite of its importance, the class dimension is limited in its ability to describe objects. First, the class view of objects is static. A class is basically a mold for making objects [26] and classifying objects [41]. Once an object is created for a class, it belongs to that class forever, hence "Once an engineer, forever an engineer." Although an object may appear to be able to change its type in a polymorphic type hierarchy, it still cannot change its base class and behavior. Second, the class centered view tends

U. Aßmann, M. Aksit, and A. Rensink (Eds.): MDAFA 2003/2004, LNCS 3599, pp. 1–16, 2005.

to place too much emphasis on encapsulation and class boundary, and drives object design like procedural design. As a result, classes are often over-specified for completeness.

The limitations of pure classes have long been recognized. As early as in 1989, Beck and Cunningham [3] already pointed out: "One of the distinguishing features of object design is that no object is an island. All objects stand in relationship to others, on whom they reply on services and control 3." To capture object relationship, they introduced *CRC* (Class, Responsibility and Collaboration) cards, an index card technique invented by Cunningham [8]. Each CRC card describes an object in three dimensions: class name, responsibilities and collaborators (Fig. 1). These three dimensions, as Beck and Cunningham 3 stated, identify the *role* of an object in a design. Hence the focal point of a CRC card is the role, the centre of object collaboration. This important connotation was made explicit when Kendall 16 renamed CRC cards as RRC (Role, Responsibility and Collaboration) cards. Wirfs-Brock [39] has recently extended her responsibility-driven approach [40] with roles, responsibilities and collaborations.

Similar to CRC cards, Reenskaug [31] developed *role models* for representing object collaborations. A role model consists of a set of roles and their interactions. Fig. 2 shows a role model consisting of three roles: Model, View and Controller. Wirfs-Brock and Johnson [38] noted that there is a many-to-many correspondence between roles and objects, in that an object may play several different roles and a given role may be played by different objects.

There is a close relationship between CRC cards and role models, as shown in Fig. 1 and Fig. 2, such that a role model corresponds to a set of related CRC cards. A role model captures a set of roles in collaboration whereas a CRC card represents a particular role in a role model. A role model hence can be used to represent an overall picture of collaboration with each role being elaborated by a CRC card.

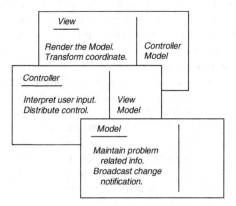

Fig. 1. CRC cards describing the responsibilities and collaborations of Smalltalk's Model, View and Controller 3

The basic idea of CRC cards and role models is to capture *patterns of object interactions*. Wirfs-Brock and Johnson [38] observed that the task in object-oriented design is to understand, describe and reuse object interaction patterns. From this viewpoint, the idea of the design patterns [11] is similar to that of CRC cards and role models. The main contribution of the design patterns, in comparison with CRC cards and role models, is that they provide a systematic way of naming and describing object interactions. The link between CRC cards, role models and design patterns has been explored by many researchers [2, 6, 9, 18, 22, 32, 35, 42]. At the core, CRC cards, role models and design patterns can be viewed as different ways of expressing *roles* and *collaborations*. Cain and Coplien [5] pointed out that the basic abstraction in object design is role, a longstanding, stable locus of associated responsibilities in a process. The role concept provides the most coherent view of object collaboration.

Yet, in spite of the above efforts, the concept of roles has not been fully understood; our experience of object-oriented design is still largely limited to class design. Coplien [7] recently made an appeal for "putting the object back into OOD." He reiterated that the central point of object orientation is the objects themselves.

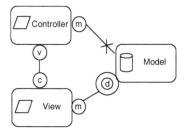

Fig. 2. A role model describing the collaboration of Smalltalk's Model, View and Controller 31

This article is motivated by two related observations. First, the role concept has not gained a widespread acceptance in the orthodox object modeling approaches owing to the lack of a proper understanding. Second, models have become increasingly important in constructing application systems. For example, OMG's Model Driven Architecture ® (MDA) uses models as building blocks to support application development. Based on the assumption that object-oriented approaches will still dominate the development of the MDA models, this article argues that the new models be oriented towards the roles, not towards the classes. We have been doing object design in a class-oriented way for so long. It is the time that we do it in a role-oriented way and focus the design on object roles, responsibilities and collaborations. With the above motivations and discussions, the aim of this article is to introduce role modeling to MDA model design.

This article is presented in the following order. Section 2 provides a survey of works on roles and establishes the thesis that roles are a central concept for object design. Section 3 relates roles to the MDA model design and demonstrates the importance of roles to the design of application domain models. Section 4 presents a simple role modeling approach and Section 5 concludes the article.

2 Working with Roles

The meaning of role, according to the Oxford English Dictionary, is an actor's part in a play; a person's or thing's characteristic or expected function. A role of a person characterizes the person's position in a particular situation, when interacting with other people to perform a particular activity [4]. Role is a natural concept for describing the dynamics of a person or an object. For example, an academic through the eyes of her students is a lecturer; a traveler in the eyes of a travel agent and an author by her readers. Lecturer, traveler and author are the three roles played by the same person. Each role characterizes the person's position in a context meaningful from a particular viewpoint. Such a viewpoint is an abstraction, which selects the detail of the person relevant to her position and suppresses the irrelevant information. Roles are therefore stereotypical, describing an object from different viewpoints.

The defining characteristic of role is responsibility: *Role is responsibility-driven.* Often a role needs to cooperate with other roles to perform some task. Thus a role can be described by a list of responsibilities and collaborators. A CRC card therefore is a perfect fit to describe a role. However, CRC cards are a design technique. A complete design method is needed to take the advantage of CRC cards. This article surveys several works on role modeling and design.

A complete role-based object design method, OOram, was developed by Reenskaug [31]. OOram supports the whole lifecycle of object development, from modeling, design to implementation. The role models described before are used for OOram role modeling. The OOram role modeling approach consists of a comprehensive notation for representing roles and role interactions. The notation contains many symbols for roles. For example, Fig. 2 shows two role symbols: Controller and View use the same symbol because they represent the tools where Model uses a different symbol because it is a database. OOram differentiates six kinds of role interaction such as unspecified interaction, synchronous interaction, asynchronous interaction and method return. OOram also offers model synthesis operations for constructing complex role models from simple ones.

Andersen [1] and Kristensen [20] have also proposed role modeling approaches and notations. Kristensen's role modeling approach separates the static and dynamic aspects of roles. Statically, roles are organized in a similar way as classes, using classification, specialization and aggregation. The dynamic relationships between the roles are represented as sequencing, overlapping and iteration. Finally, objects participated in a collaboration are grouped as a *subject*, which has the same intent as a role model. Kristensen and Østerbye [21] have also provided a theoretical definition of role and a discussion on the practical issues of role implementation.

Shams-Aliee and Warboys [36] have used roles as an abstraction above the object level to support process modeling. They define a process as a group of cooperative roles, a similar idea proposed by Cain and Coplien [5]. A process is represented in two parts. In the first part, each role of a process is represented using a formalized CRC card, which is a CRC card with added *path expressions*. A path expression represents one of the four operations – sequence, selection, concurrency and iteration – and is used to constrain the ordering of the responsibilities of a role. A formalized CRC card may contain one or more path expressions. In the second part, a process is represented as a group of collaborative roles in a Petri Net. A Petri Net shows the interactions and ordering of roles in a process, which is equivalent to a process' role model. This work demonstrates that roles can be used as an abstraction above objects to support other concepts, such as processes.

In other works, roles have been used as an abstraction for framework design [33], multiagent systems development [15, 16, 18], component composition [43] and collaborative commerce systems development [30]. Proposals have also been made to extend object-oriented languages with role constructs [12, 28, 29]. For example, in [12], the Smalltalk language is extended with a role construct and a role hierarchy construct. The role construct, similar to the class construct, defines role types; the role hierarchy construct, similar to inheritance, defines role type hierarchies. In [29], the C++ programming language has been extended with set operations to perform role specific functions.

In addition to roles, other concepts have been developed to support object design, e.g. Subject-Oriented Programming (SOP) [13] and Aspect-Oriented Programming (AOP) [19]. SOP adds a new level above the pure class level, called *subjects* to represent class groupings. A class can be grouped into more than one subject. Hence subjects are higher order classes that support multiple classifications of objects. AOP uses the notion of *aspects* to represent common behaviors of objects. In an object-oriented system (and owing to encapsulation), a class tends to be cluttered with different behaviors. Some behaviors are not specific to a class of objects, but common to objects in other classes. AOP separates out common (crosscutting) behavioral aspects from classes at design time and then attach them back to objects at a later stage. Interestingly, Kendall [17] has shown that aspects can be treated as special roles of objects whereas Kristensen [20] has used subjects as role groupings or role composition. The role concept has therefore provided a single, cohesive viewpoint from which other concepts can be understood.

In spite of the aforementioned works on roles and possibly many more, the importance of roles has only received a minor attention in the mainstream object-oriented modeling and design. For example, roles are not the first class modeling concept in UML. One reason might have been the misconception of roles, because roles are eventually *implemented* as classes of objects. This article suggests that the implementation of roles be separated from the design of roles. The mismatch between object-oriented languages (mostly class-based) and object-oriented design (object-based) means that object design should be separated from object implementation. In object design, the focus is on capturing the roles of objects, their responsibilities and collaborators, and on identifying and using patterns of object interactions. This is how object design differs from procedural design, as expressed in [3].

Another reason for not accepting the role concept in object modeling may be due to the unfamiliar and complicated notations offered by existing role modeling approaches. This article posits that role modeling should focus on the essence of roles, rather than the notations. A successful approach to role modeling should take the advantage of simple and familiar notations. The article proposes a simple role modeling approach based on CRC cards (renamed as RRC cards as Kendall [16]), role models and interaction diagrams. RRC cards are used to describe roles and interaction diagrams to show the inter-role relations. One limitation of RRC cards is that collaborations between roles are subsumed within the roles and as such the overall scope or context of role interactions is not clear at first sight [3]. To remedy this limitation, the proposed approach uses role models to represent the context of roles and collaborations. Role-responsibility matrices are provided as an alternative representation to interaction diagrams.

The proposed approach is similar to the process modeling approach of Shams-Aliee and Warboys [36] in that it also uses CRC cards for role description, but differs in two ways. First, it adopts the original CRC cards notation because the ordering of the responsibilities can be represented in interaction diagrams. Second, it uses interaction diagrams instead of Petri Nets as the former is simpler and more familiar to the object community. For simplicity our approach does not consider role specialization [20, 37].

3   Roles as a New Modeling Paradigm for Model Driven Architecture

3.1 Model Driven Architecture

OMG's Model Driven Architecture is a new architecture that uses models for software development [25]. MDA consists of three general types of models, structured into three basic layers, as shown in Fig. 3. These model types are briefly described as follows.

- *Computation independent model (CIM).* A CIM is a domain or business model which represents domain specific information, independent of implementation technologies. In Fig. 3, domain models, such as Transportation, HealthCare and E-Commerce, are structured in the outmost layer of MDA. Although not specified in [25], domain models are *vertical partitions* of application spaces.
- *Platform independent model (PIM).* A PIM is a virtual machine independent of underlying platform technologies. A PIM provides a system's services and functions, such as transactions, events and security. In Fig. 3, PIMs are structured in the middle layer. Although not specified in [25], platform independent models are *horizontal partitions* of application spaces. In other words, a PIM provides a set of generic services and functions across the application domains. For example, transaction services are applicable to many domains, such as Finance, E-Commerce and Telecom. In contrast, a CIM is specific to a particular business domain. For example, a public transport model is only applicable to the transportation domain, though it may be contained within a more general domain, such as a Geographic Information System (GIS).
- *Platform specific model (PSM).* A PSM combines the specification of a PIM with the platform specific specification. A platform specific specification is supported by a particular *platform model*, such as a CORBA or Java component model. In Fig. 3, PSMs are structured in the inner most layer.

The reason for the above model organization is to separate business logic from underlying platform technology, thereby enabling the business aspect of an application and its technological aspect to evolve independently of each other [25]. The core technologies that support MDA model development are the Unified Modeling Language

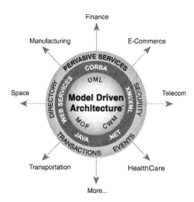

Fig. 3. Model Drive Architecture (from www.omg.com) consists of models organized into three layers. The outer layer is made of computation independent models (CIM); the middle layer is platform independent models (PIM); the inner layer is platform specific models (PSM).

(UML), the MetaObject Facility (MOF), XML Metadata Interchange (XMI), and the Common Warehouse Metamodel (CWM). UML is regarded as a standard modeling language for expressing MDA models [25].

3.2 Importance of Roles to MDA Model Design

The role concept posses certain characteristics that are required for good object design. Some of the important role characteristics are presented below.

Role is responsibility-driven. By focusing on object roles, we can express object interactions in terms of role collaborations; we can specify responsibilities for each role and achieve higher cohesion and lower coupling in the design.

Role is a natural concept for separating the concerns. By partitioning the design space into roles, responsibilities and collaborators, we can obtain a set of more or less well-separated objects, with clearly defined boundaries and meaningful inter-object relations. Each role focuses on the relevant aspect of an object and filters out the irrelevant information. When an academic takes on the role of traveler, the focus is on the responsibilities and collaborations of the traveler. Similarly, by focusing on the Author role, the non-author aspects are ignored. The role concept is therefore about separation of concerns.

Role is dynamic and flexible. An object can play different roles, change roles and take on or off roles. An academic can take on an additional role as a year tutor or change a year tutor role to an examination officer role. Each of these roles can be considered and designed independently of others. For example, the role of an academic as Traveler is independent of the role of Year Tutor. These two roles live in two different contexts and interact with different other roles; the designs of these two roles can be modified separately without affecting one another. Hence when an object is viewed by its roles, we can obtain a dynamic and flexible design.

Role is reusable and adaptable. A role is an extrinsic property of an object and may be played by different objects; likewise, an object may play several different roles. An academic may play several roles; an accountant is a role played by more than one administrative member; a travel agent is a role for all the staff working in a travel agent. Roles are therefore reusable abstractions for objects. Role collaborations are reusable abstractions for inter-object relations.

The above role characteristics are highly relevant and important to MDA model design. This article believes that the success of MDA rests on the flexibility and adaptability of its models with respect to business and technological changes. The article proposes that roles be the first-class modeling abstraction for MDA. Unfortunately the current MDA Guide [25] still focuses on the class-based design and the role concept remains to be a minor concept for naming the mappings between the classes (p.24, [25]). In the following section, a real world example from [9] is used to demonstrate the importance of roles to designing MDA domain models. Although the example is specific to a business domain, it has a general effect on the design of other types of MDA models.

3.3 Designing a Network Point Model with Roles

A public transport network is a network of bus or train services. Such a network is made of *points* and *links* between points. A point in a network can represent a whole town, a place within a town, an individual vehicle stop, or the bus bay station at a stop – depending on the level of granularity of interest to an application (See Fig. 4). Therefore, a point in a network is not simply the smallest entity in space. Rather, it is a complex entity that may contain other smaller points and links between them and that play many roles. A point is thus a complex real world entity, spatially limited in a way that can be reasonably presented as a point at one level of abstraction within the model, but not at all levels.

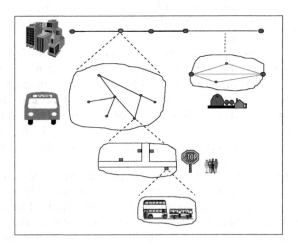

Fig. 4. A point in a public transport network (after [9])

Representing a network point is inevitably an important task in developing public transport application systems, because the structure of the points determines the structures of other components that build on the points.

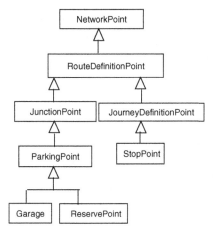

Fig. 5. A class hierarchy for point types in a public transport network. All points are by definition network points. There are already five levels of inheritance even with just seven point types. This design is inflexible because inserting a new point type will affect the application that uses it.

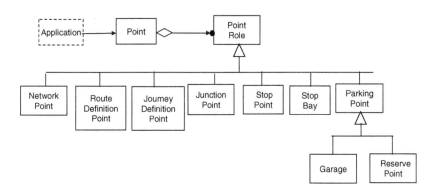

Fig. 6. Redesigning points in Fig. 5 into roles in a public transport network. A point can be attached to a specific role depending on its use in the application. This design is flexible because inserting a new point will not affect the point and the application that uses the point.

The early design of the point model was class-based; points are represented as classes and organized into a hierarchy of point types using inheritance (Fig. 5). All points are by definition *network points* and many of them overlap or intersect. Even with just seven point types there are already five levels of hierarchy. For simplicity, Fig. 5 does not show the overlapping point types. Clearly, such a representation is inflexible because inserting a new type of point in the network affects the entire network structure. Maintaining evolving points becomes a difficult task.

It was the complexity of this design problem that made the authors [9] turn away from the class concept and the class modeling paradigm. In search for a new modeling paradigm and a new concept, they decided to use the concept of role.

With role modeling, a physical point is detached from its roles in the network. When a point is used in an application, it will be attached to a role specific to that application. Fig. 6 shows this new point model, where a point role may be general, such as being a network point, or specific, such as being a junction point. A particular application system will then decide which of the point roles is to be used. Fig. 6 also conveys the following meaning: a point can take any of the roles, but not necessarily all of them; a point may take an alternative role, e.g., a point may be a parking point, which is either a garage or a reserve point. The parking point role is a general role that can be specialized into either a garage or a reserve point. In contrast to the class-based model (Fig. 5), the new point model is flexible because inserting a new point role in a network will not affect the entire network structure. Maintaining evolving points becomes easier. A detailed description and analysis of the point model can be found in [9, 42].

4 A Simple Role Modeling Approach

The proposed role modeling approach is illustrated using an academic travel service (ATS) example; the approach consists of the following steps.

1. Capturing the role collaboration context using a role model.
2. Describing roles, responsibilities and collaborators using RRC cards.
3. Representing the ordering of responsibilities and collaborations using Interaction Diagrams.

4.1 Capturing the Role Collaboration Context

The role collaboration context is determined by a specific task and the roles involved. For the ATS example, the task is about flight booking for academic travel. Typically, the task involves the following procedures:

1. An academic seeks the permission from his/her Head of the Department.
2. If the permission is granted, the Head of the Department notifies the academic and the Departmental Accountant; otherwise the travel aborted.
3. The academic then makes the flight booking through a Travel Agent.
4. The Travel Agent makes the booking and sends the invoice to the Departmental Accountant.
5. The Departmental Accountant makes the payment to the Travel Agent.
6. The Travel Agent issues the tickets and sends them to the academic.
7. The academic receives the tickets and is ready for travel.

There are four roles involved in the above task, which are:

R1: Traveler is the role of the academic who makes the request for travel.
R2: Authorizer is the role of the Head of the Department.
R3: Accountant is the role of an administrative member in the Department.
R4: Travel Agent is the role of a staff member in a Travel Agent.

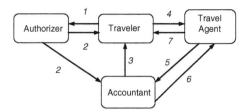

Fig. 7. A role model represents the collaboration context for the academic flight booking task. Arrows represent interactions between roles; an interaction starts from one role and ends in another; numbers show the sequence of interactions.

Traveler initiates and coordinates the whole task. We use a role model (Fig. 7) to capture the above four roles and their interactions. The role model defines the context of role collaboration in performing the flight booking task. In Fig. 7, an interaction is represented by an arrow, originated from one role and terminated in another. Interactions are numbered to show their ordering. One should note that the role model in Fig. 7 might well be replaced by a state diagram, to show the starting, ending and sequence of role collaboration.

4.2 Describing Roles, Responsibilities and Collaborators

Each role identified in a role model is described in full using a RRC card to include its responsibilities and collaborators. The role model guides the description of roles. First, according to the role model, the collaborators of a role are identified. Collaboration may not be symmetric. For example, the collaboration between Traveler and Authorizer is two-ways whereas the collaboration between Traveler and Accountant is one-way. When two roles are in a two-way collaboration, they are mutual collaborators; when two roles are in an one- way collaboration, the collaborator is the role to which another role points. Hence, Traveler has Authorizer, Accountant and Travel Agent as his/her collaborators whereas Accountant has Traveler and Travel Agent as his/her collaborators.

Having identified all the collaborators for each role, we can then assign the responsibilities to the roles. A responsibility is an action taken by a role. A responsibility may or may not result in collaborating with another role. For example, Traveler takes the travel request responsibility which will result in collaborating with Authorizer, whereas Accountant has the responsibilities of updating the account details which need no collaborators. Assigning responsibilities is an iterative process which can be directed by "what-if" scenarios as suggested by Beck and Cunningham [3]. Fig. 8 shows the four RRC cards for the role model in Fig. 7.

4.3 Representing the Order of Responsibilities and Collaborations

This final step maps a set of related RRC cards onto an interaction diagram to show the ordering of responsibilities and collaboration. Fig. 9 shows the ordering of responsibilities and collaborations of RRC cards in Fig. 8. Arrows in the interaction diagram

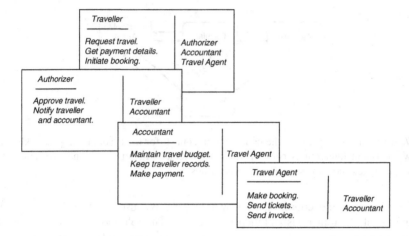

Fig. 8. RRC cards describing four roles in the academic flight booking task

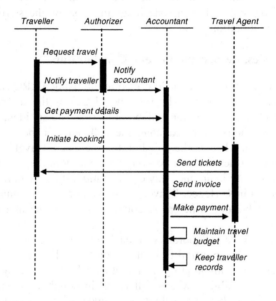

Fig. 9. An interaction diagram showing the ordering of responsibilities and collaborations, where solid bars representing the period in which roles are active and dotted lines representing the period when roles are inactive

have the same meaning as those in the role model. An interaction diagram provides a holistic view of the roles in a particular role model. It shows both internal and external views of a role. The internal view of a role is characterized by its responsibilities and the external view is characterized by its collaborations with other roles.

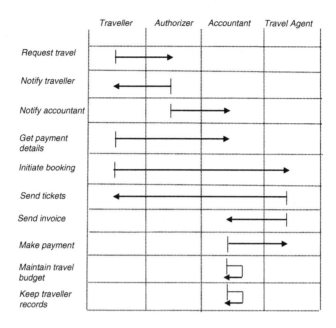

Fig. 10. A role-responsibility matrix showing roles fulfilling responsibilities through collaboration

As an alternative to interaction diagrams, we have developed role-responsibility matrices (RRM). A RRM is basically isomorphic to an interactive diagram; one tiny difference between the two diagrams (see Fig. 9 and Fig. 10) is that a RRM lines up the responsibilities explicitly and aligns them with roles in a pair-wise fashion. Such a tiny difference is intended to highlight the importance of responsibilities in collaboration and make them an important dimension in addition to roles. With this intention, the story of a RRM is that *collaboration* takes place when the *role* carries out a *responsibility*. In contrast, an interactive diagram places responsibilities in the background of roles.

5   Conclusion

This article attempts to make a claim that the class concept is static, inflexible and not suitable for object design; in contrast the role concept is dynamic, flexible and central to object design. Two facts support this claim, as found in literature survey. First, most efforts on object design have been made to remedy the problems of classes. Second, CRC cards and many other concepts are all concerned with capturing object interactions in terms of roles, responsibilities and collaborations.

With this claim, this article argues that roles are relevant and important to the design of models for MDA. The article supports this argument with a real world example and demonstrates why the class concept and the class modeling paradigm are not suitable for the domain modeling and why the role concept and the role modeling paradigm can yield a flexible design.

This article notes that the role concept has not yet gained a widespread acceptance in the orthodox object modeling approaches, such as UML, owing to the lack of a proper understanding. In order to provide a better appreciation of roles in object design, this article has illustrated the idea of roles through a simple role modeling approach.

In conclusion, this article posits that an object-oriented way of design is to focus on object interactions and drive the design from roles, responsibilities and collaborations. Modeling objects with roles not only yields a semantically rich model, but also a simple, elegant design that is flexible and adaptable. The role modeling paradigm holds much promise for MDA model design.

Acknowledgements

I wish to thank Ted Foster, Liz Kendall and Egil Andersen for many inspirational discussions on roles and objects over the past years; to Ted and Liz for working with me on roles. I am most grateful to Uwe Assmann for his encouragement and enthusiasm in this article. His valuable suggestions have helped to shape the article and bring it to the context of MDA. I am grateful to my reviewers for their expert comments and suggestions. This article owes warm thinks to all these people.

References

1. E. P. Andersen, *Conceptual Modeling of Objects: A Role Modeling Approach,* Ph.D Thesis, University of Oslo, 1997.
2. D. Bäumer, D. Riehle, W. Siberski, and M. Wulf, "The Role Object Pattern," In Proceedings of 4th Conference on Pattern Languages of Programs, 1997.
3. K. Beck and W. Cunningham, "A Laboratory for Teaching Object-Oriented Thinking," Proc the Conference on Object Oriented Programming: Systems, Languages, and Applications (OOPSLA'89), ACM Press, pp. 1-6, 1989.
4. B.J. Biddle and E. J. Thomas, *Role Theory: Concepts and Research*, New York, R. E. Krieger Publishing Co., 1979.
5. B.G. Cain and J.O. Coplien, "A Role-Based Empirical Process Modelling Environment," Proc. ICSP2, Berlin, 1993, pp. 125-133.
6. P. Coad, "Object-Oriented Patterns," Comm. ACM, vol. 35, no. 9, 1992, pp.152-159.
7. J.O. Coplien, "Teaching OO: Putting the Object Back to OOD," available at: www.artima.com/weblogs/index.jsp?blogger=cope last accessed 1 July 2004.
8. W. Cunningham, "A Diagram for Object-Oriented Programs," Proc the Conference on Object Oriented Programming: Systems, Languages, and Applications (OOPSLA'86), ACM Press, 1986, pp. 361-367.
9. T. Foster and L. Zhao. "Cascade." *Journal of Object-Oriented Programming,* vol. 11 no.9, February, 1999, pp. 18-24.
10. M. Fowler, *UML Distilled,* Reading: Addison-Wesley, 1997.
11. E. Gamma, R. Helm, R. Johnson and J. Vlissides, *Design Patterns, Reading*, MA: Addison-Wesley, 1995.
12. G. Gottlob, M. Schrefl, and B. Rock, "Extending Object-Oriented Systems with Roles," ACM Transactions on Information Systems, vol. 14, no. 3, 1996, pp.268-296.

13. W. Harrison and H. Osher, "Subject-Oriented Programming (a critique of pure objects)," Proc the Conference on Object Oriented Programming: Systems, Languages, and Applications (OOPSLA'93), Washington, D. C. September 1993. pp. 411 - 428.

14. B. Henderson-Seller, *A Book of Object-Oriented Knowledge*. Prentice Hall, 1992.

15. A. Karageorgos, N. Mehandjiev, S. Thompson, "Designing Agent Organizations Using Role Models," Knowledge Engineering Review, Special issue on Co-ordination and Knowledge Engineering, vol.17, no. 4, 2003.

16. E.A. Kendall, "Agent Roles and Role Models: New Abstractions for Multiagent System Analysis and Design," International Workshop on Intelligent Agents in Information and Process Management, Germany, September 1998.

17. E.A. Kendall, "Role Model Designs and Implementations with Aspect-Oriented Programming," Proc the Conference on Object Oriented Programming: Systems, Languages, and Applications (OOPSLA'99), ACM Press, 1999.

18. E.A. Kendall and L. Zhao: "Role Models and Patterns for Agent Collaboration", Workshop on Behavioural Modelling, In OOPSLA '98 Addendum, October, 1998.

19. G. Kiczales, et al, "Aspect Oriented Programming," Proc. European Conference on Object-Oriented Programming (ECOOP'97), Springer Verlay, 1997, pp. 220-242.

20. B.B. Kristensen, "Object-Oriented Modeling with Roles," Proc. Second Int'l Conf. Object-Oriented Information Systems (OOIS'95), Springer, London, 1996, pp. 57-71.

21. B. B. Kristensen and K. Østerbye, "Roles: Conceptual Abstraction Theory & Practical Language Issues," Theory and Practice of Object System (TAPOS), vol. 2, no. 3, pp. 143-160, 1996.

22. B. B. Kristensen and J. Olsson, "Roles & Patterns in Analysis, Design and Implementation," Pro. 3rd International Conference on Object-Oriented Information Systems (OOIS'96), London, England, 1996.

23. B. Liskov, "Data Abstraction and Hierarchy," SIGPLAN Notices, vol. 23, no.5, 1988, pp.17-34.

24. B. Liskov and S. Zilles, "Programming with Abstract Data Types," SIGPLAN Notices, vol. 9, no. 4, 1974, pp.50-59.

25. MDA Guide Version 1.0.1, Document Number: omg/2003-06-01, 12th June 2003. Available at www.omg.com.

26. B. Meyer, *Object-Oriented Software Construction*. 2nd Ed. NJ: Prentice Hall, 1997.

27. S. Meyers, *Effective C++*. 2nd Ed. Reading:Addison-Wesley, 1998.

28. L. T. Nguyen, L. Zhao and B. Appelbe, "A Set Approach to Role Modeling", Proc. 37th International Conference on Technology of Object-Oriented Languages and Systems (TOOLS-Pacific 2000), Sydney, Australia, 20-23 November 2000.

29. L. T. Nguyen, D. Taniar, B. Appelbe and L. Zhao, "Role Model Design and Implementation Using a Set Approach," ISCA Journal, vol. 11, no. 2, June 2004.

30. H. Park, W. Suh and H. Lee, "A Role-Driven Component-Oriented Methodology for Developing Collaborative Commerce Systems," Information and Software Technology, 2004.

31. T. Reenskaug, P. Wold, and O.A. Lehne, *Working with Objects, The OOram Software Engineering Method*, Greenwich: Manning Publications Co, 1996.

32. D. Riehle, "A Role-Based Design Pattern Catalog of Atomic and Composite Patterns Structured by Pattern Purpose," Ubilab Technical Report 97.1.1. Zurich, Swizerland, Union Bank of Swizerland, 1997.

33. D. Riehle and T. Gross, "Role Model Based Framework Design and Integration," OOPSLA'98, Proceedings of the 1998 Conference on Object Oriented Programming Systems, Languages and Applications, ACM Press, 1998.

34. J. Rumbaugh, M. Blaha, W. Premerlani and F. Eddy, *Object-Oriented Modeling and Design*, Prentice-Hall, 1991.
35. F. Shams-Aliee and B. Warboys, "Roles Represent Patterns," Workshop on Pattern Languages of Object-Oriented Programs, ECOOP'95, 1995.
36. F. Shams-Aliee and B. Warboys, "Applying Object-Oriented Modelling to Support Process Technology." Proc. the 1st World Conference on Integrated Design & Process Technology, University of Texas, Austin, USA, December 1995.
37. M. Snoeck and G. Dedene, "Generalisation/Specialisation and Role in Object Oriented Conceptual Modeling", Data and Knowledge Engineering, vol. 19, no. 2, 1996.
38. R. Wirfs-Brock and R. Johnson, "A Survey of Current Research in Object-Oriented Design," Communication of ACM, vol. 33, No. 9, pp. 104-124, 1990.
39. R. Wirfs-Brock and A. McKean, *Object Design: Roles, Responsibilities and Collaborations.* Addison-Wesley, 2003.
40. R. Wirfs-Brock and B. Wilkerson, "Object-Oriented Design: a Responsibility-Driven Approach," Proc the Conference on Object Oriented Programming: Systems, Languages, and Applications (OOPSLA'89), ACM Press, pp. 71-76, 1989.
41. L. Zhao and J.O. Coplien, "Symmetry in Class and Type Hierarchy," in Conferences in Research and Practice in Information Technology, 10. James Noble and John Potter, Eds. Australian Computer Society, January 2002, pp. 181-190.
42. L. Zhao and T. Foster, "Modelling Roles with Cascade", IEEE Software, vol. 16, no. 5, 1999, pp.86-93.
43. L. Zhao and E.A. Kendall, "Role Modelling for Component Design", in Proc. 33rd International Conference on Technology of Object-Oriented Languages and Systems (TOOLS Europe 2000), IEEE Computer Society, 2000, pp. 312-323.

Model Bus: Towards the Interoperability
of Modelling Tools

Xavier Blanc, Marie-Pierre Gervais, and Prawee Sriplakich

Laboratoire d'Informatique de Paris 6 (LIP6), University Paris VI,
8, rue du Capitaine Scott, 75015 Paris, France
{Xavier.Blanc, Marie-Pierre.Gervais,
Prawee.Sriplakich}@lip6.fr

Abstract. MDA software development requires the interoperability of a wide
range of modelling services (operations taking models as inputs and outputs),
such as model edition, model transformation, and code generation. In particular,
software development life cycle requires the interoperability of different
modelling services. In particular, this interoperability concerns how to
"connect" services (how to send an output model produced by one service as an
input to another service). Today, the notion of modelling services is not yet well
defined. Moreover, CASE tools, which implements different services, have
heterogeneous interfaces. For this reason, the service connection is costly and
cannot be automated. Currently, there are few works addressing this problem.
Therefore, we propose an architecture and a prototype enabling the services of
different tools to be connected.

1 Introduction

According to Model Driven Architecture (MDA), models are treated as first-class
elements in software development [21]. MDA application requires a wide range of
modelling services such as model edition [15], model storage [15], model
manipulation [22][14], code generation [9] and model transformation [4][7][8]. We
can mention also model execution and model validation as some work are now
ongoing at the OMG (execution semantics defined in UML 2.0 [25], Object
Constraint Language 2.0 [24]). For precision, we define the term *modeling service* as
an operation having models as inputs and outputs. Hence, the users of modeling
services are software developers that want to apply different modeling services to
their models in order to, for example, analyze, design and implement software.

Several CASE tools, implemented by different vendors (or developer groups), offer
various modelling services. For example, NetBeans Metadata Repository [18],
ModFact [17], Eclipse Modeling Framework (EMF) [10], and Univers@lis [3]
propose model storage and model manipulation. Rational Rose [30], Objecteering
[19], EclipseUML [11], Poseidon [29] and ArgoUML [2] propose UML model
edition and code generation. ArcStyler [1], MIA [16], and UMT-QVT [32] propose
model transformation. Although these tools cover a lot of modelling services, some
services, such as UML model execution [31], OCL constraint verification [13], deep
model copy [28], are not commonly supported by commercial tools.

U. Aßmann, M. Aksit, and A. Rensink (Eds.): MDAFA 2003/2004, LNCS 3599, pp. 17–32, 2005.

According to the MDA vision, software development life cycle requires the interoperability of tools. In particular, the **connection** between the services of different tools must be enabled. This problem concerns how to send an output model produced by one service as an input to another service (which may be offered by a different tool). For example, connecting a model storage service to a model transformation service will enable the model transformation service to retrieve its input or to store its output in the model storage service.

Connecting modelling services is a difficult problem. We identified two main concerns regarding this problem: *functional connection* and *concrete connection.* Functional connection ensures that the service inputs and outputs have compatible types so that the services can exchange data. It particularly concerns the type compatibility of models. Concrete connection ensures that modelling service connections can be realized at run-time. In particular, the connected services must agree in a model representation form and in a mechanism for exchanging models.

Today service connection cannot be done in an automated way. As a result, users must spend a lot of technical efforts to realize the connection. Neither functional connection nor concrete connection can be automated. The functional connection (i.e. type compatibility checking) is not automated because today tools are only documented informally in natural languages (in manuals), so the information about input/output types may be insufficiently precise and can not be exploited.

Moreover, each tool has its own model representations for encoding its services' inputs and outputs. A model representation can be either a textual form (e.g. XML Metadata Interchange (XML) [27], Human-Usable Textual Notation (HUTN) [20]) or an object form (e.g. Java Metadata Interface (JMI) [14], EMF Repository [10]). Also, each tool provides different interfaces. Some tools provide graphical user interfaces [30][19], some are executed via command lines [17] and others propose APIs for calling services [10]. To connect services of different tools, a dedicated conversion is required for each pair of tools. This effort is costly and can only be done manually. For this reason, concrete connection is not automated.

Despite the needs for connecting modelling services, there are currently few works concerning this problem. The Eclipse platform has been developed for connecting tools. But Eclipse does not take into account the particularity of modelling domain. Although the EMF offers the integration of modelling tools into Eclipse, it does not address at all the functional connection problem and the way tool connections are realized is limited to the use of the EMF's Java API.

We propose here the Model Bus architecture for addressing the functional connection and the concrete connection problems. Model Bus is mainly based on middleware technologies such as CORBA and Web Services but it adds new features for dealing with modelling aspects. Model Bus enables the automation of modelling service connections. We have implemented a prototype of Model Bus on the Eclipse platform and we have connected several modelling services proposed by the ModFact tools.

This paper is organized as follows. Section 2 discusses the difficulties of modelling service connection. Section 3 presents Model Bus architecture and explains how Model Bus can automate modelling service connection. In section 4, we show how to use Model Bus in an example scenario. Section 5 validates our concepts by presenting our prototype. Section 6 compares our approach with others. The last section concludes our work and presents research perspectives.

2 Service Connection Problem

First of all, let us illustrate the notion of service connection through an example (c.f. figure below). In this example, a user (software developer) wants to perform a UML to Enterprise Java Bean (EJB) transformation. To do this, he does the following scenario: First he will find a UML model in a *UML Repository* service. This service requires a model name as an input and returns a UML model as an output. This output is connected to the input of a *Transformation* service for transforming the UML model to an EJB model. The output of the transformation service (i.e. EJB model) will be connected to the input of a *Code Generation* service for generating an EJB application (i.e. code).

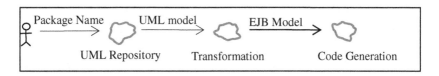

Fig. 1. A service connection example: A software developer wants to use three modelling services (UML Repository, Transformation, Code Generation) provided by three different tools conjointly.

This kind of scenario seems to be common in MDA software development. However, we will show you that there are significant difficulties in service connection.

2.1 Functional Connection: Checking Type Compatibility

To ensure that the service connection is possible, the type compatibility between an output of a service and an input of another service must be checked. The previous example requires the following checking: UML Repository's output and Transformation's input, Transformation's output and Code Generation's input.

The type compatibility is a well-known problem; however it has not been addressed in the modelling domain. Unlike classical data type, the model type compatibility is not a trivial problem because nowadays there is no well-known, precise definition of model types. Finding such a definition is also difficult because there are uncountable kinds of models (e.g. UML models, SPEM models, CWM models …). We will identify that model types have several characteristics. Then we will illustrate why these characteristics are important to the model type compatibility problem.

Model type characteristics and example of type checking rules
Metaclasses: It is a common practice to use a metamodel to define *model types* - input and output types of a service. In other words, the service's inputs or outputs can be anything conforming to a metamodel. However, currently there is no precise definition of metamodels: Is it a set of metaclasses (MOF classes) or a set of metapackage (MOF packages)? We propose that model types should be defined in terms of metaclasses rather than metapackages. This is because most services are

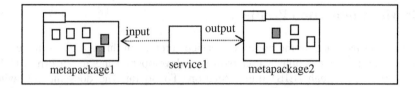

Fig. 2. Roles of metaclasses in the model type definition: The gay rectangles represent the metaclasses whose instances are inputs and outputs of a modelling service.

capable of processing instances of some metaclasses. A metapackage may contain metaclasses whose instances are not acceptable by services. The figure below shows how model types are defined. The grey rectangles in metapackage1 represent the metaclasses whose instances can be processed by the service and the metaclass in metapackage2 whose instances are produced by the service.

"Any" vs. specific model types: A model type is said to be specific if the corresponding models can contain only instances of some specific metaclasses. On the contrary, for the "any" model type, the corresponding models can contain instances of any metaclasses. The "any" model type is necessary because there are several services that operate on this type. For instance, the MOF QVT proposal [23] defines *generic* transformation that can be applied to any kinds of models. The input and output of this transformation is "any" model type.

Model granularity: A model can contain either a single instance of a metaclass (e.g. a UML package, a UML class) or a collection of instances (UML packages, UML classes). Therefore, the model type definition must specify the allowed number of instances, for example, "a single instance", "no more than two instances", or "any number of instances". Moreover, for collection-granularity model types, the order of instances in the collection may have meanings. Therefore, the type definition should specify whether the instances are required to be ordered.

The characteristics presented above are required for checking the type compatibility. We present some checking rules that use those characteristics. Then we will show that those rules cannot be verified in the UML-to-EJB example.

Metaclasses: An output model type (T1) is compatible to an input model type (T2) if all the T1's metaclasses are included in the set of T2's metaclasses.
As regards the example, UML Repository does not specify the return type. It may return either a UML package (instance of metaclass *Package*) or classes contained in the package (instances of metaclass *Class*), or other things (UseCase, Sequence Diagramme etc). Consequently, we cannot check whether its return type is compatible to Transformation's input.

"Any" vs. specific model types: All specific model outputs are compatible to an "any" model input. On the other hand, an "any" model output does not always compatible to a specific model input depending on the actual type (at runtime) of that "any" model output. Therefore, the metaclass checking is necessary at runtime.

As regards the example, it is not specified whether Transformation service is generic or specific to particular kinds of models. As consequent, we cannot know whether the type checking must be performed statically or at runtime.

Model granularity: The instance number range of the output model type must be included in the range of input model type. For example, "only single instance" is included in "from zero to two instances".

As regards the example, Transformation service does not specify how many instances (of metaclasses) the result model will contain. If the result model contained multiple instances while Code Generation service can handle only one instance, the service connection would cause errors.

We conclude that the type compatibility verification requires precise service description, especially the input/output types of services. Moreover, if this description were specified in a well-defined format, the automation of the checking rules would be feasible. However, this is not the case in current practice because such description is usually written in natural languages (i.e. in tool manuals). For this reason, the functional connection is an unsolved problem.

2.2 Concrete Connection: Executing Connected Services

As previously explained, to execute connected services, the services must agree in a model representation form and in a mechanism for exchanging models. However, tools providing services are heterogeneous. Therefore, two tools can hardly exchange models. We identify two kinds of tool heterogeneity: model representation forms and interface styles (i.e. the way services receive inputs and return outputs).

Model representation forms: Tools have their own model representation forms. On one hand, some tools use models represented in textual formats. For example, Poseidon and ArgoUML store models in the XMI format. On the other hand, some other tools require models in object forms. For example, model edition services in EclipseUML operate on model objects in the EMF repository.

Interface styles: The way services receive inputs and return outputs vary from a tool to another. For example, Rational Rose offers to users a graphical user interface (GUI) for applying code generation services on a UML model. ModFact provides a command line interface for applying a DTD generation on a MOF model. EMF provides an API for using the model manipulation service on an EMF repository. Moreover, tools that support multi-users can provide remote access. For instance, ModFact repository allows the model manipulation service to be accessible through the CORBA RPC. We can also anticipate tools offering Web Service access to their services.

Both kinds of heterogeneity cause difficulties in concrete connection. If services use different model representation forms, an output of a service can not be understood by one another. Furthermore, some interface styles, such as command lines or GUIs, do not support automatic interaction. To connect the services offering such interfaces, users must manually transfer a model from one service to another. In this case, automating service connection is not possible.

Although this heterogeneity problem is a well-known problem and several solutions have already been proposed (e.g. CORBA, Web Service), none those solutions addresses the particularity of modelling domain. They do not define model representation forms and interface styles that are appropriate to modelling services.

3   Model Bus

3.1   Describing Functional Connection

Our design principle is to provide well-formed service description. In particular, service inputs and outputs must be precisely defined in order that the service connection can be checked. The next figure contrasts the current practice and our solution. In the current practice, as we have mentioned that today there is no well-known, precise definition of model types, the view of modelling services is unclear. Our approach proposes a uniform view where services are similar to software components having precise input and output definitions.

We propose a metamodel, called *Functional Description* (c.f. the next figure). This metamodel describes the signatures of modelling services in an abstract way. Modelling services are similar to classical operations that have input and output parameters. However they have a new important feature: their input and output types can be models.

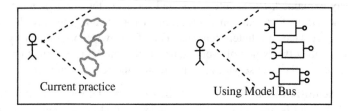

Fig. 3. Modelling services viewed as software components: Our goal is to provide a precise definition of modelling services. This definition must enable users to identify compatible services that can be connected.

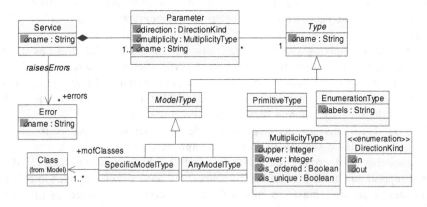

Fig. 4. Functional Description metamodel: We can describe each modelling service by creating an instance of this metamodel.

The Functional Description metamodel addresses the problem of the type compatibility verification by allowing services to be sufficiently described. The model characteristics presented in 2.1 can be precisely specified as follows.

Metaclasses: The metaclass *SpecificModelType* references MOF metaclasses whose instances can be contained in input and output parameters. For example, in the description of a service requiring a UML use case, the SpecificModelType will point to the metaclass *UseCase* in the UML metamodel. This approach is unambiguous since *SpecificModelType* allows users to obtain, for example, the complete definition of UML use cases (in a particular version of the UML metamodel).

"Any" vs. specific model types: The "any" and specific model types can be distinguished using metaclasses *SpecificModelType* and *AnyModelType*. SpecificModelType points to the metaclasses whose instances are expected while AnyModelType indicates that the parameter can contain instances of any metaclasses of any metamodels.

Model granularity: *MultiplicityType* allows model granularity to be specified using the *upper* and *lower* attributes. For example, [2..2] (i.e. lower=2, upper=2) and [1..*] (i.e. lower=1, upper= -1) denote that the model must contain respectively "exactly two" and "one or more" instances. Moreover, the *isOrdered* attribute specifies whether the order of instances (in a multi-instance model) must be respected.

The Functional Description is similar to the operation definition in MOF 1.4 [22]. However, it introduces two new features. Firstly, in MOF operations, a parameter type is limited to be a single metaclass. Therefore we cannot define, for example, a model including both UML classes and UML packages. In the Functional Description, *SpecificModelType* can define more flexible types because it can reference more than one metaclass. Secondly, in MOF operations, the "any" model type parameter doesn't exist. Thus, the Functional Description can describe a wider range of services.

Our approach supports type checking automation. A service description repository can be built from our metamodel, based on technologies such as Java Metadata Interface (JMI) [14] or Eclipse Modelling Framework (EMF) [10]. This repository offers an API for manipulating service descriptions. This API allow us to write type compatibility checking rules in Java.

3.2 Describing Concrete Connection

In section 2.2, we have already explained that the tools heterogeneity causes difficulty for users. However, it is not practical in the real world to limit all tools to only one model representation form and one interface style. Moreover, each model representation form and interface style has its own advantages. For instance, object forms (e.g. JMI, EMF) provide model manipulation facilities while XMI format is better for model exchange. As for interface styles, it is simple and convenient to call local tools' services via an API while remote access mechanisms such as CORBA or Web Service are suitable for multi-user tools. This trade-off leads us to the following design principles:

EntryPoints: We provide a set of *EntryPoints* – concrete methods to call modelling services - allowing tool implementers to choose an EntryPoint suitable for their tools. EntryPoint definition will include model representation definition and interface style definition.

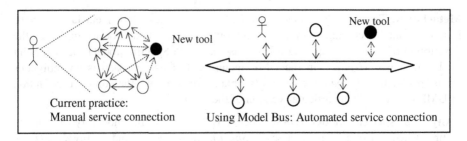

Fig. 5. How Model Bus enables concrete connection: Our goal is to generate code allowing services to be invoked. Thanks to this automated generation, the user does not need to be aware of tool heterogeneity.

Generation rules: For each EntryPoint, we also provide rules for generating 1) skeleton codes allowing services to be invoked and 2) service invocation codes for connecting an output of a service to an input of another service. Thanks to this automated generation, users who want to connect services do not need to be ware of service implementation.

The figure below illustrates how Model Bus solves the concrete connection problem. Without Model Bus, when a new tool is added, users will need to develop a dedicated method for connecting it with each existing tool. By using Model Bus, a new tool can automatically connect to others through the EntryPoints: the codes for connecting services will be generated using our generation rules.

EntryPoints: We propose a metamodel (c.f. next figure), for describing EntryPoints. The *EntryPoint* metaclass associates the concrete aspect with the abstract aspect of services. In other words, it specifies how the services defined abstractly in the Functional Description can be concretely invoked.

EntryPoint is specialized for representing each EntryPoint. We identify here three EntryPoints: *WsEntryPoint, CorbaEntryPoint, JmiEntryPoint*. Each EntryPoint is briefly defined in the table below according to model representation forms and interface styles.

Table 1. EntryPoint summary

EntryPoint	Model Representation Form	Interface style
WsEntryPoint	XMI	WSDL (Using SOAP message for invocation)
CorbaEntryPoint	CORBA objects (based on MOF-IDL)	CORBA (Using IIOP protocol for invocation)
JmiEntryPoint	Java objects (based on JMI)	Local Java API (Using Java method invocation)

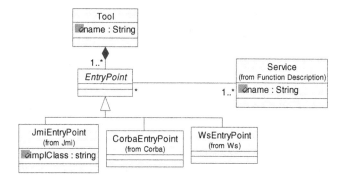

Fig. 6. EntryPoint metamodel: This metamodel describes how modelling services can be concretely invoked

All EntryPoints follows the similar principles: specifying the representation of service parameters (which are models) and specifying the service invocation mechanism via a specific interface style. In the rest of the article, we focus on the JmiEntryPoint. Our work concerning the WsEntryPoint is presented in [6].

Generation rules: For automating service access, we provide the generation rules which are used by both tool providers and users. First, they enable tool providers to generate skeleton codes allowing the services to be invoked. These skeleton codes will be used either for implementing the services or for delegating to existing implementation. Then, users can generate codes for invoking the services.

For JmiEntryPoint, a service description will be mapped to a Java interface. This interface will serve for both tool providers and users: It allows tool providers to provide the service implementation conforming to JmiEntryPoint. For users, it will be used in the generated codes that connect services (as we will later demonstrate in 4.2).

The rules for generating this Java interface are defined in terms of the correspondences between service description metaclasses and Java constructs as briefly shown the following table.

Table 2. Correspondences between service description elements and Java constructs

Service description elements		Java constructs
JmiEntryPoint		A singleton Java Interface <JmiEntryPoint.implClass>
Service		A Java method : Java.util.Map <Service.name>(java.util.Map inputMap)
Parameter	Input	A map entry (<Parameter.name>, value) in inputMap
	Output	A map entry (<Parameter.name>, value) in returned Map
Multiplicity	lower>=1	Corresponding map entry is required
Type	lower=0	Corresponding map entry is optional
	upper>1 or upper=*	Value must be instance of java.util.Collection
Type	PrimitiveType	Basic Java types (e.g. java.lang.String, java.lang.Boolean)
	EnumerationType	javax.jmi.reflect.RefEnum
	ModelType	javax.jmi.reflect.RefObject

A JmiEntryPoint is mapped to a Java interface. Each service referred by the *JmiEntryPoint* will be mapped to a Java method "java.util.Map <Service.name> (java.util.Map inputMap)". *inputMap* allows the service's input parameters to be passed as name-value pairs in the map data structure (java.util.Map). Likewise, the returned map will contain the name-value pairs of all output parameters.

The rest of the metaclasses (Parameter, Multiplicity, Type) serve as constraints on parameter values: *PrimitiveType* is mapped directly to Basic Java types (e.g. java. lang.String, java.lang.Boolean). For *ModelType*, the parameter values must be objects representing metaclass instances in JMI repositories (i.e. java.jmi.reflect. RefObject). For the optional parameter (i.e. MultiplicityType.lower>0), the map entry representing the parameter's value can be absent. For the parameter containing multiple objects (i.e. MultiplicityType.upper>1), the class java.util.Collection is used for holding the objects.

4   Model Bus Example

We take the same example UML-to-EJB for illustrating how Model Bus can solve the service connection difficulties.

4.1   Solving Functional Connection

For solving functional connection problem, we define each tool (UmlRepository, UmlToEjb, CodeGeneration) using the Functional Description metamodel. The result is shown in the following table.

The first tool, **UmlRepository**, offers two services: *findClass* and *findPackage*. The former returns a UML class from a given name while the latter returns a UML package. The second tool, **UmlToEjb**, offers the *transform* service that transforms UML packages (instances of metaclass *Model_Management::Package* in the UML

Table 3. Example of Functional Descriptions

Tool	Service	Parameter	Direction /Multipicity	Type
Uml Repository	findClass	className	In [1..1]	PrimitiveType (String)
		class	Out [1..1]	SpecificModelType (Foundation::Core::Class)
	findPackage	packageName	In [1..1]	PrimitiveType (String)
		package	Out [1..1]	SpecificModelType (Model_Management::Package)
UmlToEjb	transform	sourceModel	In [1..*]	SpecificModelType (Model_Management::Package)
		targetModel	Out [1..*]	SpecificModelType (ejb::EjbComponent)
Code Generation	generateSingle Component	ebjComponent	In [1..1]	SpecificModelType (ejb::EjbComponent)
	generate Components	ebjComponents	In [1..*]	SpecificModelType (ejb::EjbComponent)

metamodel) into instances of *EbjComponent* (defined in the EJB metamodel). The last tool, **CodeGeneration**, offers two services: *generateSingleComponent* and *generateComponents*. The former requires a single *EbjComponent* instance while the latter requires a collection of *EbjComponent* instances.

For connecting the services, users must choose one service for each tool. Since the UmlRepository tool and CodeGeneration tool propose more than one service, appropriate choices must be made. The next figure shows the choices that the user makes (i.e. *findPackage, transform, generateComponents*).

To verify that the choices are correct, the user can use the following rules to check automatically the type compatibility of the inputs and outputs of the connected services.

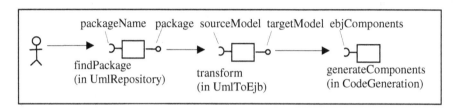

Fig. 7. Example of modelling service connections: When the modelling services are precisely described, we can identify whether the inputs and outputs of them are compatible and can be connected.

The *findPackage* & *transform* services: The output parameter *package* is connected to the input parameter *sourceModel*. The model types of both parameters correspond to the same metaclass (Model_Management ::Package) and hence are compatible. Their granularities are also compatible ([1..1] → [1..*]). Therefore, the service connection is correct.

The *transform* & *generateComponents* services: The output parameter *targetModel* is connected to the input parameter *ebjComponents*. The model types of both parameters correspond to the same metaclass (ejb::EbjComponent). Their granularities are also compatible ([1..*] → [1..*]). Therefore, the service connection is correct.

If the user made bad choices, the similar analysis as above could detect bad service connections. For example, the connection of the *findClass* service to the *transform* service would be incorrect because the model types of their parameters are incompatible (metaclass Foundation::Core::Class vs metaclass Model_Management ::Package). The connection of the *transform* service to the *generateSingleComponent* service would also be incorrect because the granularities of their parameters are incompatible ([1..*] → [1..1]).

4.2 Solving Concrete Connection

As described, EntryPoint is used for specifying how to invoke services. We will illustrate how to connect services via *JmiEntryPoint*. By using the generation rules, Java interfaces can be generated from the service descriptions as shown below:

```
public interface UmlRepository {
  public Map findPackage(Map inputMap);
  public Map findClass(Map inputMap);                      }
public interface UmlToEjb {
  public Map transform(Map inputMap);                      }
public interface CodeGeneration {
  public Map generateSingleComponent(Map inputMap);
  public Map generateComponents(Map inputMap);        }
```

To execute all the service connections, only a simple code is needed for connecting them. For brevity, only the connection of *transform* service and *generateComponents* service is shown below. The two services are connected by linking the *targetModel* output to the *ebjComponents* input. To connect them, first the service producing the output (i.e. *transform*) is invoked (line a). Then, the output is extracted from the map data structure (line b). Next the output is linked to the input by putting it in the map (line d). Finally, the service consuming the input (i.e. *generateComponents*) is invoked (line e).

```
a.  Map transformOutput = UmlToEjb.transform(transformInput);
b.  Collection targetModel = (Collection)
    transformOutput.get("targetModel");
c.  Map generateComponentsInput = new Hashtable();
d.  generateComponentsInput.put("ebjComponents", targetModel);
e.  Map generateComponentsOutput =
    CodeGeneration.generateComponents(CodeGenerationInput);
```

The codes for linking other parameter pairs follow the same pattern. For this reason, by specifying a parameter pair to be linked, we can automatically generate the code.

5   Proof of Concepts: Model Bus Integrated Environment (MBIE)

We have implemented a Model Bus prototype on the Eclipse platform. This prototype is called Model Bus Integrated Environment (MBIE). MBIE provides two facilities. Firstly, it allows users to browse all service descriptions. In particular, users can examine the signature of each modelling service. Secondly, MBIE automatically generates a GUI from service descriptions. Users can then use this GUI for invoking any service. This implementation proves that 1) service descriptions can be automatically processed and 2) The invocation of any service can be automated in the sense that users need not writing codes.

The following figure illustrates the MBIE architecture. MBIE is connected to the bus like other tools. Instead of accessing the bus directly, users can alternatively use the GUI facilities provided by MBIE to interact with tools. MBIE contains two components: Functional Management and EntryPoint Management. The Functional Management allows users to browse service descriptions. The EntryPoint Management allows users to invoke the chosen service via an automatically generated GUI.

Functional Management provides a GUI, called *Functional View* (c.f. the next figure), which lets users explore tools' Functional Descriptions (i.e. modelling service signatures) and then select a service to be invoked.

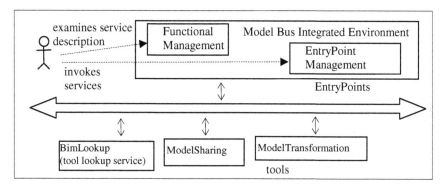

Fig. 8. MBIE Architecture: MBIE is an environment that allows users to use modelling services of any tools. It has two parts. Functional Management allows users to examine available services and to determine functional connection. EntryPoint Management allows users to invoke services transparently form service implementation.

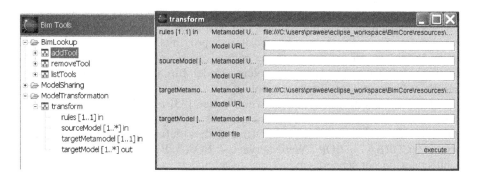

Fig. 9. GUI of MBIE: Functional Management (left) and EntryPoint Management (right)

As shown in the figure 9, three tools are available: *BimLookup,* which provides lookup services for service descriptions, *ModelSharing*, which offers a model storage service, and *ModelTransformation,* which proposes a transformation service based on Transformation Rule Language [8]. This Functional View also shows that the *ModelTransformation* tool offers the *transform* service having four parameters (rules, sourceModel, targetMetamodel and targetModel).

EntryPoint Management allows users to invoke a modelling service through the *Service Call Dialog,* which is automatically generated from the signature of the service. Firstly, this GUI takes inputs from users. Then the service is invoked using the appropriate EntryPoint. Finally, the results are returned to users.

Figure 9 shows a Service Call Dialog for invoking the *transform* service. This dialog allows users to supply three inputs parameters (rules, sourceModel, and targetMetamodel) and to receive the result (targetModel).

6 Related Works

The works related to Model Bus concern frameworks where tools can be integrated. Our previous work, Integrated Transformation Environment (ITE) [5], allows users to use many transformation engines in the same environment. Compared to Model Bus, the ITE approach is more restrictive. Firstly, ITE limits integrated tools to be model transformation tools having one input model and one output model. Model Bus can describe more flexible functionalities (i.e. any number of inputs and outputs). Secondly, ITE uses metamodels for defining model types. Model Bus proposes a more precise definition of model types using metaclasses.

The providers of some repository implementations such as Netbeans Metadata Repository [18], Eclipse Modeling Framework [10], and Univers@lis [3] propose frameworks where all tools share the same central repository. This approach allows tools to be tightly integrated: all models are stored in the same repository and hence can be shared among all tools. For example, model visualization, transformation and code generation tools are integrated in the same Univers@lis repository. However this approach has two disadvantages. Firstly, it does not address how functional connection can be checked. On the other hand, Model Bus offers a metamodel for describing modelling service signatures and also rules for checking the model type compatibility. Secondly, the central repository approach is not suitable for distributed environments: the remote access to the central repository is costly and can expose security risks. To overcome this problem, Model Bus includes the Web Service EntryPoint for supporting distributed tools.

Middleware architectures such as Web Service [33] and CORBA are similar to Model Bus in the sense that they allow services (or services) to be described (e.g. CORBA - IDL, Web Service - WSDL) and they define interfaces for invoking services (CORBA - IIOP, Web Service - SOAP Bindings). However, those architectures do not support services that have models as inputs and outputs. Model Bus is dedicated to the modeling domain. It defines model types and model representation forms to be used in modelling services.

The workflow process definition language (WPDL) [33] allows process connections to be specified. Some work for applying WPDL for connecting modeling tools [12] has been made. However this work did not address the functional and concrete connection problems. For this moment, Model Bus does not have a metamodel for expressing how services are connected. We think that a subset of WPDL can be reused for expressing service connection in Model Bus.

7 Conclusion and Perspectives

Model Bus allows modelling services to be connected. To connect services, the functional connection and the concrete connection problems must be solved. To solve the functional connection problem, we proposed the Functional Description metamodel for describing modelling service signatures. In particular a precise model type definition was described. As a result, type compatibility of the connected parameters can be automatically checked. To solve the concrete connection problem, we defined a set of EntryPoints allowing services to be invoked. We have shown how the service descriptions can be used to automatically generate a Java interface for tool providers to implement the services and for users to invoke the services. We have also demonstrated how to generate codes for automating service connections.

The Model Bus prototype is implemented in Eclipse Platform. It offers users the high-level facilities for browsing services and invoking any services. This prototype proves that modelling service description can be described and Model Bus automates the service invocation.

For future work, we plan to advance this research particularly in two aspects. At this time, modelling services are described in terms of model element types and model granularities. However, some services require model types to be more specific, for example, a service that requires a UML class having at least one attribute, a service that requires a UML class with stereotype «Table». Therefore, we plan to augment model type semantics with Object Constraint Language (OCL). We think that this improvement will ensure better the correctness of service connections.

For the second aspect, we want to propose a method for rigorously expressing how services are connected. For example, "output A of service S1 is connected to input B of service S2". In particular, we need a metamodel for describing the structure of this information. This metamodel will allow us to specify software development scenarios involving many modelling services. We also look forwards to automating the execution of those scenarios.

References

1. ArcStyler, http://www.io-software.com
2. ArgoUML, http://www.argouml.tigris.org
3. M. Belaunde: A Pragmatic Approach for Building a User-friendly and Flexible UML Model Repository, 2nd International Conference on The Unified Modelling Language (UML'99), 1999.
4. J. Bézivin et al.: First experiments with the ATL model transformation language: Transforming XSLT into XQuery, 2nd OOPSLA Workshop on Generative Techniques in the context of MDA, 2003.
5. X. Blanc et al.: Towards an Integrated Transformation Environment (ITE) for Model Driven Development (MDD), to be published in the Invited Session Model Driven Development, The 8th World Multi-Conference on Systemics, Cybernetics and Informatics (SCI 2004), July 2004.
6. X. Blanc, M-P. Gervais, P. Sriplakich: Modeling Services and Web Services: Application of ModelBus, to appear in the 2005 International Conference on Software Engineering Research and Practice (SERP'05), 2005.
7. K. Czarnecki, S. Helsen: Classification of Model Transformation Approaches, 2nd OOPSLA Workshop on Generative Techniques in the context of MDA, 2003.
8. T. Gardner et al.: A review of OMG MOF 2.0 Query /Views /Transformations Submissions and Recommendations towards the final Standard, http://www.omg.org/docs/ad/03-08-02.pdf
9. D. Hearnden, K. Raymond, J. Steel: Anti-Yacc: MOF-to-Text, EDOC 2002.
10. Eclipse Modeling Framework, http://www.eclipse.org/emf
11. Eclipse UML, http://www.omondo.com

12. G. van Emde Boas: From the Workfloor: Developing Workflow for the Generative Model Transformer, 2nd OOPSLA Workshop on Generative Techniques in the context of MDA, 2003.
13. Hamie: Towards Verifying Java Realizations of OCL-Constrained Design Models Using JML, 6th IASTED International Conference on Software Engineering and Applications, 2002.
14. Java Community Process: Java Metadata Interface (JMI) Specification, http://www.jcp.org, 2002.
15. Ledeczi et al.: The Generic Modeling Environment, Workshop on Intelligent Signal Processing, 2001.
16. MIA, http://www.model-in-action.fr
17. ModFact, http://modfact.lip6.fr
18. NetBeans Metadata Repository, http://mdr.netbeans.org
19. Objecteering, http://www.objecteering.com
20. OMG: Human-Usable Textual Notation (HUTN) Specification, document no: ptc/04-01-10, 2003.
21. OMG: MDA Guide Version 1.0.1, document no: omg/2003-06-01, 2003.
22. OMG: Meta Object Facility (MOF) Specification version 1.4, document no: formal/2002-04-03, 2002.
23. OMG: Request for Proposal MOF2.0 Query /Views /Transformations, document no: ad/2002-04-10, 2002.
24. OMG: Request for Proposal UML 2.0 OCL, document no: ad/2000-09-03, 2001.
25. OMG: UML 2.0 Superstructure Specification, document no: ptc/03-08-02, 2004.
26. OMG: Unified Modeling Language Specification version 1.4, document no: formal/01-09-67, 2001.
27. OMG: XML Metadata Interchange (XMI) Specification version 2.0, document no: formal/03-05-02, 2003.
28. Porres: M. Alanen, A Generic Deep Copy Algorithm for MOF-Based Models, Model Driven Architecture:Foundations and Applications, 2003.
29. Poseidon, http:// www.gentleware.com
30. Rational Rose, http://www.rational.com
31. D. Riehle & al.: The Architecture of a UML Virtual Machine, OOPSLA 2001.
32. UMT-QVT: http://umt-qvt.sourceforge.net
33. W3C: Web Services Architecture, http://www.w3.org/TR/ws-arch, 2004.
34. Workflow Management Coalition: Workflow Process Definition Language, document no: WFMC-TC-1025, version 1.0, 2002.

Modeling in the Large and Modeling in the Small[*]

Jean Bézivin, Frédéric Jouault, Peter Rosenthal, and Patrick Valduriez

Atlas Group, INRIA and LINA, University of Nantes,
2, rue de la Houssinière - BP92208, 44322 Nantes Cedex 3, France
`FirstName.LastName@univ-nantes.fr`
`Patrick.Valduriez@inria.fr`

Abstract. As part of the AMMA project (ATLAS Model Management Architecture), we are currently building several model management tools to support the tasks of modeling in the large and of modeling in the small. The basic idea is to define an experimental framework based on the principle of models as first class entities. This allows us to investigate issues of conceptual and practical interest in the field of model management applied to data-intensive applications. By modeling in the small, we mean dealing with model and metamodel elements and the relations between them. In this sense, ATL (ATLAS Transformation Language) allows expressing automatic model transformations. We also motivate the need for the "ModelWeaver" which handles fine-grained relationships between elements of different metamodels with a different purpose than automatic model transformation. By modeling in the large, we mean globally dealing with models, metamodels and their properties and relations. We use the notion of a "MegaModel" to describe a registry for models and metamodels. This paper proposes a lightweight architectural style for a model-engineering platform as well as a first prototype implementation demonstrating its feasibility.

1 Introduction

Following the seminal work of Deremer and Kron in 1976 [9], we believe that the situation in the modeling area today is quite similar to the situation described at that time in the programming area. Starting from this similarity, we distinguish in this paper the two related activities of "modeling in the large" and "modeling in the small" which we illustrate with specific examples. The term "Megamodel" has been chosen to convey the idea of modeling in the large, establishing and using global relationships and metadata on the basic macroscopic entities (mainly models and metamodels), ignoring the internal details of these global entities. There is probably not going to be a unique monolithic modeling language (like UML 2.0) but instead an important number of small domain specific languages (DSLs) [6], [10] and this will only be possible if these small DSLs are well coordinated. To avoid the risk of fragmentation [19], we need to offer a global vision, which can be provided by the activity of modeling in the large. On the contrary, there will always be an important need to precisely define associations between model or metamodel elements, i.e. looking inside the

---

[*] This work is performed in the context of the "ModelWare" IST European project 511731.

U. Aßmann, M. Aksit, and A. Rensink (Eds.): MDAFA 2003/2004, LNCS 3599, pp. 33–46, 2005.

global entities. This activity of modeling in the small will be illustrated here by the two related but different examples of model transformation and model weaving.

This paper is organized as follows. Section 2 recalls the main characteristics of the MDE approach (Model Driven Engineering) and illustrates them within the particular example of the AMMA (Atlas Model Management Architecture) project. Section 3 presents model transformation operations with a focus on ATL (Atlas Transformation Language). Section 4 describes model weaving operations and their implications in the context of the ATLAS Model Weaver (AMW), another important tool in the AMMA platform. In particular, we discuss the conceptual differences between model transformation and model weaving. Section 5 describes global model management facilities and shows their practical impact with the help of the ATLAS MegaModel Management tool (AM3) that is intended to support modeling in the large activities in the AMMA platform.

2 AMMA: The Atlas Model Management Architecture

AMMA consists of two main sets of tools, one set of tools for modeling in the small (model transformation and model weaving) and another set of tools for modeling in the large based on what we call megamodels [5].

2.1 Models

A model is an artifact that conforms to a metamodel and represents a given aspect of a system. These relations of conformance and representation are central to model engineering [3]. A model is composed of model elements and conforms to a metamodel. This means that the metamodel describes the various kinds of contained model elements and the way they are arranged, related and constrained. A language intended to define metamodels is called a metametamodel.

In November 2000, the OMG proposed a new approach to interoperability named MDA™ (Model Driven Architecture) [20]. In MDA, the metametamodel is MOF [15] (Meta Object Facility) and the transformation language is based on the QVT 1.0 (Query View Transformation) specification [16]. MDA is one example of a much broader approach known as Model Driven Engineering (MDE), encompassing many popular research trends such as generative programming [8], domain specific languages, model integrated computing, model driven software development, model management and much more.

A basic principle in MDE is to regard models as first class entities. Besides the advantage of conceptual simplicity, it also leads to clear architecture, efficient implementation, high scalability and good flexibility. As part of several projects, open source platforms are being built with the intention to provide high interoperability not only between recent model based tools, but also between legacy tools.

There are other representation systems that may also offer, outside the strict MDA or even MDE boundaries, similar model engineering facilities. We call them technical spaces [13]. They are often based on a three-level organization similar to the metametamodel, metamodel and model of the MDA. One example is grammarware [12] with EBNF, grammars and programs, but we could also consider XML documents, Semantic Web, database systems, ontology engineering, etc. A Java program may be viewed as a model conforming to the Java grammar. As a consequence, we may consider, in the OMG scope, strict (OMG)-models (i.e. MOF-based like a UML model); but we may also consider outside of this scope more general models such as a Java source file, an XML document, a relational database schema, etc. A strict OMG-model may be externalized as an XMI document and conforms to MOF-conforming metamodel. In our approach we deal with OMG-models but also with non-OMG models, based on other metametamodels.

2.2 Open Platforms for MDE

The advantage of using a model-based platform is that it allows many economies of scale. For example model and metamodel repositories may handle efficient and uniform access to these models, metamodels and their elements in serialized or any other mode. Transactional access, versioning and many other facilities may also be offered, whatever the kind of considered model: executable or not, product or process, transformation, business or platform, etc. An MDE platform is primarily intended for tool integration. Several tools are usually available on such a platform.

AMMA defines a lightweight architectural style for MDE platforms. It is based on the classical view of the software bus, adapted to the basic model engineering principles, and may support local or distributed implementations. A local platform is conceptually similar to a software factory as described in [10]. Most of the tools available in our current implementation of AMMA, that will be described later, are open source tools, such as ATL, AWM, ATP and AM3. More than tools, these represent minimal functional blocks in the abstract platform architecture. There is a set of conventions, standards and protocols for plugging or unplugging MDE tools from the AMMA platform. As an example, XMI is one standard for exchanging models and metamodels in serialized formats. Many other conventions will however allow other forms of communication between tools operating on a platform.

The AM3 tool described in Section 5 defines the way metadata on a given platform is managed in AMMA (registry on the models, metamodels, tools, services and all other global entities accessible at a given time in a given scope). The fact that these metadata are externally handled by megamodels allows achieving simplicity of the MDE platform. Extending the scope of a local platform to a given distributed environment may be performed by operations on the connected megamodels. The use of a megamodel allows keeping the architecture of the software bus very simple because the complexity is mainly handled externally by these megamodels conforming to specific and adapted metamodels. The megamodel will typically describe artifacts (models, metamodels, transformations, etc.), tools and services available in a given scope. The management of tools and services may borrow ideas from the Web service area (WSDL, UDDI, etc.) but we don't wish to reinvent heavyweight stream-based and event-based CORBA-like protocols for handling model-management tool interoperability on top of the Web. Instead, in the spirit of model engineering, we prefer simple, adaptive and extensible solutions, based on generative approaches and borrowing their power from the handling of metadata outside of the platform itself, in these well-defined megamodels.

3 ATL: The Atlas Transformation Language

This section presents the ATLAS model Transformation Language (ATL) and its environment: an execution virtual machine and an IDE. ATL provides internal MDE transformations, but we may also need facilities for handling external specific external formats. This is handled by the way of projectors described at the end of the section.

3.1 Model Transformation Languages

A model transformation language is used to define how a set of source models is visited to create a set of target models. The language defines how the basic operations on models can be performed using a specific set of language constructs (declarative rules, imperative instruction sequences, etc.).

More complex transformation scenarios can be expressed using this simple definition. The set of source models can include a parametric model used to drive the transformation on a specific path: this is the equivalent of the command line options given to UNIX tools. Among target models, there can be such models as trace models. In the context of model transformation, traceability is the process of collecting information on a running transformation for later use. There are different kinds of traceability ranging from the simple (and heavy) recording of every action performed to lighter, more specialized and abstract traces which only keep links between some source and target elements of interest.

3.2 ATL

ATL is a model transformation language, which has its abstract syntax defined using a metamodel. This means that every ATL transformation is in fact a model, with all the properties that are implied by this. For instance, a transformation program can be the source or the target of another model transformation. ATL has been designed as an answer to the QVT RFP [16] and is consequently in the MDA space. However, we have ongoing work on M3 level independence: enabling the possibility to write transformations for any MDE platform.

ATL is a hybrid of declarative and imperative constructs. While the recommended style to write transformations is declarative, imperative concepts are implemented to let the transformation writer decide which style is the more appropriate depending on the context. The expression language is based on OCL 2.0 (Object Constraint Language).

In declarative ATL, a transformation is composed of rules. Each rule specifies a set of model element types (coming from the source metamodels), which are to be matched, along with a Boolean expression, used to filter more precisely the set of matched elements (e.g. all classes with a name beginning with a "C"). This constitutes the source pattern, or left-hand side, of the rule. The target pattern, or right-hand side, is composed of a set of model element types (coming from the target metamodels). To each of them is attached a set of bindings which specifies how the properties of the target element are to be initialized. These declarative rules are named *matched rules*.

Imperative constructs in ATL can be specified in several places. An imperative block can be added to any declarative rule to conveniently initialize target elements requiring complex handling. Procedures, which are named *called rules* in contrast with the declarative *matched rules*, can be placed in the transformation and be called from any imperative block. Some procedures may bear the flags entrypoint or endpoint to specify that they should be executed either before or after the declarative rules are. The content of imperative blocks consists of sequences of instructions among: assignment, looping constructs, conditional constructs, etc. Complex algorithms can therefore be implemented imperatively if necessary.

A hybrid language is interesting because it can be used declaratively whenever possible. This means that some parts of a transformation and even full transformations, depending on their complexity, can be simply expressed. It is however possible to revert to a more classical all-purpose imperative language when the declarative constructs are not sufficient. However, we may then loose interesting properties that come with the use of declarative constructs. This is why it is planned to define several classes of ATL transformations, such as: declarative-only, imperative-only, hybrid, etc. Specific tools depending on the class of the transformation will use constraints to check whether a given model belongs to the class it supports. Thus, a transformation reverser that generates the opposite of a given transformation may only accept declarative transformations.

3.3 The Execution Virtual Machine

There are several practical solutions to implement ATL. We chose to define a Virtual Machine (VM) for different reasons. The main advantage we see in this approach is flexibility. As a matter of fact, AMMA is a research project and as such, ATL is constantly evolving to explore new advanced possibilities. A single low-level implementation makes it possible to work on high-level transformation language concepts while being rather independent of the actual tools used. For instance, the execution engine was first written to use the Netbeans/MDR model handler but it now can also work on Eclipse/EMF [7].The only part that had to be changed is the VM, since the ATL compiler and related tools run on top of it. Besides, despite the fact that our implementation has not been developed with performance in mind, the principal work to do to have a faster execution of ATL transformations is to write a new machine with less stringent flexibility requirements. It is of course still possible to develop a native code (or even Java bytecode to benefit from its portability) compiler later if necessary.

Among other interesting aspects, the use of a stack-based instruction set makes compiling OCL expressions quite simple. Moreover, other languages can also be compiled to our virtual machine. We use this to bootstrap several tools including the ATL compiler.

The ATL VM is a stack machine that uses a simple instruction set, which can be divided into three subsets. The first one is composed of instructions that perform model elements handling: creation, property access and assignment, operation call. The second one contains control instructions: goto, if, collection iteration instructions. There is also a set of stack handling instructions to push, pop and duplicate operands.

The primitive types are implemented by a native (meaning: part of the VM, actually in Java) library based on the OCL 2.0 standard library. All operations on primitive types are handled through operation calls to this library, e.g. 1+2 is performed as 1.+(2), the same way it is defined in the OCL specification.

While the choice of OCL as a navigation language for ATL has initially been made, other alternatives may be considered later without impacting the global architecture. Furthermore, the OCL part of ATL is being reworked to be pluggable. This means that it will be possible to reuse it in other languages for diverse purposes. One of our first experiments will be with a constraint-based language to express well-formedness rules on models. It will, for instance, be used to define the different classes of ATL transformation.

3.4 The ATL IDE

In order to ease the transformation writing process, we developed an Integrated Development Environment (IDE) for ATL on top of Eclipse [11]: ATL Development Tools (ADT) [1]. It provides several tools usually present in such environments. There is a syntax-highlighting editor synchronized with an outline presenting a view of the abstract syntax of the currently edited transformation program. We also developed wizards to create ATL projects for which a specific builder compiles ATL transformations.

A launch configuration is available to launch transformations in run or debug mode. In the latter, the execution can be debugged directly in Eclipse. The accompanying documentation tutorial can be used to show usage of all these features. Most of the ATL IDE components [1] behave the same way as their Java Development Tools (JDT) counterpart in Eclipse. Developers used to any modern IDE should not be lost when using ADT, which is illustrated in Figure 1.

3.5 Projectors

There are quite a lot of peripheral tools that are also useful to actually perform some model transformation work in relation with other technical spaces. We have grouped these tools under the name ATP (ATLAS Technical Projectors). Among these tools, we have identified a very important subset which we call injectors and extractors tools. As a matter of fact, there is a very large amount of pre-existing data that is not XMI [17] compliant but that would greatly benefit from model transformation. This data needs injection from its technical space (databases, flat files, EBNF, XML, etc.) to the MDE technical space. The need for extraction is also quite important: many existing tools do not read XMI. A simple example is the Java compiler. What we need here is code generation, which may be seen as a specific case of model extraction. The ATP goal is to host, in an organization as regular as possible, all drivers for external tool formats. It is an alternative to defining ad-hoc solutions for a lot of bridges with MDE-models usually named for example Model2Text, Text2Model, Model2EBNF, EBNF2Model, Model2SQL, SQL2Model, Model2XML, XML2Model, Mode2Binary, Binary2Model, etc.

Fig. 1. A view of ATL Development Tools (ADT)

Besides, even when dealing with MDE-based tools, it may be convenient to use simple textual representations rather than always using a complex ad-hoc tool or meta-tool. We designed the Kernel Metametamodel (KM3) to this end. It is a simpletextual concrete syntax to represent metamodels. Although there are quite a lot of tools to draw UML diagrams and although some of them actually export valid metamodels in XMI, we came to the conclusion, after much experimentation, that an additional simple textual tool for metamodel representation is really useful.

4 AMW: The Atlas ModelWeaver

In order to provide a naive description of the ModelWeaver, let us suppose we have two metamodels *LeftMM* and *RightMM*. We often need to establish links between their related elements. There are many occasions when we need such functionality in a MDE platform as will be discussed later. Concerning the set of links the following issues have to be considered:

- The set of links cannot be automatically generated because it is often based on human decisions or heuristics.
- It should be possible to record this set of links as a whole, in order to use it later in various contexts.
- It should be possible to use this set of links as an input to automatic or semi-automatic tools.

As a consequence, we come to the conclusion that a model weaving operation produces a precise weaving model *WM*. Like other models, this should be based on a specific weaving metamodel *WMM*. The produced weaving model relates to the source and target metamodels *LeftMM* and *RightMM* and thus remains linked to these metamodels in a megamodel registry.

Each link instance has to be typed conforming to a given *WMM*. There is no unique type of link. Link types should provide weaving tools with useful information. Even if some links contain only textual descriptions, these are valuable for tools supporting documentation, manual refinements or performing heuristics.

4.1 Motivating Examples

In software engineering practices, the "Y organization" sometimes called the 2TUP (Two Tracks Unified Process) has often been proposed as a methodological guide. The OMG has promoted this idea in the MDA proposal where a Platform Independent Model (PIM) should be weaved with a Platform Definition Model (PDM) to produce a merged Platform Specific Model (PSM).

Let us suppose we have a PIM for a bank containing the class *BankAccountNumber*. Suppose we have a PDM for an implementation platform containing classes *LongInteger* and *String*. One of the most important events in the software development chain is to take design decisions. One such design decision here would be for example to establish that the *BankAccountNumber* should be implemented using a *String* instead of a *LongInteger*. We will not discuss here the validity of this decision. However, we would like to ensure that this decision is well recorded, with the corresponding author, date, rationale, etc. Furthermore this decision is probably based on previous decisions and further decisions will be based on it.

What we see here is that a metamodel for design decisions would be most useful with several properties and links associated to each design decision. We can understand also that it would be very improbable to have an automatic weaving algorithm since this is most often a human decision based on practical know-how. Of course the user deciding of the weaving actions should be guided and helped by intelligent assistants that may propose her/him several choices. These helpers may be sometimes based on design patterns or more complex heuristics.

Let us take another example inspired by the work of Ph. Bernstein [2], [18]. We have two address books to merge and we get both metamodels *LeftMM* and *RightMM*. In *LeftMM* we have the class *Name* and in the second one the classes *FirstName* and *LastName*. Here we need to establish a more complex link stating that these are related by an expression of concatenation.

4.2 Extensible Metamodels

One may assume that there is no standard metamodel for weaving operations since most developers define their own. However, most often a given weaving metamodel will be expressed as an extension of another weaving metamodel that allows building a general weaving tool.

The ModelWeaver tool in AMMA reuses part of the infrastructure of the ATL IDE based on the Eclipse Platform [1]. We suppose there is a stub weaving metamodel and this is extended by specific metamodel extensions. The important goal is not to have to build a specific tool for each weaving task or use case. The two notions on which we are basing the design are metamodel extensions and Eclipse plugins.

The main idea of the implementation is that the GUI of the weaving tool is simple and may be partially generated. From the left part, one can select any class or associa

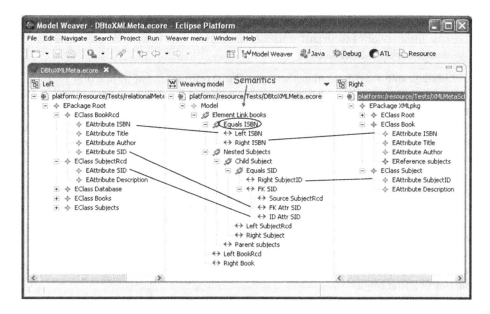

Fig. 2. First prototype for Atlas Model Weaver (AMW)

tion of the left metamodel and from the right part one can similarly select any class or association of the right metamodel. In the central part appear all the main elements of the weaving metamodel. Selecting a triple thus means creating a weaving link in the resulting weaving model.

Proceeding in this way, we get a generic weaving tool, adaptable to any kind of left, right and weaving metamodels. Of course, many design alternatives are being explored in the actual building of this tool. An initial prototype has been built and may give an idea of the user interface of AMW (see Figure 2).

As may be inferred from this prototype, a typical weaving session starts by uploading the weaving metamodel. From this metamodel, part of the tool GUI may be automatically generated. Then the left and the right metamodel may be chosen and the weaving work may proceed.

4.3 Weaving Rationale

One question often asked is why we need model weaving operations in addition to model transformations. This question raises at least the following issues:

- Issue of "arity": Usually a transformation takes one model as input and produces another model as output, even if extensions to multiple input and output may be considered. In contrast, a model weaving takes basically two models as input plus one weaving metamodel.

- Issue of "automaticity": A transformation is basically an automatic operation while a weaving may need the additional help of some heuristics or guidance to assist the user in performing the operation.

- Issue of "variability": A transformation is usually based on a fixed metamodel (the metamodel of the transformation language) while there is no canonical standard weaving metamodel.

Although one may argue that there may be several levels of abstraction in transformations (e.g. specifications and implementations of transformations), these three mentioned issues allow concluding that transformation and weaving are different problems. The first experiments with ATL and AMW confirmed this conclusion. In some particular cases however, a weaving model may be itself transformed into a transformation model.

Many research efforts like [22] are presently starting to investigate the relations between aspect-oriented programming and model engineering. This will be an important source of inspiration for weaving metamodels in the future.

One important open research issue that will be addressed later is how to integrate user guidance and domain dependent heuristics [11] in a model weaver. At this point of the research we have yet no hint on how to integrate this kind of knowledge as independent models. It is likely that those heuristics will have to be coded as Eclipse plugins in a first stage.

5   AM3: The Atlas MegaModel Management Tool

The Atlas MegaModel Management, AM3, is an environment for modeling in the large. With the macroscopic angle, models or metamodels are considered as a whole together with tools, services and other global entities.

Connected to an open platform, tools will exchange models. But tools may also be considered as models. A tool implements a number of services or operations. Each service or operation is also represented as a model. An operation may have input and output parameters, each being considered as a model. The interoperability platform may be organized as an intelligent model exchange system according to several principles and protocols such as the classical software bus or even more advanced architectures. To facilitate this exchange, the platform may use open standards such as XMI (XML model Interchange), CMI (CORBA Model Interchange), JMI (Java Model Interchange), etc.

Each time a given tool joins or leaves the platform, the associated megamodel is updated. There are also plenty of other events that may change the megamodel like the creation or suppression of a model or a metamodel, etc. Within one platform (local or global), the megamodel records all available resources. For each platform, we suppose there is an associated megamodel defining the metadata associated to this platform. For the sake of simplicity, we shall suppose that a local platform may be connected to another remote platform. This connection may be implemented by extension operations applied to the related megamodels.

5.1   Motivating Examples

To illustrate our purpose, we start by mentioning some situations, which one could find useful to get macroscopic information on models. By macroscopic, we mainly mean relations that consider models as wholes and not their elements. Of course this is a point-of-view related consideration since we are talking about elements of mega-models.

A well-known global example of global link is the conformance relation between a model and its metamodel. This is often considered as an implicit link, but we suggest that this could also be explicitly captured in a megamodel with many advantages. One interesting property of this global conformance relation between a model and its metamodel is that it may be viewed as summarizing a set of relations between model elements and metamodel elements (a relation we often name the "meta" relation). One can clearly see here the coexistence between global model level relations and local element based relations. In some cases, one is not interested in the local element level relations because the global relation provides sufficient reliable information on what is actually needed.

Another example is related to transformations. Recall that in our MDE landscape, a transformation is a model, conforming to a given metamodel. So, if a model Mb has been created from a model Ma by using transformation Mt, then we can keep this global information in the megamodel. Supposing the transformation model Mt has a link to its reverse transformation Mt^{-1}, the memorized information can be used for reverse engineering (from a modified model Mb) or for consistency checks. Being stored in a repository, a given transformation Mt will have no meaning if the three links are not provided to the source and target metamodels and the transformation metamodel itself.

There is a whole set of information that could be regarded as global metadata. For example, we could associate to a model the information of who has created it, when, why, what for, who has updated it and the history of updates, etc. To a metamodel we can associate its goal, the place where we can find its unique original definition, alternate definitions, its authors, its history, its previous and next versions, etc. A very naive implementation idea, for example, would be to imagine using a CVS for different versions of a metamodel. The notion of megamodel goes much beyond this kind of facilities, with a very low implementation cost and a much more regular organization.

The idea of model driven architecture has sometimes been presented with mega-models as described in [4] from where the diagram of **Fig. 3** is extracted. What is conveyed there is that a PSM is a model, in relation with a given PIM and with a given PDM (Platform Description Model). From a PIM, it should be possible to know which PSMs are available and to what platform they correspond. In simple cases, the

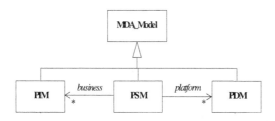

Fig. 3. Extended MDA classification

description of the process that produced the PSM from the PIM and the PDM could also be explicitly defined. Although somewhat idealized, these illustrations show how megamodels may be used beyond mere documentation of architectural and process approaches. The megamodel captures the idea of a "MDA component" as originally presented in [4], but allows going much beyond this proposal. In its present state it also allows to take into account solutions like the RAS OMG specification (Reusable Asset Specification).

5.2 Use Cases for the Megamodel Manager

Let us consider a use case with two MDE platforms installed in specific organizations, one in Nantes and one in Oslo, for example. Within each organization, there are different tools for capturing (Rational XDE, Poseidon, etc.) and storing/retrieving models and metamodels. Some tools may be common. Each platform has been initialized and whenever a tool is plugged or unplugged, the local megamodel is updated. Also, each tool has the possibility/responsibility to update the local megamodel upon achievement of specific operations. Examples of these operations may be:

- a user has created a model with a modeling tool such as Poseidon or Rational XDE,
- a user has created a metamodel in KM3 format with a textual editor,
- a user has modified a metamodel,
- a user has created a transformation in ATL,
- a user has created a new model by running an ATL transformation,
- etc.

Let us suppose a user in Oslo wishes to generate a list of contacts in a given database from a set of 5000 contacts contained in his/her local Microsoft Outlook system. The first action would be to look on the local Oslo platform if there is a metamodel for Microsoft Outlook available. If the metamodel is available in Oslo, the user will look for a corresponding injector able to act as a driver to transform Outlook into MDE formats. If these correspond exactly to his/her needs, then they will be used as is. Otherwise they will be adapted. After that, the user will do the same for the target database (metamodel and extractor). Finally the local platform will be queried for a suitable transformation. If none corresponds, one will be built or adapted with the help of suitable browsing/editing tools. In case of local unavailability, platforms that have links with the Oslo platform will be queried, for example the Nantes platform. The actions will be applied on this new platform. Alternatively, the user may consider his/her platform to virtually correspond to all components available on the Oslo or Nantes platform by a simple extension operation.

The problem of modeling in the large is related to several issues like typing [21], packaging, tool integration and interoperability, etc. Uniform access to local and remote resources may be facilitated by a megamodel-based approach as presented here. A resource may be a model, a metamodel, a transformation, a process, a service, a tool, etc. The first implementation of AMMA mainly deals with local platforms, but several extensions to distributed environments are already considered. One particular goal is to consider that professional modelers will exchange metamodels, transformations, etc.

like other exchange music or video. As a consequence, peer-to-peer architectures will be studied as an important alternative way to implement the MDE platform.

7 Conclusion

In this paper, we have presented the main tools that are being progressively integrated in the current AMMA prototype. Even if the development status of these tools is different, they share the common principle of models as first class entities and they have been designed to collaborate in a complementary way.

Our work on the design implementation and first use of the AMMA platform has led us to consider two kinds of activities in MDE: modeling in the large and modeling in the small. The corresponding operations have been illustrated by four tools at different levels of maturity: ATL, AMW, ATP and AM3. Model transformation has been recognized as an essential operation in MDE, but a lot of work yet remains to establish the exact application domain for QVT-like tools. Model weaving is presently in search of recognition, but when one considers how active this subject has been in the past in knowledge, data, and software engineering, it is very likely that applying model engineering principles to this field will bring important results in the future. As for megamodel management, it is probably the most recent question raised in the MDE field. Here again, there are a lot of examples of successful usages of this global approach in related domains and it is very likely that global registries will soon be considered essential for dealing with the management of an increasing number of global entities.

What we have tried to achieve with the AMMA platform is a balanced integration of these complementary aspects. The idea of considering models as first class entities has been the key principle to reach this goal. The AMMA experimental implementation of an MDE platform has allowed a first level of validation in the separation between the activities of modeling in the small and modeling in the large. There remains, however, a considerable amount of research effort yet to be done before these ideas translate into mainstream engineering platforms.

Acknowledgements

We would like to thank F. Allilaire, M. Didonet del Fabro, T. Idrissi, D. Lopes and G. Sunye for their contributions to the AMMA project.

References

[1] Allilaire, F., Idrissi, T. ADT: Eclipse Development Tools for ATL. EWMDA-2, September 2004, Kent, http://www.cs.kent.ac.uk/projects/kmf/mdaworkshop/

[2] Bernstein, P.A., Levy, A.Y., Pottinger, R. A.: A Vision for Management of Complex Systems. MSR-TR-2000-53, Microsoft Research, Redmond, USA ftp://ftp.research.microsoft.com/pub/tr/tr-2000-53.pdf

[3] Bézivin, J.: In search of a Basic Principle for Model Driven Engineering. Novatica/ Upgrade, Vol. V, N°2, April 2004, pp. 21-24, http://www.upgrade-cepis.org/issues/ 2004/2/up5-2Presentation.pdf

[4] Bézivin, J., Gérard, S., Muller, P.A., Rioux, L.: MDA Components: Challenges and Opportunities. Metamodelling for MDA, First International Workshop, York, UK, November 2003, http://www.cs.york.ac.uk/metamodel4mda/onlineProceedingsFinal.pdf

[5] Bézivin, J., Jouault, F., Valduriez, P.: On the Need for Megamodels. OOPSLA & GPCE, Workshop on best MDSD practices, Vancouver, Canada, 2004

[6] Booch, G., Brown, A.W., Iyengar, S., Rumbaugh, J., Selic, B.: An MDA Manifesto. Business Process Trends/MDA Journal, May 2004.

[7] Budinsky, F., Steinnberg, D., Merks, E., Ellersick, R., Grose, T.J.: Eclipse Modeling Framework, EMF, The Eclipse series, ISBN 0-13-142542-0, 2004

[8] Czarnecki, K., Eisenecker, U.: Generative Programming: Methods, Tools and Applications. Addison-Wesley, Reading, MA, USA, June 2000

[9] Deremer, F., Kron, H.: Programming in the Large versus Programming in the Small. IEEE Trans. On Software Eng. June 1976, http://portal.acm.org/citation. cfm?id=390016.808431

[10] Greenfield, J., Short, K., Cook, S., Kent, S.: Software Factories, Wiley, ISBN 0-471-20284-3, 2004

[11] Heuvel, W.J.: Matching and Adaptation: Core Techniques for MDA-(ADM)-driven Integration of new Business. Applications with Wrapped Legacy Systems. MELS, 2004

[12] Klint, P., Lämmel, R., Kort, J., Klusener, S., Verhoef, C., Verhoeven, E.J.: Engineering of Grammarware. http://www.cs.vu.nl/grammarware/

[13] Kurtev, I., Bézivin, J., Aksit, M.: Technical Spaces: An Initial Appraisal. CoopIS, DOA'2002 Federated Conferences, Industrial track, Irvine, 2002 http://www.sciences.univ-nantes.fr/lina/atl/publications/

[14] Lemesle, R.: Transformation Rules Based on Metamodeling. EDOC,'98, La Jolla, California, 3-5, pp.113-122, November 1998

[15] OMG/MOF: Meta Object Facility (MOF) Specification. OMG Document AD/97-08-14, September 1997. http://www.omg.org

[16] OMG/RFP/QVT: MOF 2.0 Query/Views/Transformations RFP. OMG document ad/2002-04-10. http://www.omg.org

[17] OMG/XMI: XML Model Interchange (XMI) OMG Document AD/98-10-05, October 1998. http://www.omg.org

[18] Pottinger, R.A., Bernstein, P.A.: Merging models Based on Given Correspondences, Proc. 29th VLDB Conference, Berlin, Germany, 2003

[19] Schmidt, D.: Model driven Middelware for Component-based Distributed Systems. Invited talk, EDOC'2004, Monterey, Ca., September 2004

[20] Soley, R.: OMG staff Model-Driven Architecture. OMG document. November 2000. http://www.omg.org

[21] Willink, E.D. OMELET: Exploiting Meta-Models as Type Systems. EWMDA-2, Canterbury, England, September 2004

[22] Wu, H., Gray, J., Roychoudhury, S., Melnik, M. Weaving a Debugging Aspect into Domain-Specific Language Grammars. ACM, 2004

Model-Driven Development of Reconfigurable Mechatronic Systems with MECHATRONIC UML*

Sven Burmester**, Holger Giese, and Matthias Tichy

Software Engineering Group, University of Paderborn,
Warburger Str. 100, D-33098 Paderborn, Germany
{burmi, hg, mtt}@upb.de

Abstract. Today, advanced technical systems are complex, reconfigurable mechatronic systems where most control and reconfiguration functionality is realized in software. A number of requirements have to be satisfied in order to apply the model-driven development approach and the UML for mechatronic systems: The UML design models must support the specification of the required hard real-time event processing. The real-time coordination in the UML models must embed the continuous control behavior in form of feedback-controllers to allow for the specification of discrete and continuous hybrid systems. Advanced solutions further require the dynamic exchange of feedback controllers at runtime (reconfiguration). Thus, a modeling of rather complex interplays between the information processing and the control is essential. Due to the safety-critical character of mechatronic systems, the resulting UML models of complex, distributed systems and their real-time behavior must be verifiable in spite of the complex structure and the embedded reconfigurable control elements. Finally, an automatic code synthesis has to map the specification correctly to code. In this paper, we will present our MECHATRONIC UML approach, which fulfills all these requirements. The approach is motivated and illustrated by means of a running example.

1 Introduction

An emerging field of software engineering research concerns complex, reconfigurable mechatronic systems. Mechatronic systems [1] combine technologies from mechanical and electrical engineering as well as from computer science. They are *real-time systems* because reactions to the environment usually have to be completed within a specific, predictable time and they are *hybrid systems* because they usually consist of discrete control modes as well as implementations of continuous feedback controllers. As incorrect software can lead to failures with fatal consequences, they are also *safety-critical* systems.

---

* This work was developed in the course of the Special Research Initiative 614 - Self-optimizing Concepts and Structures in Mechanical Engineering - University of Paderborn, and was published on its behalf and funded by the Deutsche Forschungsgemeinschaft.
** Supported by the International Graduate School of Dynamic Intelligent Systems. University of Paderborn.

U. Aßmann, M. Aksit, and A. Rensink (Eds.): MDAFA 2003/2004, LNCS 3599, pp. 47–61, 2005.

Mechatronic systems, which had been single, autonomous systems, have been used in distributed settings, which require extensive coordination, in recent times. Due to the new requirements stemming from distribution and coordination scenarios, a new generation of *reconfigurable* mechatronic systems has emerged. Those reconfigurable mechatronic systems change their behavior in order to comply with certain roles, which result from coordination and contracts with other mechatronic systems.

This reconfiguration leads to an increased complexity and thus makes it more difficult to fulfill safety-critical requirements. To guarantee safety for reconfigurable mechatronic systems, we extend in this paper the Model Driven Architecture (MDA) approach [2] for the design of hybrid mechatronic real-time systems with reconfiguration.

The today existing UML specification languages for technical systems [3,4,5,6,7,8] only provide solutions for either modeling, verification, or code generation, but fail to provide seamless support for all three requirements, which would be necessary for the model-driven development of reconfigurable mechatronic systems. Therefore, a specification language (model) is required, that contains at first sufficient information to specify the real-time behavior of the system in such a manner that high level modeling, verification, and semantically correct source code generation are possible. Methods for verification are required that guarantee the correctness of the whole distributed, hard real-time system. Reconfigurable mechatronic systems are typically too complex to directly verify the whole system using model checking. Instead, the model must enable the compositional model checking which considers just the component's external visible behavior to verify the real-time coordination. When specifying the details of the component's behavior within the model, it must be possible to guarantee that adding the details does not invalidate the component's external behavior taken into account during verification.

In this paper, we present the MECHATRONIC UML approach which allows the model-driven development of complex, distributed, safety-critical real-time systems which supports modeling, verification, and code generation by employing earlier inventions namely hybrid mechatronic components [9] and real-time coordination patterns [10]. Two different views need to be distinguished: the structural view and the behavioral view. The structural view describes the overall system that consists of multiple component instances, which are possibly distributed, interconnected with each other, and which are exchanging messages via communication. In the behavioral view, the behavior of single components is specified. As proposed in the MDA approach, structure and behavior are specified with platform independent models which are transformed to platform specific code, later. We apply UML diagrams [3] as platform independent models. UML state machines are extended by more expressive constructs for the description of real-time behavior [11,12]. Component diagrams are refined such that block diagrams [13], which are the most common description technique in the domain of feedback control engineering, can be smoothly integrated [9].

The required steps during the model-driven development with the MECHATRONIC UML approach can basically be divided into three phases which will be described in detail in Section 3 (see Figure 1). In the first two phases a correct platform independent model (PIM) is specified: In the first phase (steps 1-3), the system structure is defined which is used to identify where in the system communication is required. Each

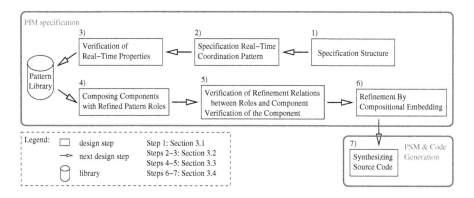

Fig. 1. Seamless support for the design of mechatronic systems

communication is described by an individual *real-time coordination pattern*. These co-ordination patterns have different roles, which contain the real-time logic for the coordination, and a real-time constraint, which is proven w.r.t. certain communication network properties. If such a coordination pattern has been designed and successfully verified, it is added to a pattern library for reuse.

In the second phase (steps 4-6), the mechatronic components are built using the pre-fabricated already verified coordination patterns, stored in the library of patterns. The real-time behavior of the component is a refinement of the combination of pattern roles and additional specified behavior. The employed refinement notion ensures the verified real-time properties. In addition, the component's internal coordination has to be verified to exclude inconsistent behavior or deadlocks. In the next step further components (e.g. hybrid ones) are embedded into the superordinated component. Simple consistency checks ensure again that the verified real-time properties of the coordination patterns are still valid in spite of the embedding. Thus, a complete verification of the system is not necessary, because the verification results of the individual patterns and components still hold for the complete system. In the last phase, the platform specific model (PSM) and finally platform specific source code is synthesized in step 7.

In the next section, we present the application scenario, which is used within this paper to exemplify the application of our approach. In Section 3, we present our approach w.r.t. system structure, real-time behavior, real-time coordination, and the integration of hybrid behavior. Our approach is then compared with the UML 2.0 specification [3] in Section 4 and other related work in Section 5. We finally conclude in Section 6 and present current and future work.

2   Application Example

As concrete example, we present the design of a self-optimizing version of the software for the RailCab research project[1] which aims at using a passive track system with self-optimizing shuttles that operate individually and make independent and decentralized operational decisions. The vision of the railcab project is to provide the comfort of

---

[1] http://www-nbp.upb.de/en

individual traffic concerning scheduling and on-demand availability of transportation as well as individually equipped cars on the one hand and the cost and resource effectiveness of public transport on the other hand. The modular railway system combines sophisticated undercarriages with the advantages of new actuation techniques as employed in the Transrapid[2] to increase passenger comfort while still enabling high speed transportation and (re-)use of the existing railway tracks.

One particular problem is to reduce the energy consumption due to air resistance by coordinating the autonomously operating shuttles in such a way that they build convoys whenever possible. Such convoys are built on-demand and require a small distance between the different shuttles such that a high reduction of energy consumption is achieved. Coordination between speed control units of the shuttles becomes a safety-critical aspect and results in a number of hard real-time constraints, which have to be addressed when building the control software of the shuttles.

When shuttles approach each other, they use wireless communication to coordinate the building of the convoy. Dependent on the position within the convoy they have to change their behavior. For example a rear shuttle will no longer hold the velocity on a constant level, but the distance to the front shuttle. Therefore, it dynamically has to exchange the feedback controller which controls its acceleration. Further, a shuttle will reduce the intensity of braking when another one drives in a short distance behind to avoid a rear-end collision. Consequently, the shuttle design must ensure on the one hand that the communication fulfills all safety requirements (e.g. safe coordination when building or breaking convoys, no deadlocks) and that the exchange of the dynamic controller (*reconfiguration*) guarantees safety and stability.

As a running example within this paper we consider a simplified version of the convoy building problem. Namely we assume that only convoys of two shuttles are built.

3   Model-Driven Development with MECHATRONIC UML

For the component-based development of mechatronic systems with UML, we extend the UML by notions for the specification of continuous and real-time behavior. The real-time extensions for the UML are specially geared towards verification of safety-critical properties. In the following, we will describe our approach in detail using the above mentioned example.

3.1   System Structure

UML component diagrams are used for the specification of the structure of our systems. Component diagrams specify components and their interaction in form of connectors. We distinguish component types and their instances during runtime. Connectors model the communication between different components via the ports and interfaces and the communication properties w.r.t. message loss, latency, etc. Ports are distinct interaction points between components and are typed by provided and required interfaces.

---

[2] http://www.transrapid.de/en

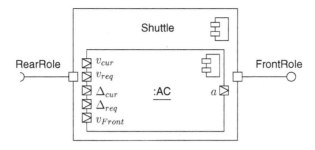

Fig. 2. Type specification of component Shuttle

For our example scenario, Figure 2 shows the component type for the shuttle. The Shuttle component contains a hybrid AccelerationControl (AC) component instance. This component computes the acceleration needed to achieve a specific goal (keeping a specified distance or keeping a specified speed level). The AccelerationControl component has five incoming continuous ports for the current velocity v_{cur}, the current distance Δ_{cur}, and the velocity of the front shuttle v_{Front} provided by sensors, and the required velocity v_{req} and the required distance Δ_{req} which are parameterized reference inputs. Further, AccelerationControl has one outgoing continuous port that sends the acceleration values to the appropriate hardware actuator devices. In addition (the details are presented in Section 3.4), the AC component contains discrete behavior to switch between keeping distance or keeping velocity on a constant level, and, thus, is a hybrid component. For clearer presentation, the sensors and actuators connected to the input ports and the output port of the AC component have been hidden.

3.2   Real-Time Coordination

Interaction between component instances during runtime is a major part in the design of complex, reconfigurable, mechatronic systems. In our scenario, a shuttle forms a convoy with another shuttle via the RearRole and FrontRole interfaces. In the domain of mechatronic systems, an autonomous unit like a shuttle reacts in a local environment and the interfaces to its environment are strictly defined (as e.g. a shuttle trying to build a convoy has to interact only with one other shuttle and not with a third one which is a few kilometers away). This domain-specific restriction is the reason why usually only relative simple coordination patterns have to be constructed, i.e. patterns with simple coordination protocols between roles, limited numbers of input signals and a fixed number of roles.

The interaction between two shuttles w.r.t. building a convoy is one such simple coordination pattern. Figure 3 shows the ConvoyCoordination pattern between two shuttles. The protocol for building and breaking convoys is specified in the roles of this pattern (see Figure 4). Components in the domain of mechatronic systems must meet real-time requirements. Therefore, we use our real-time variant of UML state machines called *Real-Time Statecharts* [11,12] for the specification of role behavior. They allow to apply constructs from timed automata [14,15] like clocks, time guards, time invariants and further annotations like worst case execution times and deadlines (see

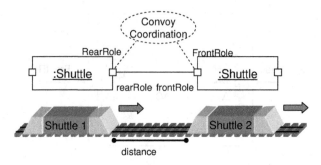

Fig. 3. Component Diagram and Patterns

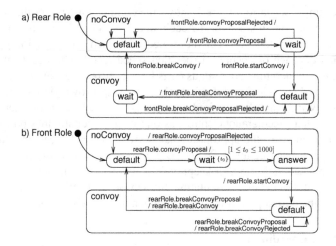

Fig. 4. Statechart of the **RearRole** role and the **FrontRole** role

Section 3.3). As shown in [11], these annotations enable an automatic implementation on a real physical machine with limited resources.

If an event has the form interface.message it means that the transition is triggered when message is received via the interface interface. Side-effects of the form interface.message describe the sending of message to a receiver which is connected via interface. Later, we will use events where no interface is specified. Then message is local and sent or received within the same statechart.

Initially, both roles are in state noConvoy::default, which means that they are not in a convoy. The rear role non-deterministically chooses whether to propose building a convoy or not. After having chosen to propose a convoy, a message is sent to the other shuttle resp. its front role. The front role chooses non-deterministically to reject or to accept the proposal after max. 1000 msec. In the first case, both statecharts revert to the noConvoy::default state. In the second case, both roles switch to the convoy::default state.

Eventually, the rear shuttle non-deterministically chooses to propose a break of the convoy and sends this proposal to the front shuttle. The front shuttle chooses non-deterministically to reject or accept that proposal. In the first case, both shuttles remain in convoy-mode. In the second case, the front shuttle replies by an approval message, and both roles switch into their respective noConvoy::default states.

For the connector which represents the wireless network we do not apply an explicit statechart, but instead specify its QoS characteristics such as throughput, maximal delay etc. in the form of connector attributes. In our example, we assume that the connector forwards incoming signals with a delay of 1 up to 5 msec. The connector is unsafe in the sense that it might fail at any time, such that we set our specific QoS characteristic reliable to false.

To provide safe behavior, the following RT-OCL [16] constraint must hold. It demands that a combination of role states where the front role is in state noConvoy and the rear role is in state convoy is not possible. This is required because such a situation would allow the front shuttle to brake with full intensity although another shuttle drives in short distance behind, which causes a rear-end collision.

```
context DistanceCoordination inv:
    not (self.oclInState(RearRole::Main::convoy) and
        self.oclInState(FrontRole::Main::noConvoy))
```

It is shown in [10], that this property holds. As mentioned there, those patterns are individually constructed and verified. In the next section, we show how components are developed without compromising the verification results by composing roles of different coordination patterns and refining their behavior. In our example, the Shuttle component is a combination of refined versions of the RearRole and the FrontRole. For a component, which combines different patterns respective the roles, the verified properties still hold due to the approach presented in [10]. Thus, components for mechatronic systems are developed in a way similar to a construction kit using several proven and verified building blocks and refine them to suit different requirements.

3.3 Local Real-Time Behavior

Figure 5 depicts the behavior of the Shuttle component from Figure 2, taken from [10] and extended with real-time annotations. The Real-Time Statechart consists of three orthogonal states FrontRole, RearRole, and Synchronization. FrontRole and RearRole are refinements of the role behaviors from Figure 4 and specify in detail the communication that is required to build and to break convoys. Synchronization coordinates the communication and is responsible for initiating and breaking convoys. The three sub-states of Synchronization represent whether the shuttle is in the convoy at the first position (convoyFront), at second position (convoyRear), or whether no convoy is built at all (noConvoy). The whole statechart is a refinement of both role descriptions as it just resolves the non-determinism from the roles from Figure 4 and does not add additional behavior.

As mentioned above, components in the domain of mechatronic systems must meet real-time requirements. In the specific example it needs not only to be specified that, e.g. RearRole has to send a startConvoy message after receiving convoyOK, but also that this has to be finished within a specific, predictable time. Therefore, we apply our *Real-Time Statecharts* [11] for specification. Real-Time Statecharts respect that the firing of transitions consumes time and that real physical, mechatronic systems can never react

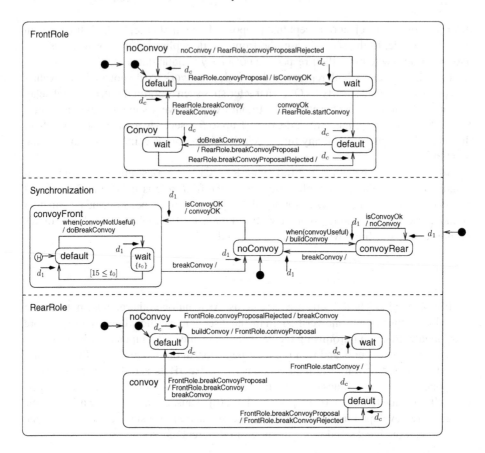

Fig. 5. Behavior of the Shuttle component

in *zero time*, but always with a delay. To represent this in the model, we make use of the deadline construct:

In Figure 5 so called *deadline intervals* d_c and d_1 are used to specify a minimum and a maximum duration for the time between triggering a transition and finishing its execution. E.g. sending the message convoyProposalRejected to RearRole has to be finished within the time specified by d_c after receiving the message noConvoy in state FrontRole::noConvoy::wait. As another example for predictable timing behavior (real-time behavior) the change in Synchronization from noConvoy to convoyFront has to be finished within d_1.

3.4 Controller Integration

The Acceleration Control (AC) component contained in the Shuttle component (cf. Figure 2) is a hybrid component. It consists of two discrete control modes which represent whether the shuttle is under velocity control or under distance control (see Figure 6). Further it has continuous in- and outputs. Dependent on the active discrete mode either the current and the required velocity are used for the velocity controller or the cur-

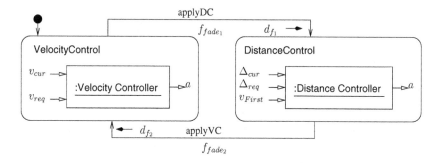

Fig. 6. Behavior of the AC component

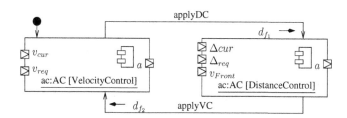

Fig. 7. Interface Statechart of the AC component

rent and required distance to the front shuttle as well as the velocity of the first shuttle are used for the distance controller. The output a is the acceleration in any mode.

In order to embed the continuous controllers into the discrete states, the Real-Time Statecharts are extended to hybrid ones. In Hybrid Statecharts each discrete state is associated with a configuration of embedded component instances [9]. In this example, each configuration consists of just one single feedback controller.

When a change occurs between the discrete states, a discrete switch between the controllers could lead to an unsteadiness in the output signal a. This unsteadiness will stimulate additional excitations which could lead to instability even when both controllers are stable on their own. In order to avoid these unsteadinesses, output cross-fading is applied [9]. This is specified by a *fading function* f_{fade_1} resp. f_{fade_2} and a minimal and a maximal *fading duration* (d_{f_1} resp. d_{f_2}) which is specified as an interval as well.

Although the hybrid AC component has five different continuous input signals, never all of them are required. When the component is in velocity control mode only v_{cur} and v_{req} are required, in distance control mode only Δ_{cur}, Δ_{req}, and v_{First} are required. These dynamic interfaces are visualized by the so called *Interface Statechart* in Figure 7.

The Interface Statechart abstracts from the component's internals as it just contains the externally relevant behavior: the different control modes, the modes' continuous in- and outputs, and the deadline information for switches between the control modes. Whether fading is required and which kind of fading function is applied and which components are associated to the discrete states is not important for the external view.

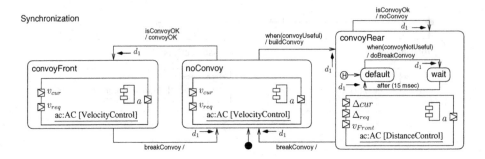

Fig. 8. Behavioral embedding

This interface representation is used when the different components are embedded into each other (see below).

The Shuttle and the AC component, which have been designed independent of each other, are embedded hierarchically from the structural point of view (cf. Figure 2). As their behavior is executed concurrently, we say AC is *hierarchically, parallel embedded* into Shuttle. As it makes no sense for AC to be in state DistanceControl while Synchronization is in state convoyFront, which represents the situation when there is no further shuttle before, the two behavior descriptions have to be coordinated.

Therefore, the Shuttle statechart from Figure 5 is extended to a Hybrid Statechart. Figure 8 depicts the orthogonal Synchronization state, whose sub-states embed different configurations each consisting of one AC instance *and its current internal state and continuous interface.* So in Figure 8 is specified that AC has to be in state DistanceControl when Synchronization is in state convoyRear. If Synchronization is in state noConvoy or convoyFront, AC has to be in state VelocityControl. Consequently, a state change within the orthogonal Synchronization state implies a state change in its embedded AC component. As only the external visible information of the AC component is important when it is embedded, the form of the embedded component is equal to the single states of the Interface Statechart from Figure 7.

This kind of modeling has the advantage that it supports the decomposition into multiple components that is required to handle the complexity in mechatronic systems. Further the control engineering know-how is separated from the software engineering know-how: The discrete coordination and communication is specified by the statechart from Figure 5, the continuous behavior and the restrictions of the controller exchange is specified in Figure 6 and the later integration is specified in Figure 8. Another advantage is the support for flexible continuous interfaces.

In order to ensure that the results of the compositional verification are not invalidated by the detailed realization of the Shuttle component, the component realization has to be a refinement of the role behavior (see Section 3.2). The statechart from Figure 5 is a refinement of the roles from Figure 4. Consequently, it needs to be ensured that the embedding of AC still just refines the specified real-time behavior from Figure 5 and is not adding additional behavior or is in conflict with the real-time specification of this superordinated component.

Assume, for example, in Figures 5 and 8 is specified that a change from state no-Convoy to convoyRear has to be finished after 200 msec and that this change implies a change of the embedded AC component from VelocityControl to DistanceControl. Then in Figure 7 the minimal fading duration may not be above 200 msec.

This example demonstrates how consistency is approved by simple syntactical checks between the superordinated component and the Interface Statecharts of the embedded components: In the above example $d_{f_1} \subseteq d_c$ must be satisfied. Such checks have to be enforced for every possible change of the global state (the current global state consists of the current states of all components). Due to the hierarchically, parallel embedding, the global state space is restricted: Although Synchronization consists of 3 states and AC of 2 states, the hierarchical parallel composition does not consist of $2 * 3 = 6$ states, but just of 3 states.[3] This information is contained in the specification in Figure 8 and does not need to be derived by a costly reachability analysis. Consequently, the number of consistency checks to be enforced are thus not exponential in the number of states. If these consistency checks are successful, the results of the compositional model checking presented in Section 3.2 are valid even for components that embed further components in the hierarchical, parallel manner (cf. [9]).

4   MECHATRONIC UML and Standard UML

The UML 2.0 [3] can be considered as the currently evolving *de facto* standard for modeling complex software systems. Event though the standard UML 2.0 is not specifically tailored for technical systems, it is frequently applied also in this domain (cf. [17,4,18,19]) and actually includes most of the concepts of the Real-Time Object-Oriented Modeling (ROOM) approach [20]. However, as the ROOM concepts focus on architectural design and do not address the real-time or hybrid behavior of the operational model at all, UML supports real-time aspects only rudimentarily and hybrid behavior not at all. In the presented MECHATRONIC UML approach, the architectural design must employ standard UML components and patterns in a well-defined rigorous manner. The real-time communication protocols of each port or pattern role have to be specified. While UML 2.0 offers so called *Protocol State Machines* (PSM) to do so, we require that our real-time extension of the UML state machines named *Real-Time Statecharts* are employed.

A relevant UML extension w.r.t. real-time is the *UML Profile for Schedulability, Performance, and Time* [4]. The profile defines general resource and time models which are used to describe the real-time specific attributes of the modeling elements such as schedulability parameters or quality of service (QoS) characteristics. Besides an abstract *logic model*, a more concrete *engineering model* can be specified by using these extensions. The engineering model is later used for the required model analysis and code generation. However, appropriate concepts for the real-time modeling at the logic model level are missing and real-time aspects are only present at the level of the engineering model. Thus, the developer has to map his logical model onto the technical concepts such as threads and periods manually. Then, he has to test and adjust the logical model as well as its mapping to the engineering model manually until the engineering model mets all real-time constraints.

---

[3] This is because the state combinations (convoyFront, DistanceControl), (noConvoy, DistanceControl), and (convoyRear, VelocityControl) are not reachable.

The presented approach in contrast addresses real-time aspects at the logical model level. The employed Real-Time Statecharts support deadlines, worst case execution times, clocks, clock resets, time guards, and time invariants. Therefore they provide powerful abstract means to specify complex timing requirements. A formally defined semantics for them further enables the compositional verification by means of model checking. MECHATRONIC UML thus really enables the model-driven development of real-time systems as all required timing requirements are contained in the (logical) model and the synthesis of the mapping to threads and their periods can be done automatically.

A request for proposals for *UML for System Engineering (UML for SE)* [21] by the OMG currently address UML in the context of technical systems. The idea of UML for SE is to provide a language that supports the system engineer in modeling and analyzing software, hardware, logical and physical subsystems, data, personnel, procedures, and facilities. The presented approach addresses some of these issues, but mainly focuses on the specific requirements of hybrid, reconfigurable, mechatronic systems.

One distinguishing proposal for UML for SE is the *Systems Modelling Language (SysML)*,[4] which extends a subset of the UML 2.0 specification. One extension, related to the design of continuous and hybrid systems are *Structured Classes*, that describe the fine structure of a class extended by continuous communication links between ports. In *Parametric Diagrams* the *parametric* (arithmetic) *relations* between numerical attributes of instances are specified and the nodes of Activity Diagrams are extended with continuous functions and in- and outputs. This enables to model simple difference equations, but using this approach to model complex feedback-controllers leads to an overwhelming complexity. The specification or the integration of continuous behavior in form of continuous components is not supported. Further SysML does not support reconfiguration, as the specification of parametric relations is always static.

In contrast to UML 2.0 and the SysML proposal, our approach provides the required support for modeling of hybrid, reconfigurable systems by first refining UML ports into discrete, continuous, and hybrid ones such that hybrid components can be modeled with UML components. To specify the reconfiguration and hybrid behavior of these components, we extended Real-Time Statecharts towards Hybrid Statecharts which employ UML instance diagrams of the subordinated components to specify the state-dependent embedding and coordination. The formal definition of the embedding for Hybrid Statecharts enables to check efficiently whether an embedding is consistent. A consistent embedding further ensures, that the real-time properties, verified through compositional model checking, still hold for the more detailed hybrid system behavior.

5   Related Work

Besides UML and its profiles, a number of proprietary approaches for the modeling of technical systems with UML exist.

Within the IST project AIT-WOODDES *hierarchical timed automata* (HTA) [5] have been invented to enable the modeling and verification of complex real-time behavior. HTA are a hierarchial extension of timed automata [15] and they provide most

---

[4] http://www.sysml.org

of the powerful modeling concepts of statecharts as well as clocks. A mapping to multiple parallel running flat timed automata permits to verify the model by using the model checker UPPAAL [14]. Code synthesis has also been addressed in [22], however, the approach is restricted to flat automata and does not take into account the delays that occur when transitions are fired. Our approach for code generation respects hierarchy, parallelism, and the real-time specifications [11,23].

The aim of the IST OMEGA project [6] is to ensure the correctness of embedded systems. In the approach, the UML has been extended by additional time constructs and a formally defined semantics is intended. However, unlike our approach, there is no support for hybrid behavior and compositional verification. Verification is only supported for the semi-automatic verification via theorem proving.

Like the presented approach, HyROOM [7] and the underlying HyCharts [8] support the component-based modeling of hybrid systems. The software's architecture is specified similar to ROOM/UML-RT and the behavior is specified by statecharts whose states are associated with systems of ordinary differential equations and differential constraints or Matlab/Simulink block diagrams. These approaches provide means for the reconfiguration of systems in terms of changing the continuous behavior. But it is only possible to reconfigure the model inside a component on one hierarchy-level. In contrast to that, our approach allows for a complex reconfiguration altering the structure and concerning more than one hierarchy-level. Support for compositional verification of models is not addressed by any of these approaches.

6   Conclusion and Future Work

Reconfigurable mechatronic systems in the domain of safety-critical distributed systems must be designed with great care. MECHATRONIC UML not only supports the model-driven development of such systems respecting real-time requirements, but also allows for a mixture of discrete event-based as well as continuous behavior. In addition, the applied modeling approach contains means for the compositional verification of safety-critical properties. Finally, source code is synthesized from the models, which respects the real-time constraints and safety requirements of the model.

MECHATRONIC UML further refines the industry standard UML where possible and provides a well defined UML subset as well as a guideline how to develop safety-critical reconfigurable mechatronic systems.

Tool support (in form of a number of plug-ins for the Fujaba Tool Suite[5]) for the specification, verification and automatic source code synthesis of the Real-Time Statecharts and the real-time coordination patterns exists. For the support of hybrid behavior a prototypic implementation exists and we are currently working on the tool support.

In the future, we plan to employ graph transformations [24] to describe the reconfiguration of the behavior w.r.t. the online addition or removal of coordination pattern roles. By this reconfiguration, the hybrid components reconfigure themselves to different coordination scenarios to optimize their memory and processing power footprints. These reconfigurations specified by graph transformations are also targets for the verification of safety-critical properties.

---

[5] http://www.fujaba.de

We further plan to integrate MECHATRONIC UML with our approaches for automatic deployment [25] and dependability [26] with UML.

Acknowledgements. The authors thank Oliver Oberschelp for the support in the control engineering domain.

References

1. Bradley, D., Seward, D., Dawson, D., Burge, S.: Mechatronics. Stanley Thornes (2000)
2. Object Management Group: Model Driven Architecture (MDA) Edited by Joaquin Miller and Jishnu Mukerji. (2001)
3. Object Management Group: UML 2.0 Superstructure Specification. (2003) Document ptc/03-08-02.
4. OMG: UML Profile for Schedulability, Performance, and Time Specification. OMG Document ptc/02-03-02 (2002)
5. David, A., Möller, M., Yi, W.: Formal Verification of UML Statecharts with Real-Time Extensions. In Kutsche, R.D., Weber, H., eds.: 5th International Conference on Fundamental Approaches to Software Engineering (FASE 2002), April 2002, Grenoble, France. Volume 2306 of LNCS., Springer (2002) 218–232
6. Graf, S., Hooman, J.: Correct Development of Embedded Systems. In Oquendo, F., Warboys, B., Morrision, R., eds.: Proceedings of the First European Workshop on Software Architecture, EWSA2004. Volume 3047 of Lecture Notes in Computer Science., St Andrews, UK, Springer Verlag (2004) 241–249
7. Stauner, T., Pretschner, A., Péter, I.: Approaching a Discrete-Continuous UML: Tool Support and Formalization. In: Proc. UML'2001 workshop on Practical UML-Based Rigorous Development Methods – Countering or Integrating the eXtremists, Toronto, Canada (2001) 242–257
8. Stauner, T.: Systematic Development of Hybrid Systems. PhD thesis, Technische Universität München (2001)
9. Giese, H., Burmester, S., Schäfer, W., Oberschelp, O.: Modular Design and Verification of Component-Based Mechatronic Systems with Online-Reconfiguration. In: Proc. of 12th ACM SIGSOFT Foundations of Software Engineering 2004 (FSE 2004), Newport Beach, USA, ACM (2004)
10. Giese, H., Tichy, M., Burmester, S., Schäfer, W., Flake, S.: Towards the Compositional Verification of Real-Time UML Designs. In: Proc. of the European Software Engineering Conference (ESEC), Helsinki, Finland. (2003)
11. Giese, H., Burmester, S.: Real-Time Statechart Semantics. Technical Report tr-ri-03-239, University of Paderborn, Paderborn, Germany (2003)
12. Burmester, S., Giese, H.: The Fujaba Real-Time Statechart PlugIn. In: Proc. of the Fujaba Days 2003, Kassel, Germany. (2003)
13. Ogata, K.: Modern Control Engineering. Prentice Hall (2002)
14. Larsen, K., Pettersson, P., Yi, W.: UPPAAL in a Nutshell. Springer International Journal of Software Tools for Technology 1 (1997)
15. Henzinger, T.A., Nicollin, X., Sifakis, J., Yovine, S.: Symbolic Model Checking for Real-Time Systems. In: Proc. of IEEE Symposium on Logic in Computer Science. (1992)
16. Flake, S., Mueller, W.: An OCL Extension for Real-Time Constraints. In: Object Modeling with the OCL: The Rationale behind the Object Constraint Language. Volume 2263 of LNCS. Springer (2002) 150–171

17. Bichler, L., Radermacher, A., Schürr, A.: Evaluation uml extensions for modeling realtime systems. In: Proc. on the 2002 IEEE Workshop on Object-oriented Realtime-dependable Systems WORDS'02, San Diego, USA, IEEE Computer Society Press (2002) 271–278
18. Gu, Z., Kodase, S., Wang, S., Shin, K.G.: A Model-Based Approach to System-Level Dependency and Real-Time Analysis of Embedded Software. In: The 9th IEEE Real-Time and Embedded Technology and Applications Symposium, Toronto, Canada. (2003)
19. Masse, J., Kim, S., Hong, S.: Tool Set Implementation for Scenario-based Multithreading of UML-RT Models and Experimental Validation. In: The 9th IEEE Real-Time and Embedded Technology and Applications Symposium, Toronto, Canada. (2003)
20. Selic, B., Gullekson, G., Ward, P.: Real-Time Object-Oriented Modeling. John Wiley and Sons, Inc. (1994)
21. Object Management Group: UML for System Engineering Request for Proposal. (2003) Document ad/03-03-41.
22. Amnell, T., David, A., Fersman, E., Pettersson, M.O.M.P., Yi, W.: Tools for Real-Time UML: Formal Verification and Code Synthesis. In: Workshop on Specification, Implementation and Validation of Object-oriented Embedded Systems (SIVOES'2001). (2001)
23. Burmester, S., Giese, H., Gambuzza, A., Oberschelp, O.: Partitioning and Modular Code Synthesis for Reconfigurable Mechatronic Software Components. In: Proc. of European Simulation and Modelling Conference (ESMc'2004), Paris, France. (2004) (accepted).
24. Rozenberg, G., ed.: Handbook of Graph Grammars and Computing by Graph Transformation. Volume 1. World Scientific, Singapore (1999)
25. Tichy, M., Schilling, D., Giese, H.: Design of Self-Managing Dependable Systems with UML and Fault Tolerance Patterns. In: Proc. of the Workshop on Self-Managed Systems (WOSS) 2004, FSE 2004 Workshop, Newport Beach, USA. (2004)
26. Tichy, M., Giese, H.: A Self-Optimizing Run-Time Architecture for Configurable Dependability of Services. In de Lemos, R., Gacek, C., Romanovsky, A., eds.: Architecting Dependable Systems II. Volume 3069 of Lecture Notes in Computer Science. Springer Verlag (2004) 25–51

Model Transformation Language MOLA

Audris Kalnins, Janis Barzdins, and Edgars Celms

University of Latvia, IMCS, 29 Raina boulevard, Riga, Latvia
{Audris.Kalnins, Janis.Barzdins, Edgars.Celms}@mii.lu.lv

Abstract. The paper describes a new graphical model transformation language MOLA. The basic idea of MOLA is to merge traditional structured programming as a control structure with pattern-based transformation rules. The key language element is a graphical loop concept. The main goal of MOLA is to describe model transformations in a natural and easy readable way.

1 Introduction

The Model Driven Architecture (MDA) initiative treats models as proper artifacts during software development process and model-to-model transformations as a proper part of this process. Therefore there is a growing need for model transformation languages and tools that would be highly acceptable by users. Though model transformations would be built by a relatively small community of advanced users, the prerequisite for broad acceptance of transformations by system developers is their easy readability and customizability.

Model transformation languages to a great degree are a new type of languages when compared to design and programming languages. The only sound assumption here is that all models in the MDA process (either UML-based models or other) should be based on metamodels conforming to MOF 2.0 standards.

The need for standardization in the area of model transformation languages led to the MOF 2.0 Query/Views/Transformations (QVT) request for Proposals (RFP)[1] from OMG.

To a great degree the success of the MDA initiative and of QVT in particular will depend on the availability of a concrete syntax for model-to-model transformations that is able to express non-trivial transformations in a clear and compact format that would be useful for industrial production of business software [2].

QVT submissions by several consortiums have been made [3, 4, 5], but all of them are far from a final version of a model transformation language. Currently the proposal most likely to be accepted seems [3] – actually a merge of several initial proposals. Several serious proposals for transformation languages have been provided outside the OMG activities. The most interesting and complete of them seem to be UMLX [6] and GReAT [7]. Some interesting transformation language proposals use only textual syntax, e.g., [15].

According to our view, and many others [2], model transformations should be defined graphically, but should combine the graphical form with text where appropriate. Graphical forms of transformations have the advantage of being able to represent

U. Aßmann, M. Aksit, and A. Rensink (Eds.): MDAFA 2003/2004, LNCS 3599, pp. 62 – 76, 2005.

mappings between patterns in source and target models in a direct way. This is the motivation behind visual languages such as UMLX, GReAT and the others proposed in the QVT submissions. Unfortunately, the currently proposed visual notations make it quite difficult to understand a transformation.

The common setting for all transformation languages is such that the model to be transformed (**source model**) is supplied as a set of class and association instances conforming to the **source metamodel**. The result of transformation is the **target model** - the set of instances conforming to the **target metamodel**. Therefore the transformation has to operate on instance sets specified by a class diagram (actually, the subset of class notation, which is supported by MOF).

Approaches that use graphical notation of model transformations draw on the theoretical work on graph transformations. Hence it follows that most of these transformation languages define transformations as sets of related rules. Each rule has a pattern and action part, where the pattern has to been found (matched) in the existing instance set and the actions specify the modifications related to the matched subset of instances. This schema is used in all of the abovementioned graphical transformation languages. Languages really differ in the strength of pattern definition mechanisms and control structures governing the execution order of rules [8].

It should be mentioned that an early pioneer in the area (well before the MDA era) is the PROGRES language [9]. This semi-graphical language offered pattern-based graph rewrite rules applicable to "models" described by schemas (actually, metamodels). The execution of rules is governed by the traditional structured control constructs – sequence, branch and loop, though in the form of Dijkstra's guarded commands.

The current MDA-related graphical transformation languages – UMLX and GReAT use relatively sophisticated pattern definition mechanisms with cardinality specifications (slightly more elaborated in GReAT). The control structure in UMLX is completely based on recursive invocations of rules. The control structure of GReAT is based on hierarchical dataflow-like diagrams, where the only missing control structure is an explicit notation for loops (loops are hidden in patterns). The proposal [3] also offers elaborated patterns, which are combined with a good support for recursive control structures. Since the PROGRES project is now inactive, there currently is no transformation language based on traditional control structures.

This paper proposes a new transformation language **MOLA** (**MOdel transformation LAnguage**). The prime goal of MOLA is to provide an easy readable graphical transformation language by combining traditional structured programming in a graphical form (a sort of "structured flowcharts") with rules based on relatively simple patterns. This goal is achieved by introducing a natural graphical loop concept, augmented by an explicit loop variable. The loop elements can easily be combined with rule patterns. Other structured control elements are introduced in a similar way. In the result, most of typical model transformation algorithms, which are inherently more iterative than recursive, can be specified in a natural way. The paper demonstrates this on the traditional MDA class-to-database transformation example and on the statechart flattening example – an especially convincing one. Some extensions of MOLA are also sketched.

2 Basic Constructs of MOLA

This section presents a brief overview of basic constructs of MOLA. The MOLA language is a procedural graphical language, with control structures taken from traditional structured programming. The elements specific to model transformations can easily be combined with traditional language elements such as assignment statements. A **program** in MOLA is sequence of graphical statements, linked by dashed arrows:

A **statement** can be an assignment or a rule – an elementary instance transformation statement, however the most used statement type in MOLA is a loop. There are two types of **loops**, which will be depicted in the following way:

(the first type) or   (the second type).

A loop body always contains one or more sequences of graphical statements. Each body sequence starts with a **loop head** statement declaring the **loop variable** for this sequence. In MOLA the loop variable represents an instance of the given class. In order to distinguish it from other class instances defining its context, the loop variable is shown with a **bold** frame: c:Class   . The loop head statement, besides the loop variable, typically contains also instance selection conditions, which constrain the environment of a valid loop variable instance. The UML object (instance specification) notation is used both for the loop variable and its environment description – it expresses the fact that any valid instance from the instance set of the given class in the source model must be used as a loop variable value during the loop execution.

The semantics of both types of loops differ in the following way. A type one loop is executed once for each valid instance from the instance set – but the instance set itself may be modified (extended) during the loop execution. The type two loop continues execution while there is at least one valid variable instance in the instance set (consequently, the same loop variable instance may be processed several times). In an analogy to some existing set and list processing languages, it is natural to call type one loops **FOREACH** loops and type two loops - **WHILE** loops in MOLA.

Another important statement type is the **rule** – the specification of an elementary instance transformation. A rule contains the pattern specification – a set of elements representing class instances and association instances (links), built in accordance with the metamodel. In addition, the rule contains the action specification – what new class instances are to be built, what associations (links) drawn, what instances are to be deleted, what attributes are to be assigned value etc. Its semantics is obvious – locate a pattern instance in the source model and perform the specified actions. When a rule has to be applied – it is determined by the loop whose body contains the rule. A rule can be combined with the loop head – a loop head can also contain actions, which are performed for each valid loop variable instance.

All MOLA statements, except loops, are graphically enclosed in grey rounded rectangles: ⬭ .

Further, more precise definitions of MOLA syntax and semantics will be given on toy examples.

Let us assume that a toy metamodel visible in Fig.1 is used.

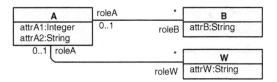

Fig. 1. Metamodel for the toy example

Then a MOLA program, which sets the attribute *attrA1* to 1 for those instances of the class *A* that are linked to at least one instance of class *B*, is shown in Fig. 2. The loop (FOREACH type) contains two statements – the loop head and a trivial rule which sets the value of attribute *attrA1* in the loop variable. First, some comments on the loop head statement. The selection condition consisting of an instance of *B* linked by the only available association (*roleB*) to the loop variable (*a:A*) requires that at least one such instance of *B* must exist for a given instance of A to be a valid loop variable instance. We want to emphasize that an **association** with no constraints attached in the loop head (or in a rule pattern) always means – there **exists at least one instance** (link) of such an association. The loop head in MOLA is also a kind of pattern.

The second statement in the loop **references** the same instance of *A* – the loop variable, this is shown by prefixing the instance name by the @ character.

The second program example (in Fig.3) finds how many instances of *B* are linked to each instance of *A*.

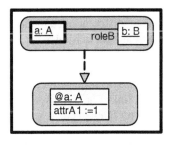

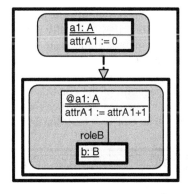

Fig. 2. Program finding *A*'s linked to a *B*   **Fig. 3.** Program counting *B*'s linked to an *A*

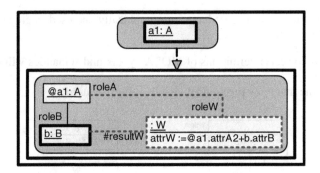

Fig. 4. Program building *W* for each *B*

This example demonstrates a natural use of nested loops. The outer loop (with the loop variable *a:A*) is executed for every instance of *A*. The loop head sets also the initial value of the attribute *attrA1*. The nested loop, which is executed for those instances of *B* which are linked to the current *A*, performs the counting.

The next more complicated task is to build an instance of *W* for each *B* which is linked to an *A*, link it by an association (*roleW*) to the *A* and assign to its string parameter (*attrW*) the concatenation of string parameters in the corresponding instances of *A* and *B*. Fig. 4 shows the corresponding MOLA program.

The same nested loops as in the previous example are used. But here the inner loop head is also a rule with more complicated action – building an instance of *W*, linking it to the current loop variable instance of the outer loop and setting the required value of *attrW*.

The new elements – instances and links are shown with **dotted** lines (and in red color) in MOLA. The expression for *attrW* references the attribute values from other instances – they are qualified by the corresponding instance names. The association linking the instance of *W* to the instance of *B* is a special one – it is the so called **mapping association** (which actually should also be specified in the metamodel). Mapping associations are typically used in MDA-related transformations for setting the context of next subordinate transformations and for tracing instances between models (therefore they normally link elements from different metamodels). Role names of mapping associations are prefixed by the # character in MOLA.

Two more MOLA constructs should be explained here. The first one is the **NOT** constraint on associations in patterns – both in loop heads and ordinary rules. It expresses the negation of the condition specified by the association – there must be no instance with specified properties linked by the given link. Fig. 5 shows an example where an instance of *W* is built for those *A* which have no *B* attached.

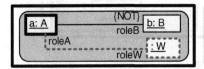

Fig. 5. NOT constraint

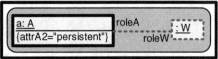

Fig. 6. Attribute constraint

Another one is attribute constraints. Fig. 6 shows an example where an instance of *W* is built for those *A* where the attribute *attrA2* has the specified value. The Boolean expression in braces in general uses OCL syntax (in addition, it may contain also explicit qualified references to other instances in the pattern).

There are some more elements of MOLA which are not used in the examples of this paper and therefore will not be explained in detail. Besides the attributes in the source metamodel, instances may have "temporary" computed attributes which can be used as variables for storing values during the computation. These temporary attributes are also defined in the metamodel. Similarly, there may be temporary associations. There is also one more control structure – an equivalent of the **if-then-else** (or case) statement. There is also a **subprogram** concept in MOLA and the subprogram **call** statement, where the parameters can be references to instances used in the calling program (typically, to loop variables) or simple values. The called subprogram has access to the source model and can add or modify elements in the target model.

3 UML Class Model to Relational Model Example in MOLA

Further description of MOLA will be given on the basis of the "standard benchmark example" for model transformation languages – the UML class model to relational database model transformation example. This example has been used for most of model transformation language proposals (see e.g., [3, 4, 6, 10]). However, no two papers use exactly the same specification of the example. Here we have chosen the version used by A. Kleppe and J. Warmer in their MDA book [10].

The source is a simplified class diagram built according to the metamodel in Fig. 7 (it is a small subset of the actual UML metamodel). Any class which is present in the source model has to be transformed into a database table. Any class attribute has to be converted into a table column. Attribute types are assumed to be simple data types – the problem of "flattening" the class-typed attributes is not considered in this version. We assume here that type names in class diagram and SQL coincide (in reality it is not exactly so!).

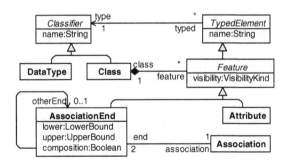

Fig. 7. Simplified class metamodel

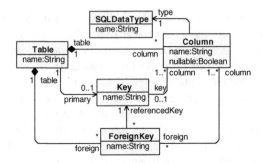

Fig. 8. Simplified relational database metamodel

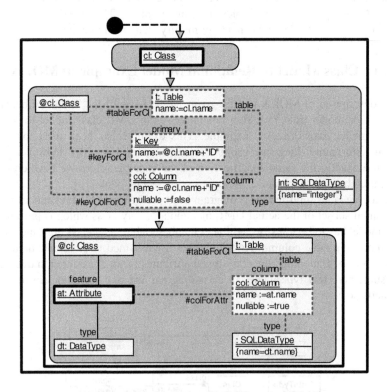

Fig. 9. Class to database transformation (part 1)

Each converted table has an "artificial" primary key column with the type *integer*. The treatment of associations is quite realistic. One-one or one-to-many associations result into a foreign key and a column for it in the appropriate table (for one-one – at both ends). A many-to-many association is converted into a special table consisting only of foreign key columns (and having no primary key). Each foreign key references the corresponding primary key.

We should remind that according to UML semantics, in the metamodel the *type* association from an *Association End* leads the *Class* at that end, but *class* association – to *Class* at the opposite end.

The resulting database description must correspond to a simplified SQL metamodel given in Fig. 8.

The metamodels and transformation specification are exactly as in [10] except that some inconsistencies and elements unused in the given task are removed.

More formally, in MOLA the source and target metamodels (Fig. 7 and 8) are combined into one common metamodel, where mapping associations can also be

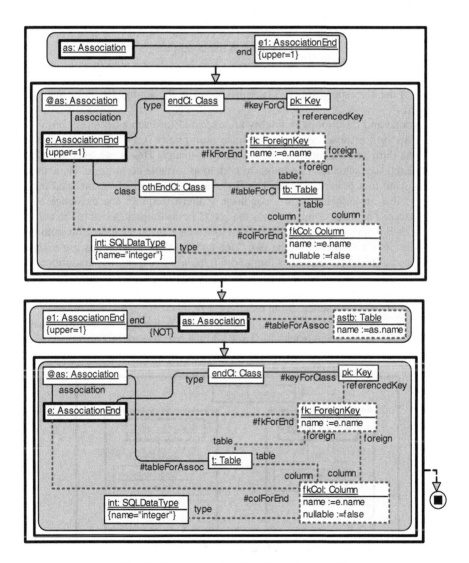

Fig. 10. Class to database transformation (part 2)

specified. We do not present this combined metamodel here, role names of mapping associations can be deduced from MOLA diagrams (Fig. 9 and 10).

Fig. 9 and 10 show the complete transformation program in MOLA. The part 1 (Fig. 9) implements the required class-to-table transformations, but the part 2 – the transformation of associations into foreign keys and appropriate columns.

A complete program in MOLA starts with the UML start symbol and ends with end symbol. In between there are statements connected by arrows; in the given program – three top-level loops (one for class instances and two for associations). All loops are of FOREACH type.

Now some more detailed comments for this program. The first loop is executed once for each class in the source set and during each loop execution the corresponding database elements – the table, the primary key and the column for it are built. The mapping association #tableForCl is used in the condition for the inner loop – to ensure that the correct *Table* instance is taken. This loop is executed once for each attribute and builds a column for each one. Here it is assumed that SQL data types (as instances of the corresponding class) are pre-built and the appropriate one can always be selected.

The second and third loops in totality are executed for each association instance – the second loop for those instances that have multiplicity 0..1 or 1..1 at least at one end and the third one for those which are many-to-many. This is achieved by adding mutually exclusive selection conditions to both loop variable definitions. These conditions are given in a graphical form. The first one uses the already mentioned in section 2 fact that an association in a condition (pattern) requires the existence of the given instance. The other condition uses the {NOT} constraint attached to the association – no such instance can exist. Then both loops have an inner loop - for both ends (even in the first case there may be two "one-ends"). Both inner loops use mapping associations built by previous rules (#keyForCl, #tableForCl) in their conditions. The type for "foreign columns" is *integer* – as well as that for "primary columns".

An alternative form of control structure for processing associations could be one loop with an if-then-else statement in the body (Fig. 11).

One more alternative representation could be to make the Fig. 10 a transformation of its own (e.g., *TransformAssociations*) and add the call statement *TransformAssocia*

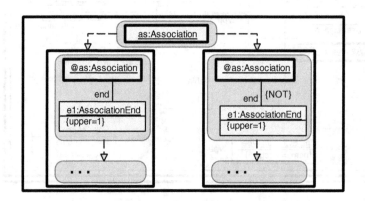

Fig. 11. Loop with an if-then-else statement

tions (this time without parameters) to the bottom of Fig. 9. In our case there is no great need in this since the whole transformation example actually fits in one A4 page. However, the subprogram mechanism in MOLA permits to define arbitrarily complicated transformations by well-proven methods of structural programming.

4 Statechart Flattening Example

This section presents another example – the flattening of a UML statechart. This example was first used in [7] to demonstrate the GReAT transformation language. Due to space limits, we use a version where the statechart can contain only composite states with one region (OR-states in terms of [7]). Composite states may contain any type of states, with an arbitrary nesting level. Such a statechart must be transformed into an equivalent "flat" statechart (which contains only simple states). The informal flattening algorithm is well known (most probably, formulated by D. Harel [11]). A version of this example with much simplified problem statement is present also in [3].

The simplified metamodel of the "full" (hierarchical) statechart is depicted in Fig. 12. There are some constraints to the metamodel specifying what is a valid statechart. There are "normal" transitions for which the event name is nonempty and "special" ones with empty event. These empty transitions have a special role for state structuring. Each composite state must contain exactly one initial state (an instance of *Init*) and may have several final states. There must be exactly one empty transition from the initial state of a composite state (leading to the "default" internal state). The same way, there must be exactly one empty transition from the composite state itself - the default exit. This exit is used when a contained final state is reached. Otherwise, transitions may freely cross composite state boundaries and all other transitions must be named. Named transitions from a composite state have a special meaning (the "interrupting" events), they actually mean an equally named transition from any contained "normal" state – not initial or final. This is the most used semantics of composite states (there are also some variations).

All states have names – but those for initial and final states actually are not used. Names are unique only within a composite state (it acts as a namespace) and at the top level.

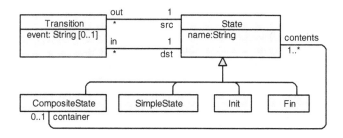

Fig. 12. Metamodel of hierarchical statechart

The traditional flattening algorithm is formulated in a recursive way. Take a topmost composite state (i.e., one not contained in another composite state). There are three ways how transitions related to this state must be modified:

1. Transitions entering the composite state itself must be redirected to the state to which the empty transition from its initial state leads.
2. Transitions leading to a final state of this composite state must be redirected to the state to which the empty transition from the composite state leads.
3. Named transitions from the composite state must be converted into a set of equally named transitions from all its "normal" states (with the same destination)

Then the name of the composite state must be prefixed to all its contained normal states and the composite state must be removed (together with its initial and final states and involved empty transitions). All this must be repeated until only simple states (and top level initial/final ones) remain.

A simple analysis of this algorithm shows that the redirection of transitions may be done independently of the composite state removal – you can apply the three redirection rules until all transitions start/end at simple states (or top initial/final). The set of simple states is not modified during the process – only their names are modified.

Namely this modified algorithm is implemented in the MOLA program in Fig. 13. It contains two top-level loops – the first one performs the transition redirection and the second – the removal of composite states.

Both top-level loops are WHILE-type – especially, in the first loop a transition may be processed several times until its source and destination states reach their final position. A closer analysis shows that the second loop actually could be of FOREACH type, but the original algorithm suggests WHILE.

The program performs a model update – source and target metamodels coincide, simply, some metaclasses cannot have instances in the target model. Mapping associations are not used in this example.

The first loop contains three loop head statements – all specify the instance *t:Transition* as a loop variable, but with different selection conditions. According to the semantics of MOLA, any *Transition* instance satisfying one of the conditions (one at a time!) is taken and the corresponding rule is applied (note that the conditions are not mutually exclusive). All this is performed until none of the conditions applies – then all transitions have their final positions. The first two rules contain a dashed line – the association (link) removal symbol. The link is used in the selection condition, but then removed by the rule. The third path through the loop contains the instance removal symbol.

Namely the use of **several lop heads per loop** is a strength of MOLA – this way inherently recursive algorithms can be implemented by loops.

The second loop – the removal of composite states also has a recursive nature to a certain degree – it implements the so-called **transitive closure** with respect to finding the deepest constituents (simple states) and computing their names accordingly to the path of descent.

It shows that transitive closure can be implemented in MOLA in a natural way (even the FOREACH loop could be used for this). The other constructs in this loop are "traditional" – except, may be, the fact that several instances may be deleted by a rule in MOLA.

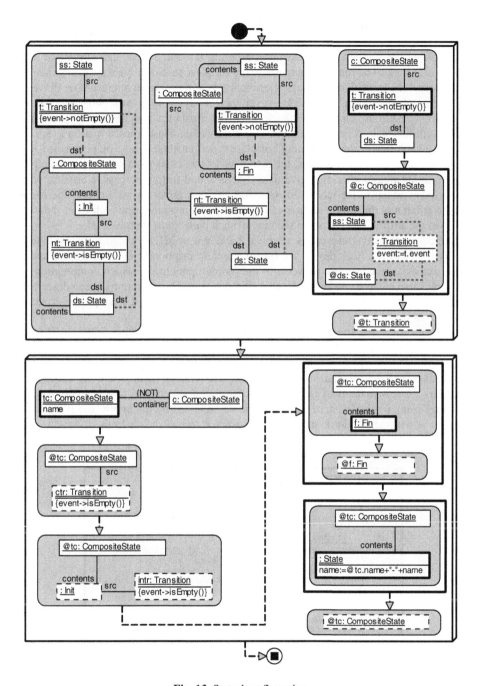

Fig. 13. Statechart flattening

5   Extended Patterns in MOLA

The rule in the previous example for computing the name of a state contained in a composite state to be removed actually is the simplest case of a typical transformation paradigm – the transitive closure. Experiments show that transitive closure in all cases can be implemented in MOLA. However, not always it is so straightforward as in Fig. 13, sometimes temporary associations and attributes and nested loops are required for this task. A typical example is the class to database transformation as specified in [3, 6], where the "flattening" of class-typed attributes must be performed – if the type of an attribute is a class, the attributes of this class must be processed and so on. If an attribute with a primitive data type is found in this process, a column with this type is added to the table corresponding to the original ("root") class. The name of the column is the concatenation of all attribute names along the path from the root class to the attribute. It is easy to see that all such paths must be traversed.

Since the transitive closure is a typical paradigm in MDA-related tasks, an extension of MOLA has been developed for a natural description of this and similar tasks. This extension uses a more powerful – the looping pattern, by which computation of any transitive closure can be implemented in one rule. This feature has been described in details in [12], here we present only the above-mentioned example with some comments.

Fig.14 shows one statement in extended MOLA which is both a FOREACH loop over *Class* instances and a rule with an extended pattern. In contrast to patterns in basic MOLA, this pattern matches to unlimited number of instances in the source model. Most of the associations in this pattern are directed (using the UML navigability mark). The semantics of this pattern is best to be understood in a procedural way. Starting from a valid instance of loop variable (selected by the undirected part of the pattern – one association), a temporary instance tree is being built, following the directed associations.

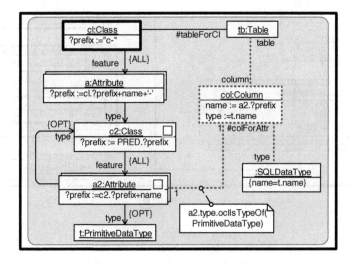

Fig. 14. Transitive closure by extended pattern

Associations in this pattern use two new qualifiers – **ALL** and **OPT**. The first one says the instance tree has to contain all possible valid links of this kind (a fan-out occurs), but the second one – that the link is not mandatory for the source instance to be included in the tree (an association without qualifier is mandatory in MOLA). The white square icons in *c2* and *a2* specify that for these pattern elements instance copies are built in the tree (but not the original source model instances used) – it is easy to see that in order to obtain all paths from the root class to primitively-typed attributes namely such copying is required. Another new pattern syntax element is the UML multiobject notation for some elements – to emphasize that a fan-out occurs at these places during the pattern match. The looping part of the pattern – the elements *c2* and *a2* actually are traversed as many times during the matching (tree building) process as there are valid candidates in the source model. The rule uses the temporary attribute *?prefix* (with the type *String*), whose scope is only this rule. The values of this attribute are computed during the building of the match tree (for each of its node) – it is easy to see that the expressions follow the building process (the special PRED qualifier means any predecessor). For this extended pattern the building action also generates many instances of *Column* – one for each instance of *a2* in the tree (it is a copy!) which satisfies the building condition in OCL.

Extended patterns have more applications, however their strength most clearly appears on complicated transitive closures like the one in Fig. 14.

6 Conclusions

MOLA has been tested on most of MDA-related examples – besides the ones in the paper, the class to Enterprise Java transformation from [10], the complete UML statechart flattening, business process to BPEL transformation and others. In all cases, a natural representation of the informal algorithms has been achieved, using mainly the MOLA loop feature. This provides convincing arguments for a practical functional completeness of the language for various model to model transformations in MDA area. Though it depends on readers' mindset, the "structured flowchart" style in MOLA seems to be more readable and also frequently more compact than the pure recursive style used e.g., in [6]. Though recursive calls are supported in MOLA, this is not the intended style in this language. For some more complicated transformation steps the extended MOLA patterns briefly sketched in section 5 fit in well.

The implementation of MOLA in a model transformation tool also seems not to be difficult. The patterns in basic MOLA are quite simple and don't require sophisticated matching algorithms. Due to the structured procedural style the implementation is expected to be quite efficient. All this makes MOLA a good candidate for practically usable model transformation language.

Initial experiments with MOLA have been performed by means of the modeling tool GRADE [13, 14], in the development of which authors have participated. A separate MOLA tool is currently in development. A graphical editor for MOLA has already been developed, the pictures for this paper have been obtained by this editor. A MOLA execution system is also close to completion.

References

1. OMG: Request For Proposal: MOF 2.0/QVT. OMG Document ad/2002-04-10, http://www.omg.org/cgi-bin/doc?ad/2002-04-10
2. Bettin J. Ideas for a Concrete Visual Syntax for Model-to-Model Transformations. Proceedings of the 18th International Conference, OOPSLA'2003, Workshop on Generative Techniques in the context of Model Driven Architecture, Anaheim, California, USA, October 2003.
3. QVT-Merge Group. MOF 2.0 Query/Views/Transformations RFP, Revised submission, version 1.0. OMG Document ad/2004-04-01, http://www.omg.org/cgi-bin/doc?ad/2004-04-01
4. Compuware, SUN. MOF 2.0 Query/Views/Transformations RFP, Revised Submission. OMG Document ad/2003-08-07, http://www.omg.org/cgi-bin/doc?ad/2003-08-07
5. Interactive Objects Software GmbH, Project Technology, Inc. MOF 2.0 Query/Views/Transformations RFP, Revised Submission. OMG Document ad/2003-08-11, http://www.omg.org/cgi-bin/doc?ad/2003-08-11
6. Willink E.D. A concrete UML-based graphical transformation syntax - The UML to RDBMS example in UMLX. Workshop on Metamodelling for MDA, University of York, England, 24-25 November 2003.
7. Agrawal A., Karsai G, Shi F. Graph Transformations on Domain-Specific Models. Technical report, Institute for Software Integrated Systems, Vanderbilt University, ISIS-03-403, November 2003.
8. Czarnecki K., Helsen S. Classification of Model Transformation Approaches. Proceedings of the 18th International Conference, OOPSLA'2003, Workshop on Generative Techniques in the context of Model Driven Architecture, Anaheim, California, USA, October 2003.
9. Bardohl R., Minas M., Schürr A., Taentzer G.: Application of Graph Transformation to Visual Languages. G. Rozenberg (ed.): Handbook on Graph Grammars: Applications, Vol. 2, Singapore, World Scientific, 1998.
10. Kleppe A., Warmer J., Bast W. MDA Explained. The model driven architecture: practice and promise. Addison-Wesley, 2003.
11. Harel D. Statecharts: a Visual Formalism for Complex Systems. Sci. Comput. Program. Vol 8, pp. 231-274, 1987.
12. Kalnins A., Barzdins J., Celms E. Model Transformation Language MOLA: Extended Patterns. To be published in proceedings of Baltic DB&IS 2004, Riga, Latvia, June 2004.
13. Kalnins A., Barzdins J., et al. Business Modeling Language GRAPES-BM and Related CASE Tools. Proceedings of Baltic DB&IS'96, Institute of Cybernetics, Tallinn, 1996.
14. GRADE tools. http://www.gradetools.com
15. Bézivin J., Dupé G., Jouault F., et al. First experiments with the ATL model transformation language: Transforming XSLT into XQuery. 2nd OOPSLA Workshop on Generative Techniques in Context of MDA, Anaheim, California, 2003.

A Graphical Notation to Specify Model Queries for MDA Transformations on UML Models

Dominik Stein, Stefan Hanenberg, and Rainer Unland

University of Duisburg-Essen, Essen, Germany
{dstein, shanenbe, unlandR}@cs.uni-essen.de

Abstract. Specifying queries on models is a prerequisite to model transformations in the MDA because queries select the model elements that are the source of transformations. Current responses to OMG's MOF 2.0 QVT RFP mostly propose to use (and/or extend) OCL 2.0 as specification language for queries. In this paper, we demonstrate that using textual notations (like OCL) quickly leads to complex query statements even for simple queries. In order to overcome this handicap, we present a graphical notation based on the UML that facilitates comprehension of query statements as well as estimation of the (ultimately) selected model elements. We advocate that queries should be specified in terms of user model entities and user model properties (rather than meta model entities and meta model properties) for the sake of feasibility and comprehensibility to the user.

1 Introduction

Model-Driven Architecture (MDA) [16] aims to assist the development process of software intensive systems by providing a standardized framework for the specification of software artifacts and integration directives. Its key idea is to install traceable relationships between software artifacts of different domains or different development phases. In that way, the MDA aims to improve software quality since software developers can directly relate the final program code to design decisions and/or requirement specifications of the early phases of software development. It allows them to validate and test the final code for compliance to particular requirements, thus making maintenance much simpler. Further, the MDA promotes reuse of existing system solutions in new application domains by means of conceptual mappings and artifact integration.

The principal software artifact of consideration in the MDA are machine-readable models. The underlying technique of the MDA is model transformation. Transformations are accomplished according to the tracing and mapping relationships established between the software artifacts (i.e., between their models).

Striving for a standardized language to define such model transformations, the OMG released the "MOF 2.0 Query / Views / Transformation (QVT)" Request For Proposal (RFP) in April 2002 [17]. It has been one of the mandatory requirements to come up with a query language to select and filter elements from models, which then can be used as sources for transformations. In response to the RFP, several proposals for general-purpose model transformation languages have been submitted (e.g., [1],

U. Aßmann, M. Aksit, and A. Rensink (Eds.): MDAFA 2003/2004, LNCS 3599, pp. 77–92, 2005.

[5], [9], and [20]). Most of them propose to use (and/or extend) the Object Constraint Language (OCL) 2.0 [18] as query language (e.g., [9] [20] [1]). Having said so, only one proposition [20] provides a graphical representation for its query language.

We think, though, that a graphical notation to specify and visualize model queries is inevitable for the MDA to drive for success. We think that software developers require a graphical representation of their selection queries, which they can use to communicate their ideas to colleagues, or to document design decisions for maintainers and administrators. A graphical visualization would facilitate their comprehension on where a transformation actually modifies their models. We think that using a textual notation (like OCL), instead, would quickly turn out to lead to very complex expressions even when defining a relatively small number of selection criteria.

In this paper we present a graphical notation to specify selection queries on models specified in the Unified Modeling Language (UML) [19], aiming to overcome the lack of most of the RFP responses when working in a UML model context. We introduce several abstraction means in order to express various selection criteria, and specify how such selection criteria are evaluated by OCL expressions. Query models built from such abstraction means are called "Join Point Designation Diagrams" [26] (or "JPDD" in short). JPDDs originate in our work on Aspect-Oriented Software Development (AOSD) [7] in general, and on the visualization of aspect-oriented concepts in particular. They are concerned with the selection of points in software artifacts that are target to modifications (so-called "join points" in AOSD). They extend the UML with selection semantics. And they make use of, and partially extend, UML's conventional modeling means.

This paper is an immediate follow-up paper of our submission [24] to the "MDA Foundation and Application" workshop [3]. We carefully revised that submission taking into account the comments and remarks that we received at the workshop. Meanwhile, JPDDs have also been presented in [26]. While there we have identified the general need to specify queries on software artifacts as a new evolving design issue, here we concentrate on the integration of JPDDs into the MDA context. In particular, we describe a generic mechanism to map JPDDs onto OCL statements, thus giving way to the integration of our approach with the current QVT submissions.

The remainder of this paper is structured as follows: In the first section we emphasize the need of a graphical notation to specify selection queries with the help of an example. After that, we briefly sketch the background that JPDDs originate from, and point to the parallels of query specification in AOSD and MDA. In section 4, we briefly describe the abstract syntax of our notation. We then present the graphical means as well as the OCL expressions by which they are evaluated. We conclude the paper with relation to other work and a summary.

2 Motivation

In order to make the motivation of this work more clear, we take a look at a hypothetical, yet easy-to-understand example (adopted from [20]): Imagine, for some arbitrary model transformation, we need a model query that selects all classes with name "cn" that either have an attribute named "an", or – in case not – that have an association to some other class with name "cn1" which in turn has an attribute named "an". Fig. 1, right part, demonstrates how such query would be expressed using the textual and graphical notation as proposed in [20]. Fig. 1, left part, shows the same query, once expressed as an OCL statement, and once expressed as a JPDD.

As you can learn from the example, even a simple model query quickly results in a complex query expression – when using a textual notation (cf. Fig. 1, top part). As a result, comprehension of the query and estimation what model elements finally will be selected is rather difficult. The graphical notation shown in Fig. 1, bottom right part, helps to keep track of what is going on in the selection query. However, since the query is specified in terms of meta model entities and meta model properties, unnecessary and distracting noise is added to the diagram: A simple association between classes "c" and "c1" is represented by three distinct entities.

Fig. 1, bottom left part, shows what the query looks like using a JPDD. JPDDs represent model queries in terms of user model entities and user model properties. Using user model entities and user model properties for query specification (rather than meta model entities and meta model properties) is to the advantage of feasibility and comprehensibility: Software developers work with abstraction means they are familiar with. They do not need to bother about meta models. Further, query models turn out to be concise and comprehensible: They specify a minimal pattern to which all ultimately selected model elements must comply.

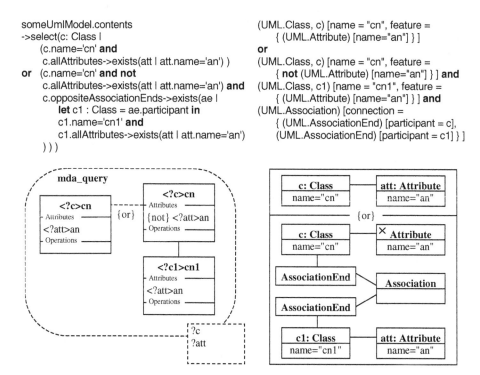

```
someUmlModel.contents
->select(c: Class |
    (c.name='cn' and
    c.allAttributes->exists(att | att.name='an') )
or  (c.name='cn' and not
    c.allAttributes->exists(att | att.name='an') and
    c.oppositeAssociationEnds->exists(ae |
        let c1 : Class = ae.participant in
        c1.name='cn1' and
        c1.allAttributes->exists(att | att.name='an')
    ) ) ) )
```

```
(UML.Class, c) [name = "cn", feature =
    { (UML.Attribute) [name="an"] } ]
or
(UML.Class, c) [name = "cn", feature =
    { not (UML.Attribute) [name="an"] } ] and
(UML.Class, c1) [name = "cn1", feature =
    { (UML.Attribute) [name="an"] } ] and
(UML.Association) [connection =
    { (UML.AssociationEnd) [participant = c],
    (UML.AssociationEnd) [participant = c1] } ]
```

Fig. 1. Selection query expressed in OCL (*top left part*), using the textual and graphical notation presented in [20] (*right part*), and with help of a JPDD (*bottom left part*)

3 Background

JPDDs originate in our work on AOSD. AOSD deals with the encapsulation of *crosscutting concerns* into separate modular units, called *aspects*. A crosscutting concern is a concern that cannot be cleanly decomposed to the primary decomposition of a program, thus leading to crosscutting code that is scattered throughout every module of the dominant decomposition. This is what became known as the *Tyranny of the Dominant Decomposition* [28]. An aspect encapsulates the crosscutting code of a crosscutting concern. Besides specifying the crosscutting code that should be injected into the primary decomposition, an aspect also specifies the conditions under which the injection shall take place.

In order to do so, aspect-oriented programming techniques rely on the concepts of *join points* and *weaving*. Join points designate *loci* (in program code) or *instants* (in program execution) at which injection takes place. Weaving defines the exact *manner* in which injection takes place. Since crosscutting usually takes place at more than one join point (in fact, this is the major case that AOSD is focused on), aspect-oriented programming techniques provide various ways to specify selections of join points. For example, join point selection is possible based on lexical similarities of join point properties [14] [15] (e.g., of their name or type declarations), based on the structural arrangement the join points reside in [8] (such as the presence of particular parameters in an operation's parameter list, or the existence of a navigable path to a particular class), or based on the dynamic context join points occur in [15] (e.g., in the scope of a particular object, or in the control flow of a particular method).

We see strong parallels between AOSD and MDA with respect to the selection of locations in software artifacts that are focus of modification. We estimate (e.g., from the examples given in [20]) that selection in MDA also depends on lexical similarities of model element properties – in particular, of their names. Further, structural arrangements, such as the existence of certain features or relationships, are deemed to play a major role in model element selection, as well. Structural constraints may also involve general statements on navigable paths, i.e., indirect associations or indirect generalizations between classifiers.

In the following, we explain the graphical elements that we provide to specify model element selections based on lexical similarities and structural arrangements with JPDDs. We briefly sketch their general syntax, and detail their semantic implications using OCL expressions.

4 Notation and Semantics

A JPDD consists of at least one selection criterion, some of which delineate selection parameters. A JPDD represents a selection criterion itself and thus may be contained in another JPDD (e.g., for reuse of criteria specifications). JPDDs can be fully integrated into the UML, making use of UML's modeling means and its meta model: Structurally, JPDDs compare to UML templates of UML namespaces (cf. Fig. 2). Note, though, that semantically JPDDs differ from conventional UML templates since they render a "selection pattern" rather than a "generation pattern". This means in particular that the parameters of JPDDs represent logical variables (which *return*

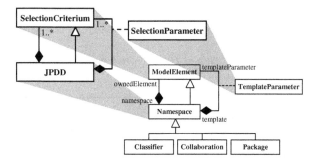

Fig. 2. Abstract syntax of JPDDs (*top part*) mapped to UML's meta model (*bottom part*) (cf.26)

values), while the parameters of a conventional UML template are *fed* with values. To emphasize this difference in meaning visually, parameters of JPDDs are summarized at the lower right corner of JPDDs – rather than at their upper right corner as with conventional UML templates (see Fig. 4 in section 5 for an example).

In the following we present the core modeling means that may be used to specify selection queries with help of JPDDs. We explain their graphical notation, and describe how they can be evaluated using OCL meta operations[1]. Such meta operations are appended to UML's meta model classes (e.g., to classifiers, attributes, operations, associations, messages, etc.). Note that not all meta operations are shown due to space limitations. At last, we sketch how the meta operations are deployed in order to retrieve an actual set of matching model elements.

4.1 Classifier Selection

Looking at the selection semantics for classifiers, we may learn about the general selection mechanism for all model elements: Principally, model elements are selected based on the values of their *meta attributes*. In case of classifiers, these are the properties "isAbstract", "isLeaf", and "isRoot" (see Table 1, block II).

Besides that, model elements are selected based on their *meta relationships* to composite model elements. In case of classifiers, for example, special regards must be given to the features they must possess in order to be selected (see Table 1, block III).

At last, note that name matching of model elements is accomplished with help of name patterns (see Table 1, block I). Name patterns may contain wildcards, e.g. "*", in order to select groups of model elements based on lexical similarities. All element names in a JPDD represent name patterns by default. In case an element needs to be referenced within the JPDD (e.g., if it needs to be defined as a JPDD parameter), the element may be given an identifier[2]. In diagrams, identifiers are enclosed into angle brackets and are prepended by a question mark (see "<?C>Con*" in Table 1 for example, or "<?c>cn", "<?c1>cn1", and "<?att>an" in Fig. 1 of section 2). They are placed in front of the element they refer to.

---

[1] We used *OCL Checker*, version 0.3 (http://www.klasse.nl/ocl/ocl-checker.html), to write the OCL statements, and *OCLE*, version 2.02 (http://lci.cs.ubbcluj.ro/ocle), to typecheck them.
[2] In that case, the name pattern is stored (technically) in a special tagged value.

Having explained these general selection principles, we concentrate on discussing the particularities of other modeling means in the following.

Table 1. OCL meta operation for matching classifiers (*left part*), and a sample class pattern that could be passed as an argument (*right part*)

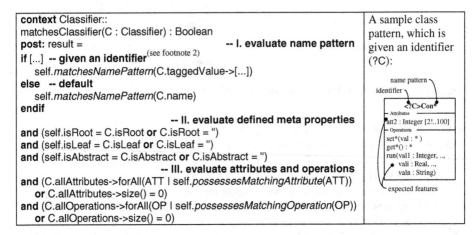

4.2 **Operation Selection**

Special regards in operation selection must be given to the usage of wildcard ".." in the operation's signature pattern. Wildcard ".." provides for the selection of operations based on their structural arrangement – that is, based on the existence of particular parameters, while others are disregarded.

Table 2 gives a detailed description on how such structural arrangements are evaluated by means of an OCL expression: Meta operation "matchesParameterList" compares (a) the *overall order* of parameters in the actual operation("self")'s parameter list to the one being passed from the JPDD (Table 2, block I), as well as (b) the *partial order* of parameters at the parameter lists' beginnings (Table 2, block II) and their ends (Table 2, block III). For that purpose, the meta operation defines a couple of sub-expressions: "ownPars" comprises all parameters of the actual operation ("self"); "patternPars" holds the parameters being passed from the JPDD, neglecting all wildcarded parameters ".."; and "matchingPars" is a subset of "ownPars", containing only those parameters that have a matching counterpart in "patternPars".

The sub-expressions are used to compare the overall order of parameter lists with help of meta operation "matchesParameterOrder" (not shown here). That operation recursively iterates over "matchingPars" and "patternPars", verifying if (subsequences of) the former contains all the elements belonging to (subsequences of) the latter. The partial order is evaluated based on "ownPars" and the parameter list being passed from the JPDD. Order evaluation stops (i.e., is always true) when the first wildcarded parameter ".." is reached in the parameter list passed from the JPDD (see collect statement at end of block II and III).

Table 2. OCL meta operation for matching parameter lists (*left part*), and a sample signature pattern whose parameter list could be passed as an argument (*right part*)

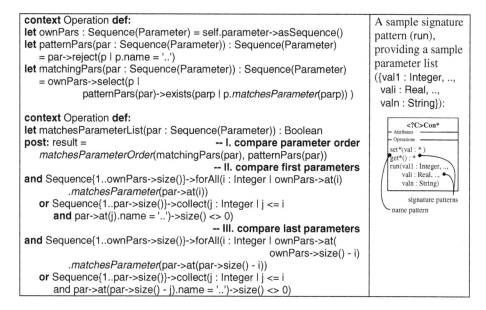

Table 3. Sample relationship patterns for (indirect) relationships, which could be passed to a meta operation as an argument (meta operations are omitted here; see [26] for further details)

4.3 Relationship Selection

When selecting relationships, special regards must be given to indirect relationships. Indirect relationships are a sophisticated means to constrain structural arrangements: Indirect relationships may be used in JPDDs to indicate that a classifier does not need to be directly connected to a particular parent, child, or associated classifier. This means in case of associations, that the particular classifier must be reachable via the designated association, but does not need to be a direct neighbor.

In diagrams, indirect relationships are rendered by a double-crossed line[3]. Table 3 (left part) states, for example, that there must be a navigable path from class "C" to

---

[3] Technically, indirect relationships are rendered by a special stereotype for associations or generalizations, respectively. Query evaluation is based on the (non-)presence of that stereotype (cf. [26]).

Table 4. OCL meta operation for matching association ends (*left part*), and a sample association end pattern that could be passed as an argument (*right part*)

context AssociationEnd::
matchesAssociationEnd(ae : AssociationEnd) : Boolean
post: result = [...]
and ((**if** [...] **-- exact limit**   **-- evaluate multiplicity**
    self.multiplicity.range.lower   = ae.multiplicity.range.lower
    else   **-- minimum bound**
    self.multiplicity.range.lower >= ae.multiplicity.range.lower
    endif
and   if [...] **-- exact limit**
    self.multiplicity.range.upper   = ae.multiplicity.range.upper
    else   **-- maximum bound**
    self.multiplicity.range.upper <= ae.multiplicity.range.upper
    endif)
or ae.multiplicity = '')
	A sample association pattern (A), comprising a sample association end pattern (aRole):

class "B" for the selection criterion to be fulfilled. The ends of that path must match with the association ends of the indirect association. In case of indirect generalizations, the particular parent or child needs to reside somewhere in the inheritance tree, but does not need to be a direct parent or child. For example, class "C" in Table 3 (right part) must be among the ancestors of class "B", and class "B" must be among the descendants of class "C", for the selection criterion to be satisfied. The respective OCL meta operations are omitted here due to space limitations. Please refer to [26] for a detailed description.

4.4 Multiplicity Restrictions

Special attention in association end selection must be paid to the association end's multiplicity specification[4]: Multiplicity of an association end may declare exact upper and/or lower limits; or it may designate the upper and/or lower bounds which the multiplicity of an association end must not exceed or underrun (respectively). Being able to declare exact limits and/or minimal and maximal bounds provides for further flexibility in query specification based on structural arrangements.

Graphically, exact multiplicity bounds are indicated by exclamation marks[5]. The lower multiplicity limit of association end "aRole" in Table 4, for example, denotes a strict limit. Accordingly, association ends are only selected, if their lower multiplicity limit equates "2". The upper multiplicity limit of "aRole", on the contrary, denotes a maximum. Association ends are selected as long as their upper multiplicity limit does not exceed "100".

4.5 Message Selection

Selection is not restrained to structural aspects of a UML model as they are specified in UML class diagrams, for example. Selection criteria may as well involve behave-

---

[4] The same counts for the multiplicity specification of attributes (see sample classifier pattern in Table 1 for an example).

[5] Technically, fix upper and lower limits are specified as stereotypes of multiplicity ranges.

Table 5. OCL meta operation for matching (indirect) messages (*left part*), and a sample message pattern that could be used as an argument (*right part*)

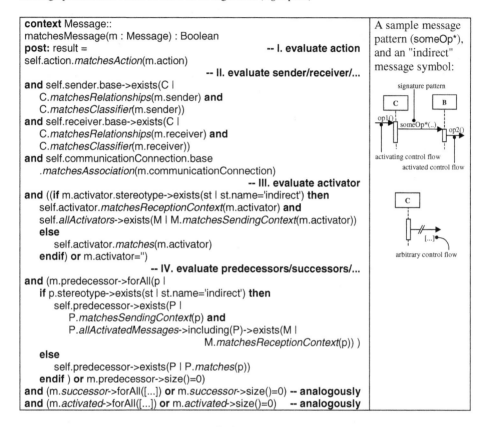

| context Message:: <br> matchesMessage(m : Message) : Boolean
 post: result =   **-- I. evaluate action**
 self.action.*matchesAction*(m.action)
      -- II. evaluate sender/receiver/...
 and self.sender.base->exists(C \|
     C.*matchesRelationships*(m.sender) **and**
     C.*matchesClassifier*(m.sender))
 and self.receiver.base->exists(C \|
     C.*matchesRelationships*(m.receiver) **and**
     C.*matchesClassifier*(m.receiver))
 and self.communicationConnection.base
     .*matchesAssociation*(m.communicationConnection)
      -- III. evaluate activator
 and ((**if** m.activator.stereotype->exists(st \| st.name='indirect') **then**
     self.activator.*matchesReceptionContext*(m.activator) **and**
     self.*allActivators*->exists(M \| M.*matchesSendingContext*(m.activator))
     else
       self.activator.*matches*(m.activator)
     endif) **or** m.activator='')
      -- IV. evaluate predecessors/successors/...
 and (m.predecessor->forAll(p \|
    if p.stereotype->exists(st \| st.name='indirect') **then**
      self.predecessor->exists(P \|
       P.*matchesSendingContext*(p) **and**
       P.*allActivatedMessages*->including(P)->exists(M \|
                M.*matchesReceptionContext*(p)))
    else
      self.predecessor->exists(P \| P.*matches*(p))
    endif) **or** m.predecessor->size()=0)
 and (m.*successor*->forAll([...]) **or** m.*successor*->size()=0) **-- analogously**
 and (m.*activated*->forAll([...]) **or** m.*activated*->size()=0)   **-- analogously** | A sample message pattern (someOp*), and an "indirect" message symbol: |

ioral requirements as they are specified in UML interaction and collaboration diagrams. Table 5 shows the notational means to specify selection criteria on messages, and how such criteria are evaluated by an OCL operation.

Messages are selected based on the action they invoke (Table 5, block I). In case of operation call actions, signature patterns may be used to restrict the operation called. Further, messages are selected based on their senders and receivers (Table 5, block II). It is important to note that the OCL operation evaluates the senders' and receivers' base classifiers rather than their role specifications. This is accomplished deeming that selections should consider the full specification of classifiers rather than restricted projections thereof. The same counts for the associations used for transmitting the messages.

Lastly, messages may be selected based on their activator message, their predecessor and successor messages, as well as based on the messages they are activating themselves (Table 5, block III and IV). This is particularly useful to constrain the (preceding) control flow in which selected messages may occur, as well as the (succeeding) control flow that selected messages may invoke. Message "someOp" in Table 5, for example, must be activated in the control flow of message "op1", and must in turn invoke message "op2".

Messages of special stereotype "indirect" can be used to indicate arbitrary control flow that may occur between two successive messages. In diagrams, indirect messages are depicted as double-crossed arrows. Technically, indirect relationships are rendered as special message stereotypes. The presence of that stereotype is checked during query evaluation (see Table 5, block III and IV, for illustration). Evaluation of indirect messages is accomplished in two steps: One step is concerned with finding messages that comply to the sending context of the indirect message (i.e. sender role, predecessors, successors, and activator messages); the other step deals with the identification of messages matching to the reception context of the indirect message (i.e. receiver role and subsequently activated messages).

4.6 Combination of Selection Criteria

By default, all selection criteria specified in a JPDD are implicitly combined with "and". That is, all such selection criteria must be fulfilled by a given model element in order to be selected by the query. In some cases, though, we may need to specify alternative, exclusive, or mutual exclusive selection criteria. In order to render such combinations of selection criteria, we may use constraint strings ("{or}", "{xor}", and "{not}"). The corresponding OCL operations specify that either at least, or exactly, one (respectively) of all model elements interrelated by such a constraint must comply to the selection criteria; or it inverts the result of matching in case the model element is constrained with "{not}". The OCL operations are omitted here due to space limitations. Please refer to [24] for further illustrations.

4.7 Retrieving Matching Model Elements

Retrieval of actual model elements from user models is accomplished using the UML meta model operations as they have been exemplified in the previous sections. A corresponding meta operation is specified for each UML meta model element (whose instances may appear in class/object diagrams or in interaction diagrams, e.g. classifiers, attributes, operations, associations, messages, etc.). In order to retrieve a set of (matching) model elements, the meta operation successively invoke one another so that all selection criteria specified in the JPDD are evaluated (see Fig. 3). The meta operations take a model element pattern from the JPDD as argument, and compare its characteristics with an actual model element instance of a user model. Starting point of evaluation is a return parameter of the JPDD. For each return parameter of a JPDD, a set of matching elements in the given user model is retrieved.

Fig. 3 exemplifies how the OCL meta operations work together in order to retrieve a set of matching model elements for a classifier pattern ("?cPattern"). The selection is initiated by a special meta operation "matchingModelElements", which is defined in the context of the JPDD parameter and that returns the set of all model elements matching to that parameter (i.e. to classifier pattern "?cPattern"; see ① in Fig. 3). The meta operation takes a UML model (or any other namespace, such as packages, collaborations, etc.) as an argument. The contents of that model (or namespace) are then matched against the selection criteria outlined by the JPDD parameter (i.e. by classifier pattern "?cPattern"), one by one (see ② in Fig. 3). The model elements contained

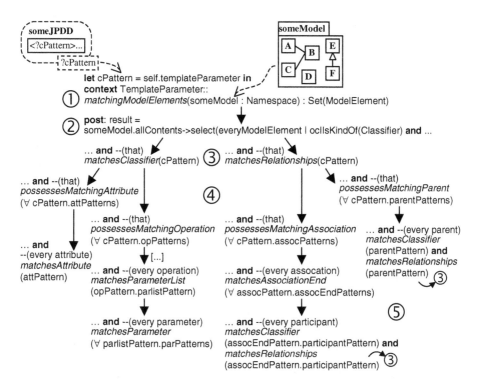

Fig. 3. Cascading evaluation of JPDDs (note that not all evaluation steps are shown)

in the model are selected if their meta attributes (in this case, "isAbstract", "isLeaf", "isRoot", etc.) as well as their meta relationships (to other model elements, such as attributes, operations, associations, and generalizations, etc.) comply to the ones defined by classifier pattern "?cPattern" (cf. also section 4.1). This is checked with help of operations "matchesClassifier" and "matchesRelationships" (see ③ in Fig. 3), which in turn make use of operations "possessesMatchingAttribute", "possesses MatchingOperation", "possessesMatchingAssociation", and "possessesMatching Parent" (see ④ in Fig. 3) – and so forth. It is important to note that relationship matching also involves matching the participating classifiers (see ⑤ in Fig. 3)[6]. That way, evaluation cascades from selection criterion to selection criterion, assessing if all selection criteria in the JPDD are fulfilled.

5 Example

With help of the notational means presented in the previous section, we now can define even complex selection queries without getting lost in its specification.

---

[6] Likewise, attribute and operation matching involves matching of their type and parameter types, respectively (not shown in Fig. 3).

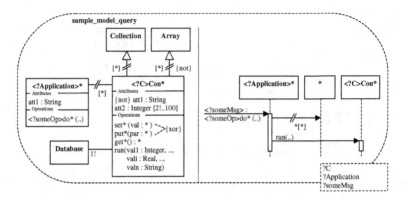

Fig. 4. A sample JPDD

Fig. 4, for example, depicts a sample JPDD that selects all classifiers (identified with "?C") (1) matching the name pattern "Con*"; (2) that do *not* have an attribute matching "att1" of type "String"; (3) that do have an array attribute matching "att2" of type "Integer" whose lower bound equates "2", and whose upper bound does not exceed "100"; (4) that either have an operation matching "set*", or an operation matching "put*" (but not both) that both take one parameter of arbitrary type; (5) that have an operation matching "get*" that returns an value of arbitrary type; (6) that have an operation matching "run" that takes (at least) three parameters: (6a) the first parameter in the operation's parameter list must be of type "Integer", (6b) the last parameter must be of type "String"; (6c) besides that, the operation must take a third parameter of type "Real" (no matter at which position in the operation's parameter list). Selected classifiers must be (7) subtypes of "Collection"; (8) but *not* subtypes of "Array"; and (9) they have to have an association to exactly one classifier matching "Database".

Furthermore, selected classifiers must possess an indirect association (i.e., a navigable path) to a classifier (identified with "?Application") (1) matching "*"; (2) that has an attribute matching "att1" of type "String"; (3) and that has an operation matching "do*" (identified with "?someOp"), which takes any number of parameters. That operation must be invoked by some message (identified with "?someMsg"[7]) (3a) which in turn invokes method "run" on the former classifier (identified with "?C") – (3b) no matter when (see "iterating" double-crossed message in right part of Fig. 4) – and (3c) using arbitrary values as parameters. While the left part of Fig. 4 is matched against classifiers in class diagrams, the right part is compared to message specifications in interaction diagrams in which matching classifiers are involved.

Having found actual model elements that comply to these selection criteria, the JPDD returns the resulting model elements via its template parameters "?C", "?Application", and "?someMsg".

---

[7] Note how the identifier of the message is separated from the identifier of the operation (which is being called) by means of a colon.

6 Related Work

MDA is closely related to the research field of graph transformations [21]. In both domains, we are concerned with the specification of model (or graph) transformations and – consequently – with the specification of model (or graph) queries. From that perspective, JPDDs compare to the left-hand side (LHS) of production rules as we find them in graph rewrite systems such as PROGRES [23] or AGG [27]. JPDDs differ from LHS specified in PROGRES in their way to specify constraints on (class/object) node attributes. In PROGRES, such constraints are either specified using textual descriptions, or they are attached to the (class/object) node which they apply to by means of a hollow fat arrow. Both representations differ considerably from the class/object notation as it is known from the UML. AGG does a better job in that respect, since attributes are listed within a special attribute compartment inside the node. On the other hand, though, AGG does not provide for the specification of paths (e.g., indirect associations) between (class/object) nodes – such as PROGRES and JPDDs do. The specification means of path expressions in PROGRES go beyond those of JPDDs: PROGRES gives developers fine-grained control over the evaluation process of path expressions (by providing conditional and iterative path expressions). Furthermore, it permits the specification of optional nodes. Selection criteria specified in JPDDs, on the contrary, must be satisfied as a whole; and their evaluation process is invariable as determined by the OCL statements presented in this paper[8].

Apart from the transformation approaches originating in the field of graph transformations, there are a couple of notations around that are explicitly dedicated to the field of MDA, e.g., the QVT approach presented in [20], or MOLA [10]. The major problem with these transformation languages is that they specify model queries in terms of meta model entities. While this may be more convenient when referring to meta properties that have a standard representation in UML diagrams, it severely hinders the overall comprehension of the queries. Apart form that, JPDDs facilitate the reuse of model queries since they consider model queries as first-class entities[9] which may be involved in multiple transformations.

Considering that most submissions to OMG's QVT RFP propose to use OCL as a query language, JPDDs also relate to existing approaches for the visualization of OCL expressions in general, such as Constraint Diagrams [11] or Visual OCL [4] [12]. Constraint Diagrams represent a graphical notation to specify invariants on objects and their associations (i.e., links) depending on the state they are in. In consequence to its strict focus on runtime constraints, the notation does not provide for the specification of model element queries, though. In particular, no means are provided to designate model elements that serve as sources for transformations. Further, the notation is not concerned with the specification of structural selection constraints, such as existence of particular features. Visual OCL is a graphical notation to express OCL constraints. It provides graphical symbols for all OCL keywords, in particular for the "select" statement as we need it for model element selection in MDA.

---

[8] Note that we abstract from evaluation problems of OCL expressions, such as the calculation of transitive closures (cf. [22]), for example. We consider these problems to be OCL-specific rather than JPDD-specific.

[9] i.e., as an autonomous entity that can exist without further reference to any other entities.

However, similar to the MDA transformation approaches mentioned above, Visual OCL does not provide for the specification of model element queries in terms of user model entities. In consequence, users are confronted with the full load of OCL complexity – in particular when specification of indirect relationships (see section 4.3) is necessary.

The idea of specifying queries in terms of user model entities we borrowed from the approach of Query-By-Example (QBE) [30], which is a common query technique in the database domain: We specify sample model entities, having sample properties, and determine how selected model elements must relate to such samples. We make use of "operator" symbols (such as wildcards, exclamation marks, and double-crossed lines and arrows) to differentiate whether selected model elements must match the samples exactly, or with a permissible degree of deviation (e.g., names may be rendered with help of patterns, and/or multiplicity boundaries may be specified to denote minimum and maximum values rather than perfect matches).

As already mentioned above and discussed in [26], AOSD is another application area for JPDDs. Here, JPDD are used to visualize selections of join points, i.e., they render those points in program code, or program execution, that are to be enhanced by an aspect. In [25], we demonstrate by example how JPDDs may be used to model join point selections in popular aspect-oriented programming languages. In particular, we describe how JPDDs may be used to represent *pointcuts* in AspectJ [2], *traversal strategies* in Adaptive Programming [13], or *concern mappings* in Hyper/J [29].

7 Conclusion

In this paper, we presented a graphical notation to specify model queries on UML models. We identified model queries to be prerequisites to model transformations as they are specified in the Model-Driven Architecture (MDA). We demonstrated that even simple query specifications tend to become excessive and complex when using a textual notation. Aiming to overcome this quandary, we introduced Join Point Designation Diagrams (JPDD) to specify and represent model queries graphically. We explained their abstract syntax, as well as the graphical means to specify the queries' selection criteria. We specified OCL operations for the evaluation of such selection criteria on actual user model elements. We exemplified the use of JPDDs using a complex model query, demonstrating that even then the query specification remains comprehensible.

The particular focus of this work has been on providing graphical means for the specification of model element queries based on lexical similarity (e.g., based on name and signature patterns) and structural arrangements (e.g., based on indirect relationships). We extrapolated the need of such selection means from the area of Aspect-Oriented Software Development (AOSD), where JPDDs were originally developed for. We think that mapping our graphical means to OCL expressions can assist developers in both AOSD and MDA when specifying and modeling selections. In particular, this allows seamless integration of our JPDDs with various submissions to the MOF QVT RFP, which are proposing to use OCL as a model query language. It is important to note, though, that JPDDs are not capable – and not intended – to represent OCL expressions in the general case. Further, it must be stated that JPDDs may specify only selections on model elements of a kind. It is not possible, for example, to collectively select UML model elements of different types into the same parameter (e.g., classes and associations, or all model elements contained in a model). Instead, a parameter must be defined for each model element type to be selected.

We think, however, that this limitation is more than outranged by the benefits of specifying model queries in terms of user models, rather than meta models, in order to facilitate their specification and comprehension to the user. In this paper, we have concentrated on a query language for the UML. We advocate for the development of further user model-based query languages in other modeling and domain-specific languages as well. That way, transformations may be specified as simple as relating one user-model-based query to another user-model-based query – for the sake of feasibility and comprehensibility to the user.

References

[1] Alcatel, Softeam, Thales, TNI-Valiosys, Codagen Technologies Corp, *Revised Submission for MOF 2.0 Query / Views / Transformations RFP*, 18. Aug. 2003

[2] AspectJ Team, *The AspectJ Programming Guide*, http://dev.eclipse.org/viewcvs/indextech.cgi/~checkout~/aspectj-home/doc/progguide/index.html, Jan. 2004

[3] Assmann, U. (ed.), Proc. of MDAFA 2004 (Linköping, Sweden, Jun. 2004), http://www.ida.liu.se/~henla/mdafa2004

[4] Bottoni, P., Koch, M., Parisi-Presicce, F., Taentzer, G., *A Visualization of OCL Using Collaborations*, in: Proc. of UML 2001 (Toronto, Canada, Oct. 2001), LNCS 2185, pp. 257-271

[5] CBOP, DSTC, IBM, *Revised Submission for MOF 2.0 Query / Views / Transformations RFP*, 18. Aug. 2003 (http://www.dstc.edu.au/pegamento/publications/ad-03-08-03.pdf)

[6] Ehrig, H., Engels, G., Kreowski, H.-J., Rozenberg, G. (eds.): *Handbook on Graph Grammars*, Vol. 2: Applications, Languages, and Tools, World Scientific, River Edge, NJ, 1999

[7] Filman, R., Elrad, T., Clarke, S., Aksit, M., (eds.), *Aspect-Oriented Software Development*, Addison-Wesley, 2005

[8] Gybels, K., Brichau, J., *Arranging language features for more robust pattern-based crosscuts*, in: Proc. of AOSD'03 (Boston, MA, Mar. 2003), ACM, pp. 60-69

[9] Interactive Objects Software, Project Technology, *Revised Submission for MOF 2.0 Query / Views / Transformations RFP*, 18. Aug. 2003

[10] Kalnins, A., Barzdins, J., Celms, E., *Model Transformation Language MOLA*, in: [3], pp. 14-28

[11] Kent, S., *Constraint Diagrams: Visualizing Assertions in Object-Oriented Models*, in: Proc. of OOPSLA 1997 (Atlanta, Georgia, Oct. 1997), ACM pp. 327-341

[12] Kiesner, Chr., Taentzer, G., Winkelmann, J., *Visual OCL: A Visual Notation of the Object Constraint Language*, TR 2002/23, Technical University Berlin, 2002

[13] Lieberherr, K., *Adaptive Object-Oriented Software: The Demeter Method with Propagation Patterns*, PWS Publishing Company, Boston, 1996

[14] Lieberherr, K., Lorenz, D., Mezini, M., *Programming with Aspectual Components*, TR NU-CCS-99-01, Northeastern University, 1999

[15] Masuhara, H., Kiczales, G., Dutchyn, Chr., *A Compilation and Optimization Model for Aspect-Oriented Programs*, in: Proc. of CC 2003 (Warsaw, Poland, Apr. 2003), LNCS 2622, pp. 46-60

[16] OMG, *MDA Guide Version 1.0*, OMG, 1. May 2003 (omg/2003-05-01)

[17] OMG, *Request for Proposal: MOF 2.0 Query / Views / Transformations RFP*, 2002 (OMG Document ad/2002-04-10)

[18] OMG, *UML 2.0 OCL Specification*, Final Adopted Specification, 2003 (OMG Document pct/03-10-14)

[19] OMG, *Unified Modeling Language Specification*, Version 1.5, March 2003 (OMG Document: formal/03-03-01)

[20] QVT-Partners, *Revised Submission for MOF 2.0 Query / Views / Transformations RFP*, 18. August 2003 (http://qvtp.org/downloads/1.1/qvtpartners1.1.pdf)

[21] Rozenberg, G. (ed.), *Handbook of Graph Grammars and Computing by Graph Transformation*, Vol. 1: Foundations, World Scientific Publishing, River Edge, NJ, 1997

[22] Schürr, A., *Adding Graph Transformation Concepts to UML's Constraint Language OCL*, Electronic Notes in Theoretical Computer Science Vol. 44(4), Elsevier, 2001

[23] Schürr, A., Winter, A., Zündorf, A., *PROGRES: Language and Environment*, in: [6], pp. 487-550

[24] Stein, D., Hanenberg, St., Unland, R., *A Graphical Notation to Specify Model Queries for MDA Transformations on UML Models*, in: [3], pp. 60-74

[25] Stein, D., Hanenberg, St., Unland, R., *Modeling Pointcuts*, Early Aspect Workshop, AOSD '04 (Lancaster, UK, Mar. 2004)

[26] Stein, D., Hanenberg, St., Unland, R., *Query Models*, in: Proc. of UML 2004 (Lisbon, Portugal, Oct. 2004), LNCS 3273, pp. 98-112

[27] Taentzer, G., Ermel, C., Rudolf, M., *The AGG Approach: Language and Environment*, in: [6], pp. 551-603

[28] Tarr, P., Ossher, H., Harrison, W., Sutton Jr., St., *N Degrees of Separation: Multi-Dimensional Separation of Concerns*, in: Proc. of ICSE 1999 (Los Angeles, CA, May 1999), ACM, pp. 107-119

[29] Tarr, P., Ossher, H., *Hyper/J User and Installation Manual*, IBM Corp., 2000

[30] Zloof, M., *Query-by-Example: A Data Base Language*, IBM Systems Journal, Vol. 16(4), 1977, pp. 324-343

Describing Horizontal Model Transformations with Graph Rewriting Rules

Alexander Christoph

Forschungszentrum Informatik (FZI), Haid-und-Neu-Str. 10-14,
76131 Karlsruhe, Germany

Abstract. The software model development process consists of a number of complex transformations. Especially horizontal model transformations that are used to restructure and re-organize software models require a lot of handiwork, since complex analysis and transformation steps have to be performed. The developer should be assisted by a tool set that supports horizontal as well as vertical model transformations in order to improve software quality and to reduce software development costs. This paper presents GREAT, a rule-based transformation framework which facilitates transformations among models on the same or different abstraction levels. The feasibility of GREAT is shown by rule-based implementations of model restructuring, refactoring, and optimization algorithms that can be used throughout the development process to improve the architecture of software models.

1 Introduction

The Model Driven Architecture (MDA) approach of the OMG aims at the automatization of the software development process. It defines a range of abstraction levels for software models and transformations, that translate models between different levels of abstraction. *Vertical* model transformations affect the abstraction level of a software specification. They are used to refine or to abstract a model during forward or reverse engineering, respectively. *Horizontal* transformations however, do not affect the abstraction level of a software model. They are used to restructure, complete, or optimize a software model in order to improve its internal structure and/or quality. In contrast to vertical transformations, which are the main focus for research and tool development in this area, horizontal transformations have only limited support. Horizontal transformations are often confined to the source code level of a system [1] and/or implemented internally [2], which restricts adaptation and extension. In order to automate the overall software development process, a model transformation system must be able to support both vertical and horizontal model transformations. Also, the developer must be able to create, extend and adapt transformation algorithms. This paper presents GREAT[1] [3], a rule-based transformation framework, which facilitates transformations among models on the same or different abstraction levels, i.e., *horizontal* or *vertical* transformations. Depending on the given set of transformation rules, GREAT can be used to

---

[1] German "*Gr*aphorientiertes *E*ntwurfsanalyse und *T*ransformationswerkzeug", English translation "Graph-oriented tool for design-analysis and transformation."

U. Aßmann, M. Aksit, and A. Rensink (Eds.): MDAFA 2003/2004, LNCS 3599, pp. 93–107, 2005.

automate complex model transformation tasks, such as model analysis, refactorings, or design pattern application. The applicability of GREAT is demonstrated with rule-based implementations of refactoring and optimization algorithms that can be applied to arbitrary software models. The next section presents an overview of GREAT. Section 3 introduces transformation rules that are used to analyse software models to support further transformations. Section 4 presents rule-based implementations of architecture refactorings for software models. Section 5 shows the implementation of an restructuring algorithm that produces an optimal inheritance hierarchy for a set of classes. Conclusions and related work are discussed in sections 7 and 6.

2   GREAT: A Model Transformation Framework

The GREAT model transformation framework facilitates UML model-to-model transformations, focusing on UML class-diagrams. GREAT is designed to ease and automate different software engineering tasks, such as refactoring and refinement; tasks that are currently part of the MDA process [4,5].

2.1   System Architecture

Figure 1 shows the structure of the framework.

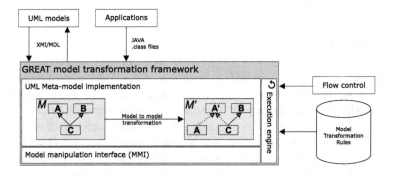

Fig. 1. The GREAT transformation framework

GREAT has three sources of input.

– The *Software models* are either UML models, which are assumed to be represented in XMI [6] or MDL[2], or Applications, which are assumed to be available in Java byte code. The usage of XMI or MDL allows the integration of GREAT into an existing tool chain, whereas byte-codes can be used for maintenance and reengineering tasks [7].
– The *model transformation rules*. These graph transformation rules are processed by OPTIMIX [8] which generates the appropriate Java-code. The Java output is used by GREAT's *execution engine*.

---

[2] Proprietary file format of *Rational Rose*.

– The *flow control*, which provides the order in which different rule sets have to be applied.

The central part of GREAT is the implementation of the UML meta-model [9]. The model manipulation interface (MMI) provides methods for accessing and manipulating UML models. The *execution engine* is responsible for loading and executing the graph transformation code generated by OPTIMIX. The GREAT framework is completely implemented in Java.

2.2 Transformation Method

GREAT uses a declarative transformation approach. The specification of a model transformation consists of a set of transformation rules together with a flow control description. The rules are translated into executable transformation code by the graph rewrite system OPTIMIX. The transformation code is executed in the context of the meta-model implementation of GREAT.

Graph Model
A software model can be defined as a set of graphs $G = (N, E)$ with nodes N and edges E. In the context of UML, graph nodes are of type $\{Class, Interface, Attribute, Method, Unit\}$. Edges represent mappings (also: *relations*) between nodes. Relations are of type $\{Generalization, Implementation, Association, Dependency, Parent\}$.

Nodes and egdes contain additional information to further specify their semantics, e.g. name, stereotype, visibility, etc. Element names must be unique with respect to the context of the element. The relations $Generalization, Implementation$, and $Parent$ are unique between two nodes A and B by definition, whereas $Association$ and $Dependency$ edges must have a unique name.

Transformation Language
Basically, transformation rules consist of two sets of predicates over the GREAT meta-model (see figure 2). The first set (above the ==> delimiter) describes a pattern to be

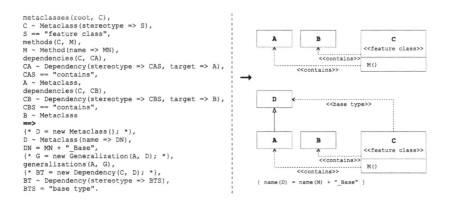

Fig. 2. Example transformation rule

matched in the software model. The pattern is a conjunction of predicates over the graph model. The second set describes the structure of the matched section, when the manipulation is finished. OPTIMIX is used to generate the navigation and manipulation code from these rule specifications. This code relies on the model manipulation interface (MMI) of GREAT. The generated code is stored in a rule repository. The GREAT execution engine loads and executes the generated rule code according to the flow control specification. Figure 2 shows a transformation rule that identifies three classes connected through stereotyped dependency edges[3]. The rule creates a new class and connects it via a generalization edge with one of the pattern classes, i.e., it creates a new base class for the pattern class. The left-hand side of the figure shows the textual representation of the rule. The right-hand side shows a graphical (UML-like) representation. In order to ease understanding, the graphical representation will be used throughout the paper.

3 Model Analysis

In order to implement complex transformation algorithms, model analysis can be used to externalize implicit knowledge contained in model elements and/or relations. This helps to keep model transformations simple and to achieve reuse of transformation steps in the sense of modularization. This section presents transformations that implement relational operations, e.g., *transitive closure*, to analyze element relationships. These operations are also used to support element analysis. Analysis results are either stored as dedicated model elements or as *tagged values* of existing model elements.

3.1 Analyzing Relations

Transitive Subgraph
Transitive closures can be used to analyse the subgraph spanned by a transitive relation R. The following rules generate a transitive closure over the generalization relation of a software model. Transitive edges are instantiated as dependency edges, stereotyped with <<tc>>.

Rule 3.1(a) produces an initial state in the model by creating transitive edges parallel to generalization edges. Rule 3.1(b) iteratively extends the transitive closure by including next neighbour nodes.

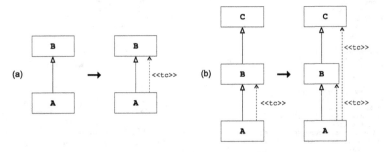

Rule 3.1: Creating a transitive closure

---
[3] Dependency edges serve as templates for user-defined relations.

The resulting transitive closure of the sample model is shown in model 3.1 (dotted edges, <<tc>> omitted).

Relation Intersection

For a number of transformations it is necessary to know the set of common members of a relation R, i.e., nodes that are contained in different branches of R. The following rules identify common base classes of a given set Sub of classes iteratively.

Rule 3.2(a) generates the set of all base classes of classes in Sub. The elements of Sub are marked with the stereotype <<Leaf>>. The (potential) base classes are marked with <<BT>>.

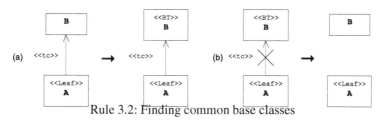

Rule 3.2: Finding common base classes

Let $Base$ be the set of potential base classes. Rule 3.2(b) identifies counter-examples, i.e., tuples of classes (A, B) with $A \in Sub$, $B \in Base$, not connected through a generalization edge. The rule removes B from $Base$, i.e., it removes its stereotype.

In the sample model, the rules identify class Base as a common base class of $Sub =$ {Member, Relationship}.

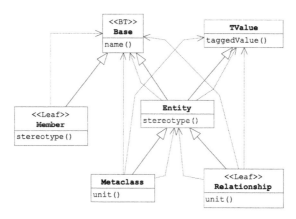

Model 3.1: Common base class of {Member, Relationship}

Shortest Edge

Once we know the set of base classes $Base$ of classes in Sub, we might be interested in a subset $Base' \subseteq Base$, that contains the nearest base classes of Sub. For this purpose, we define the distance between (A, B), $A \in Sub$, $B \in Base$ as the number of generalization edges between A and B.

Rule 3.3(a) identifies tuples (A, B, C), $A \in Sub$, $B, C \in Base$ and adds a mark to the shorter transitive edge. An edge can have multiple marks. Edges with a higher number of marks are shorter than edges with a lower number of marks.

Rule 3.3(b) pairwise compares transitive edges and removes a class from $Base$ that is connected to the edge with the lower number of marks.

In the example, Entity is the nearest common base class for $Sub = \{$Metaclass, Relationship$\}$.

3.2 Analyzing Model Elements

Feature classes are supporting model elements that are used to construct defining or containing class sets for operations and attributes.

Rule 3.4(a) creates a feature class for every operation defined in a software model. The classes are marked with <<feature class>>. Classes defining the operation are connected via a $Defines$ relation. This simple rule compares operation names only.

Rule 3.4(b) creates a $Contains$ edge between class A and a feature class C, if the base class B of A defines the operation. The rule uses the transitive closure of the generalization relation to calculate the $Contains$ relation.

In the sample model, the rules yield the following result for the operation taggedValue.

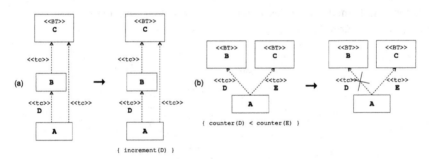

Rule 3.3: Nearest common base class

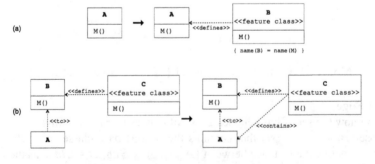

Rule 3.4: $Defines$ and $Contains$ relations

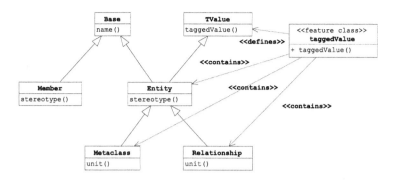

Model 3.2: *Defines* and *Contains* relations of `taggedValue`

4 Architecture Refactoring

In [10], Fowler describes a number of architectural refactorings that help to improve the internal structure of a software model. This section presents rule-based implementations of selected refactorings.

4.1 Extract Superclass

Extract Superclass identifies common features of a set of classes and moves them into a common base class. The goal of this transformation is to avoid repeated feature definitions.

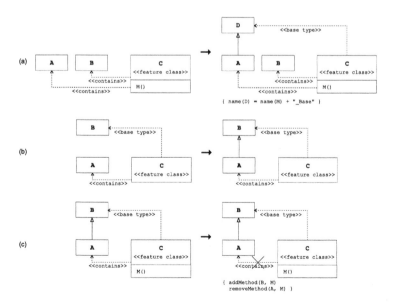

Rule 4.1: Extract Superclass: initial rule (a), iteration rule (b), final transformation (c)

Rule 4.1(a) uses feature classes to identify features that are defined by at least two classes. For matching classes, the rule creates a common base class. Rule 4.1(b) iteratively connects all the remaining classes defining the common feature to the common base class. A supporting <<base type>> edge connects the feature class with the new base class. Finally, rule 4.1(c) moves the common feature into the base class and removes its definition from the subclasses. It uses the <<base type>> relation created by rule 4.1(a).

4.2   Pull Up Feature

Pull Up Feature is a variant of Extract Superclass. It uses analysis rules presented in section 3.1 to identify an already existing common base class. In this case, the rules do not create a new base class for the common feature.

Rules 4.2(a) and (b) identify classes containing a common feature. The classes are stereotyped with <<Leaf>>. Rules 3.2(a) and (b) can then be used to find and stereotype a common base class of the set of classes stereotyped with <<BT>>. Rule 4.2(c) moves the common feature to the base class of the class set.

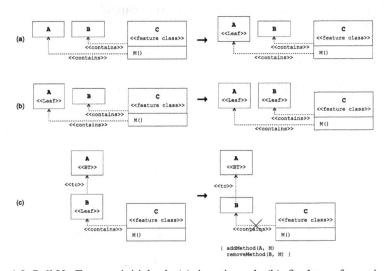

Rule 4.2: Pull Up Feature: initial rule (a), iterative rule (b), final transformation (c)

4.3   Extract Interface

Extract Interface creates an interface for a class, containing a subset of the class' methods. This is useful when client access must be restricted to a certain subset of methods, e.g. to avoid subclasses of clients to access other parts of the subject.

Rule 4.3(a) creates an interface for a class containing methods stereotyped as <<facade>>. The interface is equipped with these methods and connected to the class via an implementation edge. Rule 4.3(b) uses *call* edges to identify direct clients of the class that use the extracted methods. Associations between the clients and the class are redirected to the interface.

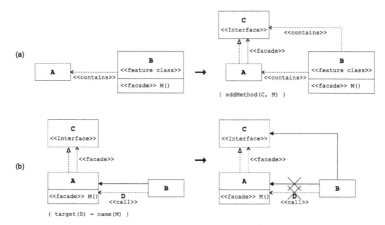

Rule 4.3: Extracting an interface: creating the interface (a), redirecting client associations (b)

5 Architecture Optimization

In [11], Snelting describes an algorithm that optimizes the inheritance tree for a set of classes[4]. The algorithm starts with a number of marked classes, that form the interface of a system or a module. The algorithm distributes class features so that every subset of features is localized in an *internal* class and multiple feature definition is avoided. This section shows a rule-based implementation of the algorithm.

The algorithm consists of the following steps.

- Model analysis is used to collect class features. Here we can use the analysis rules presented in section 3.
- After *Defines* and *Contains* relations have been calculated, containment classes are created in order to capture sets of classes with equal feature sets.
- Inheritance relations can be introduced with respect to subset relationships of the class sets described by containment classes.
- The last step of the transformation removes all intermediate and supporting classes and graph nodes.

<<INTF>> Class 1	<<INTF>> Class 2	<<INTF>> Class 3	<<INTF>> Class 4	<<INTF>> Class 5
m1() m2() m5()	m1() m2() m6()	m1() m3() m4() m7() m9()	m1() m3() m4() m7() m8() m10()	m4() m8()

Model 5.1: Example model for the IHI algorithm

---

[4] *IHI:* Inferring an optimal inheritance hierarchy.

Example Model
The algorithm assumes that the interface classes of the input model are stereotyped as
<<INTF>>. These classes must be preserved during transformation. Model 5.1 shows
an example.

Model Analysis
This step creates *Defines* and *Contains* relations for the interface classes. Here, we
can use analysis rules from section 3. Model 5.2 shows the result of this step[5].

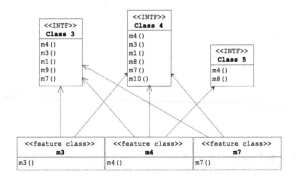

Model 5.2: *Defines* and *Contains* relations

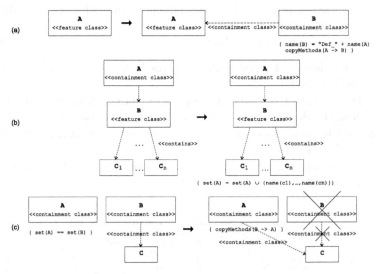

Rule 5.1: Creating containment classes: creating containment classes (a), building class
sets (b), merging identical sets (c)

---

[5] Class 1 and Class 2 were omitted due to clarity.

Containment Sets
For every feature class, rule 5.1(a) creates a supporting class that describe sets of classes containing this feature. This is necessary to allow for set operations. Rule 5.1(b) builds the set of all target classes of the *Contains* relation and stores it as a set of class identifiers in a *tagged value* of the respective containment class. Rule 5.1(c) merges identical containment sets.

Creating Inheritance
Two containment classes A and B can be connected via a generalization edge, iff $A \subset B$. Rule 5.2 finds such containment classes and connects them via a generalization edge.

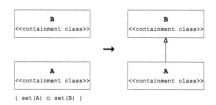

Rule 5.2: Creating generalization edges

Model 5.3 shows generalization edges between definition nodes Def_m3 and Def_m4 (classes {Class 3, Class 4} and {Class 3, Class 4, Class 5}).

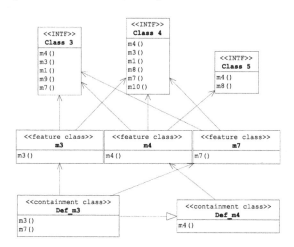

Model 5.3: Created generalization edges

Transitive generalization edges that appear because of the transitivity of the subset relationship are removed by another rule. For every interface class, rule 5.3(a) identifies a possible base class with the required set of features. Rule 5.3(b) modifies the generalization, if a base class with a lower number of features can be found.

Model Clean-up

After all transformations have been performed, clean-up rules remove all unnecessary classes and relationships. The rule is not shown here.

Model 5.4 shows the result of the algorithm. Every interface class inherits its features from an internal base class. In addition, the hierarchy avoids multiple feature declarations and reuses sets of features.

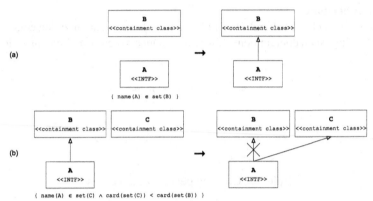

Rule 5.3: Finding base classes: initial rule (a), iterative rule (b)

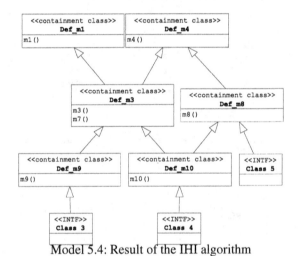

Model 5.4: Result of the IHI algorithm

6   Related Work

A lot of ideas for this work have been inspired by Assmann's work. He showed the applicability of graph rewriting systems to areas such as program analysis and optimization [12,8], and Aspect-Oriented Programming (AOP) [13].

There are several related tools available, that can be used to modify software and software specifications.

UMLAUT [14] is a design transformation framework which provides searching, retrieving and modification functionality. UMLAUT allows the developer to specify design transformations that are executed on an imported software model. Transformation specifications are based on list operations, such as selection and filtering. UMLAUT focuses on model transformations for verification and testing.

Recoder [15] is a meta-programming environment capable of transforming Java applications. Transformation programs operate on an abstract syntax tree of the imported program using the iterator API provided by Recoder. Transformed programs can be exported to source files. An example is the 'obfuscation' of programs, i.e. the renaming of classes and variables in order to make reverse-engineered code harder to understand.

The need to automate software analysis and restructuring lead to the development of several algorithms, that were mainly developed to support reverse-engineering of imperative programs.

Lundberg and Löwe describe an approach for software architecture recovery for object-oriented systems [16]. Their goal is to reconstruct a sound component model of object-oriented applications. The authors use a modified version of dominance analysis to analyse component boundaries.

The Object Management Group (OMG) plans to integrate query and transformation facilities into the UML standard. Therefore, the OMG issued a Request for Proposals (RFP) on queries, views and transformations for software specifications (QVT).

The submissions to the RFP can be split into two groups.

- Implementation-based proposals, [17,18,19] focus on the imperative description of queries and transformations. They use languages like the UML Action Semantics, list operations or path expressions to specify target elements and transformation operations.
- Rule-based proposals, [20,21] use pattern specification languages to match and transform model elements, but their submissions don't clarify how transformations are applied and executed and how critical issues like rule termination, rule and pattern selection are dealt with.

7   Conclusions

The presented work shows the applicability of graph rewriting systems for software design transformations. Even complex transformation algorithms, like architecture refactorings and optimizations can be expressed through graph transformation rules in the context of the UML metamodel.

Although the current implementation of GREAT is not optimal , the usage of GREAT in practice will free the developer from error prone, tedious, and time consuming tasks, such as model analysis and transformation.

Further work is required to improve the performance of transformation applications and to enhance the usability of GREAT.

- *Improve performance.* Measurements showed that the generated navigation and transformation code performed well together with the metamodel implementation

[7]. The most time consuming task is the identification of the rule graph patterns. The code generated by OPTIMIX uses a simple "nested loop join" algorithm. The performance of the transformation code could be improved using more efficient join algorithms, which only requires a modification of the OPTIMIX code generator. Also, a more sophisticated metamodel implementation would help to speed up transformations.

– *Improve usability.* Support for debugging and tracing transformation rules is necessary in order to enhance the usability of GREAT for real-world software engineering work.

For further information please have a look at the GREAT web-site
`http://www.the-great-system.org`.

References

1. Foundation, E.: (The eclipse platform)
2. Borland: (Together control center)
3. Christoph, A.: Graph Rewrite Systems for Software Design Transformations. In: Objects, Components, Architectures, Services, and Applications for a NetworkedWorld: International Conference NetObjectDays, NODe 2002, Erfurt, Germany, October 7-10, 2002. Volume 2591 of Lecture Notes in Computer Science., (Springer) 76–86
4. Kleppe, A., Warmer, J., Bast, W.: MDA Explained. The Model Driven Architecture: Practice and Promise. Addison-Wesley (2003)
5. Frankel, D.S.: Model Driven Architecture. Applying MDA to Enterprise Computing. Wiley (2003)
6. Group, O.M.: OMG XML Metadata Interchange (XMI) Specification (2000)
7. Christoph, A., Müller, M.M.: GREAT: UML Transformation Tool for Porting Middleware Applications. In Stevens, P., Whittle, J., Booch, G., eds.: UML 2003 - The Unified Modeling Language. Model Languages and Applications. 6th International Conference, San Francisco, CA, USA, October 2003, Proceedings. Volume 2863 of Lecture Notes in Computer Science., Springer (2003) 18–30
8. Assmann, U.: Generierung von Programmoptimierungen mit Graphersetzungssystemen. PhD thesis, Universität Karlsruhe, Fakultät für Informatik (1996)
9. Group, O.M.: UML version 1.1 (1997)
10. Fowler, M.: Refactoring: Improving the Design of Existing Code. Addison-Wesley (2000)
11. Moore, I., Clement, T.: A Simple and Efficient Algorithm for Inferring Inheritance Hierarchies. In Mitchell, R., ed.: Proceedings of the Technology of Object-Oriented Languages and Systems, Prentice-Hall, Hertfordshire, UK (1996) 173–184
12. Assmann, U.: On Edge Addition Rewrite Systems and their Relevance to Program Analysis. In J., C., H., E., G., E., G., R., eds.: 5th International Workshop on Graph Grammars and their Application to Computer Science. Volume 1073 of Lecture Notes in Computer Science., Springer (1994)
13. Assmann, U., Ludwig, A.: Aspect Weaving by Graph Rewriting. In Eisenecker, U., Czarnecki, K., eds.: Generative Component-based Software Engineering, Springer (2000)
14. Ho, W.M., Jézéquel, J.M., Le Guennec, A., Pennaneac'h, F.: UMLAUT: an extendible UML transformation framework. In: Proceedings of the 14th IEEE International Conference on Automated Software Engineering, Cocoa Beach, Florida, USA, Institute of Electrical and Electronics Engineers (1999) 275–278

15. Ludwig, A., Heuzeroth, D.: Metaprogramming in the Large. In: 2nd International Conference on Generative and Component-based Software Engineering (GCSE), Erfurt, Germany. Number 2177 in Lecture Notes in Computer Science, Springer (2000) 178–187
16. Lundberg, J., Löwe, W.: Architecture recovery by semi-automatic component identification. In: Workshop on Sofware Composition (SC) 2003, Satellite Event of ETAPS 2003, Warsaw, Poland. Volume 82 of Electronic Notes in Theoretical Computer Science., http://www.elsevier.nl/locate/entcs/volume82.html, Elsevier (2003)
17. Ltd, K.C.: MOF Query, Views and Transformations. Initial Submission to OMG RFP (2003) OMG ad/03-03-11.
18. Alcatel, Softeam, Thales, TNI-Valiosys: Response to the MOF 2.0 Query/Views/Transformation RFP (2003) OMG ad/03-03-25.
19. Corp., C.T.: MOF Query, Views and Transformations. Initial Submission to OMG RFP (2003) OMG ad/03-03-23.
20. DSTC, IBM: MOF Query, Views and Transformations. Initial Submission to OMG RFP (2003) OMG ad/03-02-03.
21. Corporation, C., Microsystems, S.: XMOF Queries, Views and Transformations on Models using MOF, OCL and Patterns (2003) OMG ad/03-03-24.

Open MDA Using Transformational Patterns

Mika Siikarla, Kai Koskimies, and Tarja Systä

Tampere University of Technology, Institute of Software Systems,
P.O.Box 553, FI-33101 Tampere, Finland
{mika.siikarla, kai.koskimies, tarja.systa}@tut.fi
http://practise.cs.tut.fi

Abstract. No generally accepted understanding on the characteristics of MDA transformation mechanisms exists. Various approaches to support such transformations have been proposed. In this paper, we discuss general requirements for MDA transformation mechanisms. We claim that, above all else, transformation mechanisms should be open, i.e. clear, transparent and user-guided. We propose a new concept, a transformational pattern, as a basis of an MDA transformation mechanism. We exploit existing tool support for this concept and show a small example of how it can be applied. Finally, we analyse the ability of the proposed technique to fill the requirements.

1 Introduction

A clearly identified long-term trend in software engineering is the introduction of higher and higher abstractions from which actual implementations are derived. OMG's Model-Driven Architecture (MDA) initiative [1] is a recent manifestation of this trend. A key idea in MDA is that system development should be based on high-level, platform independent models (PIM) from which lower level platform-specific models (PSM) and eventually implementations are derived with the support of transformation tools.

Although the vision behind MDA is generally accepted, the required tool technology is just taking its first steps. Some early tool support exists (e.g., ArcStyler [2]), but the underlying concepts and paradigms of the tools are far from well understood, if even existing.

Obviously, there are many ways to specify and execute transformations from one model to another. A straightforward approach to specify the transformations in an executable form would be a script language with access to a model repository and appropriate navigation and query capabilities. Then, transformations could be realized simply as scripts.

The real challenge of MDA transformation tool support is not in devising the computational vehicle, but rather in the collaboration of the designer and the tool. A simple black-box approach (e.g. a Python script) would hide the relationship between the source and the target model from the designer, making it very difficult to work with the result. If the path from a platform independent model to executable implementation were completely automated, this would

U. Aßmann, M. Aksit, and A. Rensink (Eds.): MDAFA 2003/2004, LNCS 3599, pp. 108–122, 2005.

not be a problem, but we argue that this is an unrealistic idea, at least in the near future. Typically, the designer has to examine the result, understand it, and apply further transformations or modifications on some parts of the result. Thus, we propose that an MDA transformation tool should be open in the sense that it allows the designer to be involved in the transformation process.

In this paper we will first discuss the required properties of an MDA transformation mechanism in more detail. As a potential approach to satisfy these requirements, we introduce the concept of a transformational pattern, which we believe can serve as the basis of open MDA transformations. This concept is an application of a generic pattern facility originally developed for supporting framework specialization [3]. We demonstrate the use of this technique by showing how a J2EE model can be generated from a platform-independent UML model for a Web Services application. Based on this example, we briefly analyse the extent to which this approach meets the requirements. Finally, we discuss related work and the future directions of our work.

2   MDA Transformation Mechanics

We see the primary role of a transformation as documenting the relations between different models of the same system. With this added information expressed in computer readable form, the models can be kept synchronized and a change in one model does not render all other models obsolete. This is absolutely vital for MDA. The description of these relations, i.e. the *record of transformation* according to [4], contains unique information about the system, and should therefore be considered a model itself.

Another important, although secondary, role is to support the designer in deriving one model from others, by alleviating the burden of at least the repetitious and trivial tasks. In some very specialized cases, such as a specific product-line, it might be possible to achieve fully automated transformations. However, it seems overly optimistic to expect fire-and-forget solutions for all possible situations any time soon. The intermediate, or derived, models do therefore contain more information than just what is derived. They have value as original artefacts and should not be considered as mere documentation.

In our view, transformation definitions are software artefacts. They are subject to evolution the same way design models or program files are. We expect, for example, that a set of model transformations can be given for a product-line platform to be used for the derivation of the designs for individual software products. Such a set of transformations is an integral part of the product-line and goes through changes and versions together with the other assets belonging to the product-line. It is likely, in fact, that the transformation mechanisms themselves need maintenance and evolve as the subject system does.

We raise *openness* as the most important property that is required of an MDA transformation mechanism. The designer should participate in the transformation process, guiding it with her decisions, rather than receive the results of a black-box operation as an outsider. The mechanism itself should be transparent, allowing the designer to follow how the models are being manipulated.

The meaning of every step in the transformation process should be clear. When using a clear and transparent machinery, the designer is better equipped to make decisions affecting the transformation. She can be trusted to make an educated choice between possible courses of action even during the transformation.

We argue that the open approach is safer, allowing the designer to understand the resulting model and modify it, if needed. In the black-box case modification of the result is risky, because the designer does not understand the purpose of different parts of the result, and therefore cannot judge the relationship elements in the target and source models. Note, that a part not dependent on the source model can be altered without compromising the relationships between the models. In the absence of fully automated transformations, it would be unreasonable to completely forbid modifications of the resulting model.

In some cases, where no single transformation process can be found for a category of systems, it is still possible to find transformation principles that apply to each of the systems. E.g. software products developed from the same product-line, or systems belonging to a particular application domain, might form such categories. The transformation mechanism should support *customisable* transformations that contain the common principles and provide variation points for customisation. Unlike with direct editing of the result, some customisation needs are foreseen and built into the transformation.

It is possible that some part in the target model resulting from applying a transformation is not considered acceptable for the particular application. Instead of trying to guess what changes in the source would lead to the desired result, it should be possible to change the result directly and produce a source model corresponding to the modified result. In cases where the source or target metamodel or the transformation itself loses information, bi-directionality cannot be fully achieved. However, the transformation mechanisms themselves should be *unbiased* as far as the direction of the transformation is concerned, and not force or encourage the transformation definitions to be unidirectional.

If a modification breaks several transformation rules and there are several ways to repair them, user-assisted repairing might be preferable to automatic repairing actions. In both cases the elements impacted by the modification should be traceable. In order to fix a problem, or to correct a mistake, it might be desirable to reverse the application of a transformation, effectively undoing it. This might prove to be challenging in practise. *Traceability* and *reversibility* are examples where knowledge of the relations between models are needed. This implies, that applying a transformation leaves a persistent record of transformation.

It should be possible to carry out the transformation one step at a time, rather than as a batch. *Incremental* transformation process contributes to the fine-grained management of the transformation, with a number of benefits. First, it contributes to openness, supporting understanding in general: the process can be better followed when divided into small pieces. Second, it allows for fine-grained backtracking: if the process appears to be going in a wrong direction, individual steps can be undone without losing the results produced so far. This is useful for steps with variation points. Third, incremental processing supports fine-grained customisability: variation points can be attached to individual steps rather than to the entire process. In this way variation points can be shown only when really needed: if a variation becomes obsolete because of earlier choices, the variation point need not be presented at all. Fourth, partial transformation processes are supported, where sensible (but incomplete) target models are produced on the basis of incomplete source models. This allows for partial evaluation of the transformation when developing or maintaining the transformation itself.

A transformation process can consist of several single, well-focused transformation steps. Therefore, mechanisms to compose configurations of individual transformation operations are needed. In these configurations, dependences and constraints between the individual operations should be supported, yielding to a need for an actual transformation language. Such *combinability* enables and promotes transformation reuse. There is also a need to relate different models together in one transformation. For instance, to form a platform-specific model, information from a platform-independent model as well as from specific platform deployment and description models might be needed. Combining information from different source models in a "concern-oriented" way would help the user to better understand and manage the dependences among the models.

Since transformation definitions are software artefacts, they need to be maintained throughout their life cycle. Therefore, transformations should be *maintainable*, implying that a transformation is specified in a manner that allows easy replacement of its parts. Customisability and combinability promote reuse and therefore improve maintainability. Many properties, especially openness, make transformations easier to understand, which helps in maintenance.

Documentation of the transformations is needed, so they can be understood and applied. Documentation is also needed for maintenance. Therefore transformations need to have an *illustrative presentation*, e.g. a visual notation that can be understood by the different parties involved. Since people comprehend examples better than rules or algorithms, it would be beneficial if examples could be constructed out of definitions and vice versa. Some visual presentation is needed for examples, too, and for visualizing mappings between models.

3   Transformational Patterns

In this work a *pattern* is an organized collection of software elements capturing any concern that is relevant for some stakeholder of the system. To be able to define a pattern independently of any particular system, a pattern is defined in terms of element *roles* rather than concrete elements; a *pattern instance* is tied to a particular context by binding its *role instances* to concrete elements. The relationship between a pattern and its pattern instance can be viewed as that of a model and its instance. Roles can then be seen as classes and role instances as objects. In this paper, we simply use the term pattern when referring to pattern instance, or role when referring to a role instance. The full term is only used when there is a risk of misunderstanding.

A role has a *role type*, which determines the kind of system elements that can be bound to the role's instances; the set of all valid role types is called the *domain* of the pattern. For example, if the domain is UML, the role types are the element types (metaclasses) of UML: there are class roles, operation roles, association roles etc. In the following we assume that the domain is UML.

Each role may have a set of *constraints*. Constraints are conditions that must be satisfied by the model element bound to a role's instance. For example, a constraint of a class role C may require that only a class stereotyped as ≪Persistent≫ can be bound to an instance of C. Constraints may also refer to other roles, e.g. a constraint on association role A may require that an association bound to A's instance must appear between classes bound to (instances of) certain class roles $C1$ and $C2$. Note that such a constraint implies (perhaps indirect) relationships between roles A and $C1$ as well as A and $C2$. Continuing with the pattern-model analogy, these relationships can be though of as associations.

A completely bound pattern instance therefore poses constraints on the elements bound to the role instances. The constraints from the pattern have in effect been joined with constraints in the domain model. For example, one of the UML well-formedness rule states that an attribute of a class may not have the same name as the class. The first pattern in the example above states that each class bound to (an instance of) the role C must be stereotyped ≪Persistent≫. Every element in the UML model must now fulfil both these constraints (although, the first still only applies to classes, and the second only to appropriately bound classes). If a model modification violates a constraint, the model must be fixed by adding, removing, or modifying elements until the constraint holds again.

In addition to constraints, *default values* can be specified for a role. For example, a class role might be given `"Breakfast"` as the default name, and `false` as the default value for the property *isAbstract*. If a role with default values needs to be bound, a new element can be generated and bound to the role. The default values do not need to be constants, and they can refer to other roles. For instance, the default name for a class role *KeyClass* might be defined as the name of the class role *Class* appended with `"Key"`. In order to make use of the default value, *Class* must of course be bound.

Exploiting the default values as a generative mechanism, a pattern can be used in any context where a collection of elements needs to be generated based on well-defined relationships between existing and the generated elements. This is the situation when a PSM is generated based on a PIM according to certain well-defined transformation rules. In this context a pattern implements a transformation rule or a set of transformation rules. We call such patterns *transformational patterns*. Assuming tool-assisted binding and element generation, patterns offer an attractive approach to realize MDA transformations.

A transformational pattern spans multiple domains. For example, consider a transformation from UML to EJB. The set of valid elements for binding contains all the elements from the UML and EJB models. The domain of the pattern contains the metaclasses from the UML metamodel and the metaclasses from the EJB metamodel. Role types include class role (UML), association role (UML), data schema role (EJB), component role (EJB), etc. From the pattern's point of

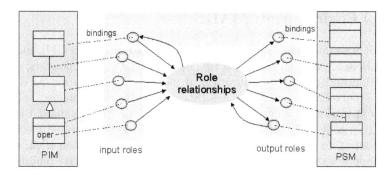

Fig. 1. A transformational pattern as a function

view, there is a single model, comprised of the UML model and the EJB model, side-by-side, but separate.

The purpose of the transformational pattern is to modify (a fragment of) the combined model so that the constraints for the pattern's roles hold for the model elements. Of course, the constraints only need to hold for elements bound to roles in the pattern. If the target model is empty, and all elements in the source model are bound, the constraints can be satisfied by creating new elements in the target model. If the default value cannot be computed, or does not exist, the constraints cannot be satisfied automatically. In a case where there are bound elements in both the source and the target model, constraint violating elements must be modified, and new elements provided for unbound roles.

To put it in a bit more formal way, a transformational pattern can be seen as a function that for a pattern instance computes the default values for unbound role instances (*output roles*) from the values of the bound role instances (*input roles*). One new element is created for each output role and the element is bound to the role. It is important to note, that the division to input and output roles does not necessarily reflect the division to source and target elements. It is very much possible to compute some source *and* target elements based on a set of existing source and target elements. Figure 1 illustrates a transformational pattern function.

The specifications of default values of roles are called *element templates*. For role r, this specification is denoted with function $Elem_r(Bound(r_1), \ldots, Bound(r_k))$, where $r_1, \ldots, r_k$ are the roles referenced in the element template specification. $Bound(r_i)$ represents the element e_i bound to role r_i. The function yields a new concrete element, assuming that the roles $r_1, \ldots, r_k$ have been bound. $Elem_o$ needs to be evaluated for each output role o. This is possible, if default values are specified and the references between the output roles imply a partial order. For any sequence $o_1, \ldots, o_n$, where o_i never depends on o_j when $i < j$, the elements for output roles can be computed with

$$Bound(o_1) = Elem_{o_1}(Bound(r_{1,1}), \ldots, Bound(r_{1,k_1})) = Elem_{o_1}(e_1, \ldots, e_{k_1})$$
$$\ldots$$
$$Bound(o_n) = Elem_{o_n}(Bound(r_{n,1}), \ldots, Bound(r_{n,k_n})) \ .$$

4 Tool Environment: MADE

MADE [5] is an integrated collection of tools for pattern-driven UML modelling. Rational Rose [6], a UML modelling tool, is one of the key components, enabling visualization and manual modification of models. We have used MADE as a prototype tool environment for transformational patterns (explained in Sect. 3). Although MADE has not been designed with transformations in mind, the underlying pattern concept is sufficiently generic to provide the required mechanisms and user interface for applying transformational patterns in the UML domain. MADE supports the specification of patterns, and the interactive binding of the roles of a pattern to UML model elements residing in Rose.

A key functionality of the environment is, that it transforms a (possibly partially bound) pattern into a task list. A task is generated for each unbound role, but only if all the other roles it depends on are already bound. The designer completes such a task by providing an element to bind to the role. Either the designer points out an existing model element or she asks the tool to generate a new element based on the default values for that role. She has full access to the UML modelling tool, Rose, and can manually create an element, e.g. a class, and then point that out to complete a task. The pattern specification can be associated with informal instructions for binding the roles, which are shown to the user when the corresponding task is to be performed.

MADE checks that role constraints are satisfied by bound elements. In the case of constraint violations, new corrective tasks are created. In many cases the tool can provide an option to correct the model automatically. Because binding information is preserved even after applying the pattern has been completed, any constraint violating changes to the model can be detected. For example, free model editing actions in Rose can cause corrective tasks. Persistent bindings also save from having to re-apply patterns when the model is changed.

The tool also maintains a list of pattern instances. Patterns with constraint violations or unbound roles are indicated with a red marker. When the designer selects a pattern, only tasks related to that pattern are displayed. This helps the user keep focused and not get distracted by concerns irrelevant to her goal. For the same reason, tasks that can not be performed at the moment are not shown.

For use with transformational patterns, the central functionality of the tool environment is the incremental, task-driven binding process, combined with the generation of default elements. This allows for stepwise performing of a transformation, keeping the designer aware and in control of each step. The designer can customize the transformation process by following different task paths. Further, a pattern stores the information about the transformation, so that it can be later retrieved and used for various purposes (e.g. tracing, comprehension, visualization). Some parts of the transformation can be easily redone later, as long as the constraints defined by the pattern still hold after the changes.

The MADE environment is still in the prototype stage, and there are shortcomings in some areas. For example, pattern combining is still under development, and currently only allows static combining. A groups of patterns can be composed and then applied instead of a single pattern. However, patterns cannot be added to a group dynamically, for example, based on properties of the model or user decisions. Also, the tool provides no real visual notation for pattern definitions or for (partially or completely) bound pattern instances. It is possible to highlight elements bound to a specified pattern instance, but that does not show which element corresponds to which role in the pattern.

MADE has not been designed explicitly for transformational patterns. Relations between pattern roles are modelled as dependencies instead of associations, and are thus directed. This is not a problem with design patterns, but it does make transformational patterns unidirectional in practice. The lack of associations also makes it impossible to navigate from a role directly to a related role with OCL. Navigation is performed by referring to the role by its name.

5   Applying Transformational Patterns in MDA: An EJB Example

The example is a transformation of a UML model (PIM) (Fig. 2) to an EJB model (PSM). Starting with a set of informal, natural language transformation rules we form transformational patterns, which are entered into the MADE tool. The patterns are then applied to the source model to produce the target model.

The UML model and the set of transformation rules were adapted from an example by Kleppe et al. [7]. The model describes a small business, Rosa's Breakfast Service, and consists of 7 classes and 5 associations. The structure of the PIM is presented in the class diagram in Fig. 2, but most attributes have been omitted to keep the diagram small. The transformation rules (in Fig. 3) have been re-worded, but should still express the idea of the original ones. Although the example is rather small, it does require roughly 40 separate invocations of the rules listed. It is therefore suitable for demonstrating our approach.

Some of the rules refer to a *root class*. In this context it means the root of the hierarchy implied by composite-associations between classes. For example, in Fig. 2, the root class of *Breakfast* is *BreakfastOrder*, and the root class of *Customer* is *Customer* itself. An EJB data schema (or an EJB component) *cor-*

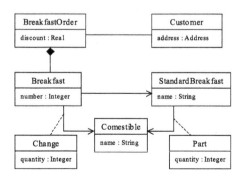

Fig. 2. PIM of Rosa's Breakfast Service (adapted from [7, Fig. 4-2, p.48])

1. (a) For each PIM class, an EJB key class is generated.
   (b) For each PIM association class, an EJB key class is generated.
2. For each root class, an EJB component and an EJB schema are generated.
3. For each PIM class, an EJB data class residing in the EJB data schema corresponding to the PIM class is generated.
4. Each PIM association is transformed into an EJB association.
5. For each PIM association class, two EJB associations and a data class are generated.
6. Each attribute of a PIM class is transformed into an EJB attribute of a data class.
7. Each PIM operation is transformed into an EJB operation of the EJB component corresponding to the PIM class of the PIM operation.

Fig. 3. Informal transformation rules (adapted from [7, p.58])

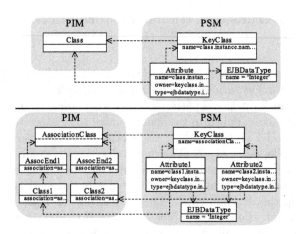

Fig. 4. Two of the transformational patterns corresponding to the informal rules

responding to a PIM class is the schema (component) that was generated by rule 2 based on the root class of the PIM class.

Each informal rule is modelled as a single transformational pattern, except for rules 1, 4, and 5, which have two alternative patterns. The rules could have, of course, been modelled in many different ways, resulting in a different set of patterns. Fig. 4 shows two of the patterns, and the rest are omitted for brevity. The top one corresponds to rule 1a, and describes the relationship between a UML class and an EJB key class. The bottom one corresponds to rule 1b. Both patterns have already been converted to a form required by the MADE tool. I.e., associations have been replaced by dependencies and OCL-constraints refer to pattern roles directly by their names instead of navigating along associations.

Each class (rectangle) in the picture represents a role and a dependence (arrow) between roles means that one role refers to the other in a constraint or a default value specification. The smaller of the two patterns in Fig. 4 contains four roles; *Class* (UML class role), *KeyClass* (EJB key class role), *Attribute* (EJB attribute role), and *EJBDataType* (EJB datatype role).

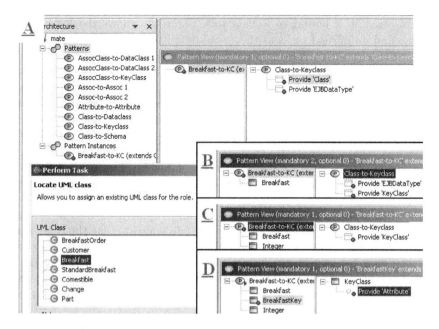

Fig. 5. Four screenshots from applying the pattern Class-to-Keyclass

KeyClass refers to *Class*, and *Attribute* refers to every other role. Constraints are shown inside the class symbols, one OCL constraint per line. For example, *Attribute* has three constraints; the first one constrains the name, the second one requires *Attribute* to be contained within *KeyClass*, and the third one states that *Attribute's* type must be *EJBDataType*. The constraints have been cut off at the edge of the class. For example, the complete constraint for *KeyClass* is `name = class.instance.name +'Key'`. The default values for attributes have been omitted, since in this case they would look exactly like the constraints.

To apply the patterns, the designer opens the source model in Rose and starts MADE. She can then select, e.g. the Class-to-KeyClass -pattern (Fig. 4, on top) and begin applying it. No roles are bound yet, and only two of the pattern's roles, *Class* and *EJBDataType*, do not depend on other roles. Therefore there will be two visible tasks: `Provide 'Class'` and `Provide 'EJBDataType'`. The designer can now select the task for *Class* and choose to locate an existing element.

Figure 5a contains a screenshot of MADE at this moment. The top left corner shows the pattern selection, as well as a list of pattern instances. The next pane to the right contains a view of the active pattern instance. This pane is empty, because there are no elements bound to the pattern instance's roles. The pane in the top right corner shows current tasks. A dialogue for selecting a UML class to be bound to the *Class* role is in the lower left corner.

The designer chooses to apply the transformation on the class *Breakfast*. The class *Breakfast* is bound to the role *Class*, satisfying the task `Provide 'Class'`, which disappears. A new task appears for *KeyClass*, because it only refers to *Class*, which is now bound. *Breakfast* appears in the list of bound elements, signifying that it is bound to a class role. Figure 5b shows the list of bound elements and unfinished tasks as they would appear.

Let us assume that the target model has already been populated with the basic data types, such as string, integer, etc. The designer can select the task for *EJBDataType* and choose to locate an existing element. The constraint (`name = 'Integer'`) is used to locate the class. The task is now completed, and disappears (Fig. 5c). *Integer* is added to the list of bound elements. No new tasks appear.

The designer highlights the remaining task and chooses to automatically complete it. Default value has been specified for role *KeyClass* and the tool creates a new class with the name *BreakfastKey* in Rose. The generated element is bound to the role, and added to the list of bound elements. The completed task disappears and a new one appears for the role *Attribute* (Fig. 5d).

The element for the attribute role, too, can be generated, and the designer chooses to have MADE do that. A new attribute is created for the class *BreakfastKey*, the name of the attribute is set to `"BreakfastID"`, and its type is set to be the class *Integer*. The task is completed, *BreakfastID* is added to the list of bound elements, and the task disappears. The pattern has now been applied successfully for *Breakfast*. For this PIM, the pattern would be applied 4 more times, once for each regular class.

For the two association classes, the pattern in the lower half of Fig. 4 is used. After choosing to apply the pattern, tasks appear for *AssociationClass* and *EJBDataType*. The latter can be automatically bound to the correct basic type (*Integer*). The designer has to select the association class manually, and she picks *Change*. Three new tasks appear, one for each of *KeyClass*, *AssocEnd1*, and *AssocEnd2*. The designer lets the tool create an element for *KeyClass*. She completes the active tasks by manually binding each association end.

The two new tasks (for *Class1* and *Class2*) could be fulfilled automatically, since an association end can only be connected to a single class. However, the automatic locating of elements in MADE works based on the value of the name field only. The designer has to choose those manually, too. The elements for *Attribute1* and *Attribute2* can be generated automatically, and that is what she decides to do. Applying the pattern is finished.

6   Evaluation

The first thing to note about the example is how much user interaction it requires. Each transformational pattern must be applied manually, and the user must initiate each generate or locate operation, even if the tool can complete it autonomously. With a source model of 41 elements (classes, attributes, etc.), as in the example, there will be 41 instances of transformational patterns applied. With the exact rules used here, this translates to 163 manual selections and 93 automatically located or generated elements. This observation, although correct, is in many ways misleading.

The numbers are in no way absolute, because they are highly dependent on how the rules are modelled. Regardless of the exact numbers, the burden on the user is far too high. However, the low level of autonomy is due to the tool, not the approach, and the user interaction could be greatly reduced with simple measures. In fact, because this particular set of rules is unambiguous, the user's participation could be limited to simply initiating the transformation. It should be noted, that we do not consider full automation as an important goal.

MADE can be instructed to automatically bind every role as soon as the roles it depends on are bound. If this option were extended to take into account more than just the name field, the user would be relieved of many monotonous tasks. If, in addition, each transformational pattern were applied automatically to each configuration of elements that satisfies the pattern's structure and other constraints, all but 14 cases of user choices could be eliminated. In those cases, a single pattern by itself does not have enough information of the transformation as a whole to locate or generate the necessary elements. In order to make the correct choices, the tool must have some idea of the way the individual patterns overlap and interact. We believe this could be achieved by expanding the experimental pattern composition functionality to allow dynamic composition.

Applying transformational patterns, even with the most basic tool support, fulfills many of the requirements discussed in Sect. 2. The approach is transparent, and does not hide transformation mechanics. The designer has full command of the process, and can change any details right down to the level of individual bindings. Even when the tool is improved to better facilitate automatic steps, they will only be engaged at the user's discretion, not the tool's. This all helps the designer to understand each step of the process, which leads to openness.

Customisability is limited to user's choices and relies on her decisions. A task can be defined as optional, and if chosen, can reveal an otherwise inaccessible path of tasks. It might also be possible to use dynamic composition of patterns to introduce more elaborate variation points. Customisability is one of the areas where better mechanisms and further research is needed.

Patterns, as implemented on MADE, are biased towards a direction, because dependencies are directed. But patterns as described in Sect. 3 use associations to express relations between roles. Forcing the user to choose in which role a symmetric constraint is placed does tilt the balance in favour of one direction over the other. Using associations, the other role(s), too, could have such a symmetric constraint. Constraints could even copied and added automatically for simple constraints, such as equality, that are easily recognised as symmetric.

MADE stores information about bindings, which makes the record of transformation persistent. Even after modifications to the models, the record can still be used as a starting point for synchronizing the models. None of the user decisions are lost, although some might have become irrelevant. Reversibility and traceability can thus be achieved. On the other hand, MADE lacks facilities, illustrative or not, to visualise these mappings. Elements that are bound to a particular pattern instance can be highlighted in Rational Rose, but there is no indication of which role an element is bound to. So, it is possible to find out information about the relations between elements of different models, but there is no easy way to study it in the tool.

Using patterns for transformations enables performing the transformation in small, incremental steps. The problems with the current machinery are in combining these steps into transformations and, further combining transformations together into bigger transformations. This has a negative effect on reusability and maintainability. Lack of visualisation also makes documenting more difficult.

To recap; our approach, as it is now, provides open, incremental, traceable, reversible, and unbiased transformations, but has problems when it comes to visualising, customising and combining transformations. The current tool environment works for evaluating the approach, but is not mature enough for real transformations. It burdens the user with some tasks it should carry out automatically and supports only unidirectional transformations. Improving facilities, both with the approach and the tool, to properly address the challenges is vital.

7   Related Work

Work by Hausmann et al. on visualizing model mappings [8] is partly driven by goals similar to ours. In their work, mappings between model elements are thought of as relations in the mathematical sense. Model mappings are expressed with extended UML class and object diagrams. The importance of comprehensible transformations and rules is one of the main issues raised and discussed. Being based on relations, the approach encourages bi-directional transformations.

QVT-Partners' response [9] to the Query / Views / Transformations (QVT) request for proposals is one of the most detailed and finished work. It describes a language for transformations and a textual and a visual representation for it. Transformations are divided into relations and mappings. Relations are birectional, but can only be used for checking whether the source and target model are properly synchronized. Mappings are used for performing a transformation, but are restricted to one direction.

Many approaches at MDA transformations are based on graph grammars. Such approaches tend to produce strictly unidirectional transformations due to the clear separation to left hand side (LHS) and right hand side (RHS) in individual rules. Also, definitions are often given only in a textual form. For example, GREAT [10] is a graph rewrite system for transformations on UML models, where LHS is defined with a textual language. RHS is defined as Java code, which manipulates the model through an API. Such transformations are, of course, unidirectional.

The theories behind VMT [11] and BOTL [12], too, are based on graphs. Both use attributed labelled graphs and offer a graphical notation for describing a source (LHS) and target template (RHS) for transformation rules. In VMT transformations can only be performed on UML models and in one direction. BOTL transformations can be bi-directional and can handle arbitrary metamodels. The expressive power of VMT's visual notation is enhanced with OCL.

Some approaches use XSLT to process models in XMI form. Due to the nature of XMI these approaches are rarely limited to a single metamodel. XSLT-based methods are often textual, but UMLX [13] is a graphical transformation language. The metamodels (called "schemas" in UMLX) is given using a subset of the UML class diagram notation. Transformations are defined with an extended class diagram notation, and are translated into XSLT form using the information about the structure of the metamodel. The XSLT is then executed on the input, which is provided in XMI form. Transformations are unidirectional.

A textual transformation language, based on rules, is described in [7]. The language is intended as a means to illustrate the sample transformations, and not as a real transformation language. Transformations are composed of small rules and can be declared as either unidirectional or bi-directional. OCL has an important role in the language.

The focus on most papers is on explaining the mechanics of the language or approach. Characteristics such as openness, customisability, maintainability, and how illustrative are the notations used, fall out of scope. It is therefore difficult to determine how much emphasis is placed on these aspects, which in our view are of great importance.

Similarly to our approach, Catalysis [14] makes use of role-based patterns (so-called "frameworks") for describing abstract collaborations of model elements. A major difference is that Catalysis emphasizes specifications of the semantics of the collaboration while we have a more pragmatic view emphasizing task-driven model (or code) generation based on the default value specifications.

8   Concluding Remarks and Future Work

In this paper we first listed and discussed what we believe to be key requirements for MDA transformations: openness, customisability, combinability, traceability, and maintainability. The new approach at MDA transformations, transformational patterns, was described and explained. A more generic pattern tool, MADE, was presented briefly. An example of performing a simple transformation using transformational patterns and the tool was presented. The approach was evaluated in light of its applicability in the example and its compliance with the key MDA requirements. Last, other groups' work on visualising and defining model transformations and mappings was discussed.

The example was very limited, but it did indicate some strengths and weaknesses of transformational patterns. We wish to pursue several related issues further. Visualisation of patterns, as well as the reverse, discovering patterns from examples are important for usability. Defining and utilizing variation points is another area of interest for us. The rule composition mechanism needs more flexibility. We are looking into implicit and explicit rule scheduling, as well as some hybrid solutions. Also, the tool support must be elevated. We are currently working on supporting arbitrary MOF-based metamodels in processing and visualisation. We hope to carry out a more realistic case study, where neither the transformation specification nor the set of models is unrealistically simple.

References

1. OMG: Model driven architecture (MDA) (2001) On-line at http://www.omg.org/cgi-bin/apps/doc?ormsc/01-07-01.pdf.
2. Interactive Objects Software: Arcstyler tool homepage (2004) on-line at http://www.arcstyler.com/.
3. Hakala, M., Hautamäki, J., Koskimies, K., Paakki, J., Viljamaa, A., Viljamaa, J.: Generating application development environments for java frameworks. In: Proceedings of the Third International Conference on Generative and Component-Based Software Engineering, Springer-Verlag (2001) 163–176
4. OMG: MDA guide version 1.0.1 (2003) On-line at http://www.omg.org/cgi-bin/apps/doc?omg/03-06-01.pdf.
5. Hammouda, I., Pussinen, M., Katara, M., Mikkonen, T.: Uml-based approach for documenting and specializing frameworks using patterns and concern architectures. In: The 4th AOSD Modeling With UML Workshop. (2003)
6. Rational: Rational Rose home page (2004) on-line at http://www.rational.com/.
7. Kleppe, A., Warmer, J., Bast, W.: MDA Explained: The Model Driven Architecture: Practice and Promise. Addison-Wesley (2003)
8. Hausmann, J., Kent, S.: Visualizing model mappings in UML. In: Proceedings of the ACM Symposium on Software Visualization. (2003)
9. QVT-Partners: Revised submission for MOF 2.0 Query / Views / Transformations RFP (2003) On-line at http://www.omg.org/cgi-bin/apps/doc?ad/03-08-08.pdf.
10. Christoph, A.: Graph rewrite systems for software design transformations. In: Revised Papers from the International Conference NetObjectDays on Objects, Components, Architectures, Services, and Applications for a Networked World, Springer-Verlag (2003) 76–86
11. Sendall, S., Perrouin, G., Guelfi, N., Biberstein, O.: Supporting model-to-model transformations: The VMT approach. In Rensink, A., ed.: CTIT Technical Report TR-CTIT-03-27, Enschede, The Netherlands, University of Twente (2003) 61–72
12. Braun, P., Marschall, F.: BOTL - the bidirectional object oriented transformation language. Technical Report TUM-I0307, Technische Universität München (2003)
13. Willink, E.D.: UMLX: A graphical transformation language for MDA. In Rensink, A., ed.: CTIT Technical Report TR-CTIT-03-27, Enschede, The Netherlands, University of Twente (2003) 13–24
14. Catalysis: Catalysis home page (2005) on-line at http://www.catalysis.org/.

"Weaving" MTL Model Transformations

Raul Silaghi, Frédéric Fondement, and Alfred Strohmeier

Software Engineering Laboratory,
Swiss Federal Institute of Technology in Lausanne,
CH-1015 Lausanne EPFL, Switzerland
{Raul.Silaghi, Frederic.Fondement,
Alfred.Strohmeier}@epfl.ch

Abstract. Model transformations are the core of the MDA approach to software development. As specified by the OMG, model transformations should act on any kind of model of any kind of metamodel, which implies the possible "reflective" use of model transformations, i.e., model transformations acting on model transformations. However, this requires transformation developers to be familiar with the metamodel of the transformation language itself, which is not always the case. In order to overcome such a frustrating impediment for the MTL language, and inspired by AOP approaches, we have designed and implemented an MTL *weaver* that modifies MTL transformations according to some *weaving behavior*, which is specified as special MTL transformations, called *MTL-aspects*, using an AOP-like extension to the MTL language. Both the weaver and the language extension are presented in this paper, and an example is used to show how transformation developers can take advantage of the proposed language extension constructs in order to write "reflective" model transformations in MTL without requiring any previous knowledge of the MTL metamodel itself.

Keywords: Model-Driven Architecture, MDA, Model Transformations, MTL, Aspect-Oriented Programming, AOP.

1 Introduction

To escape from the proliferation of middleware infrastructures and to avoid drowning in their implementation complexities, models are proposed as a far more accessible and easier means for developers to build, extend, and evaluate applications than working directly at the code level. The Model Driven Architecture (MDA) [1][2], an Object Management Group (OMG) [3] initiative, promotes the separation of concerns between two modeling dimensions: one focusing on the business functionality (resulting in *Platform Independent Models – PIMs*), and the other one focusing on the implementation of that functionality on a specific middleware platform (resulting in *Platform Specific Models – PSMs*). Since in this paper we consider the *middleware* to be our MDA platform, further on we will directly refer to the middleware instead of the general concept of (MDA) platform.

Besides the obvious importance of PIMs and PSMs in MDA, *model transformations* are undoubtedly the key technology in the realization of the MDA

U. Aßmann, M. Aksit, and A. Rensink (Eds.): MDAFA 2003/2004, LNCS 3599, pp. 123–138, 2005.

vision [4]. Among other usages, model transformations are the ones responsible for refining PIMs into PSMs (or abstracting away from PSMs to PIMs) and mapping PSMs to concrete middleware-based implementations, providing thus an elegant approach to adapt PIMs to the peculiarities of the new middleware infrastructures that do not cease to appear.

Unfortunately, there is not yet a standard language for defining model transformations. To fill this gap, OMG has issued a Request for Proposal called MOF 2.0 Query/Views/Transformations RFP [5], which has been answered by eight different initial submissions, five revised submissions, and finally two "joint" revised submissions.

A clear requirement in OMG's RFP was (and still is) that model transformations should be able to act on *any kind of model of any kind of metamodel*. Since model transformations are at the same time models compliant with the metamodel of the transformation language, model transformations should be able to *transform* other model transformations independently of their metamodels. As a consequence, all currently existing model transformation languages (to our knowledge) implement such a "reflective" behavior. However, the "reflective" use of model transformations is not trivial.

Typically, writing model transformations for driving the development process of domain-specific applications requires the transformation developer to be familiar with the metamodel of that specific domain and with the syntax of the model transformation language used – and no more than that. As a consequence, many transformation developers are not at all familiar with the metamodel of the transformation language itself, and thus they are not capable of writing "reflective" model transformations, i.e., model transformations that transform already existing model transformations.

In order to overcome this frustrating impediment for the INRIA Model Transformation Language (MTL) [6], we present in this paper a solution inspired by Aspect-Oriented Programming (AOP) [7] approaches. We have designed and implemented an MTL *weaver* that modifies MTL transformations according to some *weaving behavior* that is specified as a special kind of MTL transformations, called *MTL-aspects*. The MTL transformation produced by the MTL weaver can be immediately used for refining application models.

Like in AspectJ [8][9], which is an aspect-oriented extension to Java, the syntax defining the weaving behavior in MTL-aspects is a small AOP-like extension to the MTL language itself. In this way, relying on a few high-level AOP-like but MTL-based constructs for defining the weaving behavior, average MTL transformation developers should not have any problems using this MTL extension straightforwardly for defining their "reflective" model transformations.

The rest of the paper is structured as follows: Section 2 provides the motivation of this work by discussing concrete examples where such a weaving functionality is useful; Section 3 gives a concise overview of the MTL model transformation language; Section 4 introduces the MTL weaver, describes the AOP-like extension to MTL for defining the weaving behavior in MTL-aspects, and presents an example showing both the input and the output of a concrete weaving; Section 5 draws some conclusions and presents future work directions.

2 Motivation

Based on our experience with MTL transformations, we present in this section how currently applied MTL transformations benefit from the weaving support provided by the MTL weaver, promoting the separation of concerns paradigm even at the level of model transformations.

Separation of concerns [10] and modularization are fundamental techniques of software engineering. Decomposing software into smaller, more manageable and comprehensible parts, each of which encapsulating and addressing a particular area of interest, called a *concern*, is a well-proven method for developing applications that are easy to configure, adapt, or extend according to changes in the requirements specification.

Middleware is an essential element in large distributed systems like those that support enterprise applications and require multiple heterogeneous components to interoperate. Moreover, middleware, like software in general, is subject to concerns. Several concern-dimensions specific to middleware can be grouped into a category called Middleware Services, as middleware addresses specific concerns of a system, such as distribution, concurrency, security, or transactions. An extended list of categories that group several middleware-specific concern-dimensions can be found in [11].

In order to address such middleware services in an MDA fashion and following the separation of concerns principle, we defined the Enterprise Fondue software development method [12]. As an integral part of the Enterprise Fondue method, we propose several MDA-oriented UML profiles that address middleware-specific concerns at different levels of abstraction. MTL transformations are used to incrementally refine existing design models (within the same or between different MDA-levels) along middleware-specific concern-dimensions according to the proposed UML profiles. A complete example of applying the Enterprise Fondue method for addressing the distribution concern was presented in [13], where we considered CORBA [14] as our target implementation technology. The *UML-D Profiles* proposed in [13] address the distribution concern at three different MDA-levels of abstraction: *platform-independent* level (the `DistributionProfile`), *abstract realization* level (the `AbstractDistributionRealizationProfile`), and *concrete realization* level (the `CORBADistributionRealizationProfile`).

Based on the support provided by the MTL weaver, we refactored the MTL transformation that refined application designs along the distribution concern-dimension according to the `DistributionProfile` (as promoted by the Enterprise Fondue method). Instead of one big model transformation that performed the entire refinement, we have now a standard MTL transformation that performs the `copy` of an input model to an output model, both models being compliant with the same UML metamodel, and a very small MTL-aspect that defines the weaving behavior according to the `DistributionProfile` that has to be applied. The `MTL-Copy` transformation and the `MTL1-D-Aspect` are now fully separated from each other, just as they should be, since they address totally different concerns. Figure 1a sketches the refinement process in the presence of the `MTL1-D-Aspect`, or more

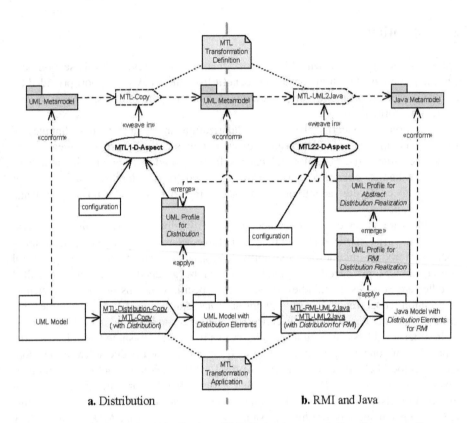

Fig. 1. Refining along the Distribution, RMI-Technology, and Java-Language Concern-Dimensions

generally in the presence of MTL-aspects. Its name, `MTL1-D-Aspect`, was chosen in accordance with the `MTL1-D` transformation defined in [13] for refining along the distribution concern-dimension. The `MTL-Distribution-Copy` transformation is the result produced by the weaver when modifying the `MTL-Copy` transformation according to the weaving directives defined in the `MTL1-D-Aspect`.

A more complex example is shown in Figure 1b, where the metamodel of the input and output models changes; we move from a UML model to a Java model that represents the concrete Java implementation. Considering as input the output model of the previous refinement process, we refine this time along the RMI-technology [15] and Java-language concern-dimensions as defined by the Enterprise Fondue method. While the `MTL-UML2Java` transformation deals with translating any UML model to its correspondent Java model (relying on their respective metamodels), the `MTL22-D-Aspect` addresses how distribution specific elements in the UML model are translated into their Java model counterparts when employing RMI as their implementation technology. For instance, interfaces marked as «Distributed» in the UML model will extend `java.rmi.Remote` in the Java model; similarly, the class of the object marked as «Servant» will extend `java.rmi.server.UnicastRemoteObject` in the Java model, and so on. Once again, the name,

MTL22-D-Aspect, was chosen in accordance with the MTL22-D transformation defined in [13] even though we considered this time another technology, i.e., we have chosen RMI instead of CORBA. The MTL-RMI-UML2Java transformation is the result produced by the weaver when modifying the MTL-UML2Java transformation according to the weaving directives defined in the MTL22-D-Aspect.

As can be seen in Figure 1, the support provided by the MTL weaver has enabled us to modularize the different concerns in stand-alone units of encapsulation represented by MTL-aspects. In this way, we give transformation developers not only the possibility, but also the means to rely on the well-proven power of separation of concerns even at the model transformation level. Moreover, the size of such MTL-aspects is very small, compared to the corresponding implementation in the initial MTL transformations, since they rely on the MTL weaver which is now the one carrying all the burden of the weaving. The example presented in Figure 1a is reconsidered in section 4.2, where we discuss in more details its complete implementation.

Besides encapsulating middleware-specific concerns into MTL-aspects as presented in this section, the number of possible usages of such MTL-aspects is unlimited since the support provided by the MTL language enables us to implement almost anything in the MTL weaver, and thus, the expressiveness power that could be provided to transformation developers through the MTL extension syntax may be very broad, covering all possible and impossible needs that developers may think of.

3   The Model Transformation Language (MTL)

This section provides a concise overview of the MTL transformation language focusing mainly on the concepts that are relevant in the context of this paper. Readers that are familiar with the MTL language may skip this section and jump directly to section 4 which presents the MTL weaver.

Many different solutions have been proposed for model transformation languages, making it very hard for the OMG to merge all ideas into one future standard. Unfortunately, standards of the future are not solutions to problems of today. The idea of the INRIA Model Transformation Language (MTL) [6] is to provide *all* model transformation facilities, including the possibility to transform MTL transformations. This makes it possible for the future QVT language standard to be mapped to an MTL transformation by means of an MTL transformation. This *pivot* approach has already been validated. The MTL itself is developed according to a bootstrap approach: a simple language, called BasicMTL [16], provides the most important facilities, such as classes or attributes, and new facilities are added by extending the abstract syntax and by making a transformation from the extended to the initial syntax, always relying therefore on the small "kernel" of BasicMTL. As an example, associations between classes have been added in this way. Moreover, the plan is to transform, or in other words, to compile the Atlas Transformation Language [17] into an MTL transformation. As a conclusion, MTL aims more at *motorizing* model transformations than proposing a new standard.

As suggested just before, MTL is an object-oriented imperative language for model transformations. Therefore, MTL transformations are defined as programs in terms of classes, methods, attributes, etc. In order not to confuse these MTL constructs with the ones that the manipulated model may contain, we will further on refer to them as MTL classes, MTL methods, MTL attributes, and so on. A special entry point, the main method, has to be defined for each MTL transformation. Pieces of MTL transformations are organized in MTL *libraries*, each library being in addition responsible for holding models. Each such model can either be a collection of instances of MTL classes from an MTL library, or a collection of model elements inside a repository.

MTL is a compiled language; Figure 2 presents the compilation process. In order to compile an MTL transformation T described in an mtl file, the first step is to parse it. A parser (①) reads the transformation as text and transforms it into an internal model that is compliant with the abstract syntax of MTL [16]. In the next step, a type checker (②) refines this model by adding information about types. For instance, in order to deal with polymorphism, the type checker will perform the analysis of MTL methods in order to reference, for each of them, other MTL methods that they are overriding. If necessary, the types used by the transformation T might need to be referred (by the type checker) from already compiled MTL libraries. For example, the MTL standard library, which defines the MTL predefined types and operations, is typically used by all MTL transformations, and thus, it participates in such library-usage dependencies. In order for the MTL transformation T to be reused by other MTL transformations, its internal model, decorated with type information, is stored in a binary file (T.tll). In the end, a code generation step is performed (③). Java source files that implement the behavior described by the internal (refined) model of the MTL transformation T are generated, and they will make use of the model repositories on which the implemented transformation was defined to act. We used two * signs in Figure 2 in order to show that many precompiled libraries (*.tll) may be needed, on one hand, and several Java source files (*.java) may be generated, on the other hand, for one single MTL transformation. If transformation T relies on other libraries, the generated Java source files for T will require the Java source files that resulted from the compilation of those libraries.

The entire compilation process relies on the model of the MTL transformation T itself, which complies with the well-defined MTL metamodel. Therefore, steps ①, ②, and ③ can be viewed as special transformations acting on the MTL model of the

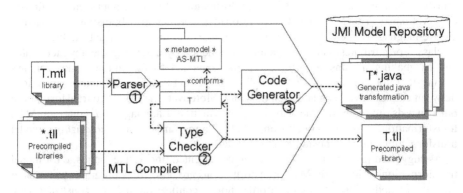

Fig. 2. The MTL Compilation Process

transformation T itself. Besides these three steps, it is at this MTL model level of the MTL transformations that new special transformations may be defined in order to change the very behavior of those MTL transformations. Following this idea, our MTL weaver is indeed implemented as such a special transformation, acting on the MTL models of the MTL transformations and transforming them according to the weaving behavior defined in MTL-aspects, as we will see in section 4.

4 The MTL Weaver

Reusability has always been an important concern in the software development industry because of its potential to reduce the cost of software development. During the last decade, different levels of reuse have been proposed, such as functions, procedures, classes, components, aspects, or even entire models. But how can we achieve the reuse of model transformations? How to adapt existing model transformations that successfully fulfill most of our needs?

The reuse of MTL transformations is currently promoted at the level of MTL libraries, which are some kind of light model transformation components. In this section, we present some implementation details and the facilities provided by an aspect-oriented support that allow transformation developers to reuse existing MTL transformations and to easily adapt them in order to address new needs, or concerns, that the application under development has to incorporate. The main concepts of the MTL weaver are introduced along with the AOP-like extension to MTL for defining the weaving behavior in MTL-aspects. We also present an example showing both the input and the output of a concrete weaving.

The standard MTL language already provides support for transformation developers to define MTL transformations that *transform* other MTL transformations. However, writing such "reflective" MTL transformations still requires transformation developers to be familiar with the metamodel of the MTL language itself, a requirement that significantly reduces the number of such developers. In order to overcome this impediment for the MTL language, we propose a solution inspired by AOP approaches. We have designed and implemented an MTL *weaver* that modifies MTL transformations according to some *weaving behavior* that is specified in terms of *weaving directives* modularized in special stand-alone MTL transformation encapsulation units called *MTL-aspects*. Like in AspectJ, which is an aspect-oriented extension to Java, the syntax defining the weaving behavior in MTL-aspects is a small AOP-like extension to the MTL language itself. In this way, relying on a few high-level AOP-like but MTL-based constructs for defining the weaving behavior, average MTL transformation developers should not have any problems using this MTL extension straightforwardly for defining their "reflective" model transformations.

The place of the MTL weaver in the MTL compilation process and the evolution of the MTL weaving process are presented in Figure 3, where the MTL transformation T is refined according to the weaving directives defined in the MTL-aspect A. The weaving process is very similar to the compilation process presented in Figure 2. First, both T and A are parsed (①) in order to transform the two text files into internal MTL models compliant with the MTL metamodel. The important change comes next, when the *MTL Weaver* (②) reads the two internal models of T and A, and produces a

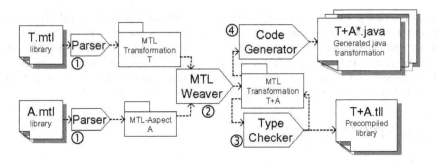

Fig. 3. The MTL Weaving Process

new model instance (of the MTL metamodel) for the new MTL transformation T+A, which represents the result of modifying T according to the weaving directives defined in A. Even though it is not explicitly shown in Figure 3, the MTL weaver itself is implemented as an MTL transformation as well. Once this weaving step is finished, the normal compilation process can continue with the type checking step (③), which produces a reusable precompiled MTL library, and the code generation step (④), which produces Java source files. One may notice that the weaving process results in a completely new MTL transformation, without making any changes to the original MTL transformation T. In this way, both transformations can independently be reused later on in order to transform application models. Moreover, the MTL-aspect A may be reused as well for refining other MTL transformations according to the same weaving directives.

4.1   MTL-Based Syntax for Describing the Weaving Behavior

There are two major requirements that an MTL-aspect must fulfill. First, it must clearly identify *where* the modifications have to be performed, and second, it must clearly define *what* are those modifications. In AOP terminology, a *join point* is a well-defined point in the execution of a program where additional functionality may be "injected". To identify such points in our weaving process, a *pattern matching* mechanism is used based on the names of the MTL libraries, MTL classes, MTL methods, etc. Both requirements can be expressed using the MTL syntax, relying on small extensions that are detailed in this section.

One of the extension mechanisms proposed by the MTL language is the tagging facility. *Tags* are key/value pairs associated either with an MTL library, an MTL class, or an MTL method. Since tags are part of the MTL metamodel, once they are analyzed by the MTL parser, they populate the internal MTL model representing the MTL transformation. This makes it possible for the MTL weaver presented in Figure 3 ② to access these tags and to use them for very different purposes. Since MTL-aspects only rely on the *tag* extension mechanism to define additional weaving directives, it is possible to use the same parser for reading both MTL-aspects and MTL transformations, as shown in Figure 3 ①.

In order to give an example of an MTL-aspect that could play the role of A in Figure 3, we show in Figure 4 some snippets of the MTL1-D-Aspect. For the sake of readability, we will further on refer to the MTL library taken as input for the weaving process as *input library*, i.e., the library that plays the role of T in Figure 3, and its elements as *input classes*, *input methods*, etc. The MTL library produced as a result of the weaving process, T+A in Figure 3, will further on be referred to as *output library*, and its elements as *output classes*, *output methods*, etc.

Each line in Figure 4 may be considered as a weaving directive for the MTL weaver. For instance, the first line defines the name of the input library in which the MTL1-D-Aspect will have to be weaved, i.e., Copy. In order not to alter the Copy input library during the weaving process and to avoid name clashes between input and output libraries, the name of the output library has to be provided. This can be achieved by defining a tag on the MTL library of the MTL-aspect. We have named this tag rename, and its value represents the name of the MTL library produced as a result of the weaving process, e.g., Distribution in this particular case.

By default, elements of the input library will be simply reproduced in the output library. However, this simple reproduction can be tuned by the rest of the MTL-aspect. For instance, in Figure 4 ①, the MTL class Copier is defined. This weaving directive indicates to the MTL weaver that if a class with the same name exists in the input library, then the reproduced class in the output library contains both the members in the input class and the ones defined in the MTL-aspect class. This process is called *class merge*. On the other hand, if such a class does not exist in the input library, then it will simply be added to the output library exactly as defined in the MTL-aspect, i.e., it will include all member definitions defined by the MTL-aspect, e.g., the servantIterfaceName MTL attribute and the initDI MTL method.

```
     library Copy;
     tag rename := specialtag [Distribution];

①  class Copier {
        servantIterfaceName : Standard::String;

        initDI(sin : Standard::String) : Copier {
           self.servantIterfaceName := sin;
           return self;
        }
     }

②  class [{Copier$}]{
        [{^getTarget (.*)}] (theSource : Standard: :ModelElement)
        tag merge := specialtag [Append] ;
        tag refactorParameters := booleantag true;  {
           theSource.toOut () ;
        }
     }
```

Fig. 4. Snippets of the MTL1-D-Aspect

A *conflict* may appear during a class merge if some members in the matching input classes and in the MTL-aspect class have the same name. If the member in the MTL-aspect is an attribute, it will be added as it is, without worrying whether the name of the attribute already exists in the input MTL library, since the rest of the compilation process will detect such a duplicate attribute, if any, and an error will be thrown. For methods, the detected conflict is registered to be solved later.

MTL-aspect developers may refer to many MTL classes or MTL methods in a single pattern by relying on "wildcard" facilities, such as an underscore "_", which matches any name, or more sophisticated regular expressions delimited by curly brackets. For instance, in Figure 4 ②, the class named {Copier$}, matches all input classes whose names end (denoted by $) with "Copier", and its method {^getTarget(.*)} matches all input methods, defined on the matched input classes, whose names start (denoted by ^) with "getTarget". However, it would be considered an abuse to use such constructs for adding new classes or methods to the output library.

The class merge process, as it is implemented in the MTL weaver, is shown in Figure 5. The libClass represents the input class, and the behaviorClass represents the MTL-aspect class. Please note that the name of the behaviorClass matches the name of the libClass as a precondition for the mergeClass method.

A method conflict may be solved according to some predefined rules. We have identified three kinds of possible rules that prescribe the MTL weaver how to manage the instructions defined by the conflicting method of the MTL-aspect:

- add MTL-aspect instructions at the very beginning of the output method,
- add MTL-aspect instructions just before returning from the output method, or
- replace input instructions with MTL-aspect instructions in the output method.

It is the responsibility of the MTL-aspect developer to indicate which alternative she desires to be chosen for a given method conflict. For this purpose, we defined the merge tag that has to be added to each conflicting method in the MTL-aspect. The three possible values corresponding to the previously described rules are Prepend, Append, and Replace respectively. If a conflict cannot be solved, the weaving process ends in failure.

```
mergeClass(libClass : BasicMtlASTView::UserClass;
           behaviorClass : BasicMtlASTView::UserClass) {
    lo : Standard::Set;
    // adding attributes
    if (isNull(behaviorClass.definedAttributes).not()) {
      foreach (at : BasicMtlASTView::Attribute) in (behaviorClass.definedAttributes) {
        libClass.appendDefinedAttributes(at);
      }
    }
    // merging operations
    foreach (bo : BasicMtlASTView::Operation) in (behaviorClass.definedMethods) {
      lo := matchingOperations(libClass, bo) ;

      if (lo.size(). [=](0)){ // to be added
          if (self.canAdd(bo)) {
            libClass.appendDefineMethods(bo);
        } else {
          bo.name.concat(' seems to be pattern; no correspondence found.'). toOut();
          'ignoring addition to class '.concat(libClass.name).toOut();
        }
      } else { // conflict, to be treated later
        self.operationConflicts := operationConflicts.including(
                              new OperationConflict().init(libClass, lo, bo));
      }
    }
}
```

Fig. 5. MTL Weaver Snippets for Class Merge (mergeClass)

The instructions in the MTL-aspect method may need to refer to some parameters of the matched input methods. The presence of the boolean tag `refactor Parameters` set to `true` makes such parameters accessible inside the MTL-aspect according to the names provided in the MTL-aspect method. Moreover, this tag requests the method matching mechanism to take into account the number of parameters of the input methods rather than just matching the names of the methods.

As an example, Figure 4 ② states that for all input methods whose names start with "getTarget" inside classes whose names end with "Copier", the first parameter, named in the MTL-aspect `theSource`, must be sent to the console by means of the MTL predefined operation `toOut`. This output must be performed before returning from the modified MTL methods, as stated by the value `Append` of the `merge` tag defined for the MTL-aspect method.

As a summary, the list of possible tags that may appear in the definition of an MTL-aspect is provided in Table 1. The first column gives the name of the tag as it must appear in the MTL-aspect. The second column indicates on which MTL element this tag may be defined. The third column indicates whether the presence of the tag is mandatory or optional; default values are indicated for optional tags. The fourth column gives a brief description of the semantics of the possible associated values.

As we showed on some concrete examples, the MTL-aspect developer does not need to have a deep knowledge of the MTL metamodel and its semantics in order to transform an MTL transformation. All s/he needs to know is the MTL syntax and some predefined tags. Moreover, with the current implementation of the MTL weaver, an MTL-aspect is about 10 times smaller (in lines of code) and about 50

Table 1. Predefined MTL-Aspect Tags

Tag Name	Base MTL Element	Presence	Description
`rename`	Library	mandatory	The name of the output library.
`merge`	Method	mandatory if conflict	`Prepend` to add instructions at the very beginning of the method. `Append` to add instructions just before returning from the method. `Replace` to replace initial instructions with MTL-aspect instructions.
`refactorPa-rameters`	Method	optional; default value is `false`	Indicates if the number of parameters has to be taken into account by the pattern matching mechanism, and if parameters have to be intercepted for further usage inside the instructions of the MTL-aspect.

times faster to develop than a standard MTL transformation that would achieve the same weaving behavior on another MTL transformation.

Please notice, however, that the MTL weaver and the aspect-oriented support provided are relatively young, still undergoing refinement and improvement as we move along. New constructs will be added in order to address MTL-aspect developer needs and to facilitate as much as possible the development of "reflective" MTL transformations. For instance, it would be very helpful to have a pattern matching mechanism for instructions or expressions, e.g., matching all *calls* to a given method. The pattern we adopted for extending the MTL language with AOP-like constructs will remain nevertheless the same, i.e., extending the language by providing new tags that change the semantics of their base element, just like UML profiles extend the UML.

4.2 Running Example

In this part, we consider weaving the MTL1-D-Aspect in the simple MTL Copy transformation in order to modify its behavior and make a system distributed by applying the stereotypes defined in the DistributionProfile [13] according to some configuration information. Since the goal is to illustrate the most important principles of the weaving process, we focus on very small parts of the example.

The input MTL Copy transformation is specialized in copying an input UML 1.4 model to an output UML 1.4 model. Snippets of the transformation are presented in Figure 6. The transformation is located in the MTL library Copy, having two variables, in and out, for referring to the input, and output models respectively. One of the MTL classes of this library is Copier, which defines the getTarget method. This method takes as parameter a UML element srcElt from the in model, and retrieves and returns the corresponding UML element inside the out model. Another MTL class, extending Copier, is UML14CreatorCopier, which defines the

```
library Copy;
model in  : RepositoryModel;  // should be a UML1.4
MetaModel
model out : RepositoryModel;  // should be a UML1.4
MetaModel
class Copier {

getTarget(srcElt : in::Core::Element) : out::Core::Element {

    r : out::Core::Element;
    ... // compute r
    return r;

    }
}
class UML14CreatorCopier extends Copier {

getTargetClass(src : in::Core::Class) : out::Core::Class {

    r : out::Core::Class;
    r := new out::Core::Class();
    trace(src, r);
    return r;

    }
}
```

Fig. 6. Snippets of the Copy Input Library

getTargetClass method. This method takes a UML class src in the in model as parameter, and is responsible for creating and returning a UML class in the out model.

We present now two of the modifications that have to be performed in order for the MTL Copy transformation to make a system distributed. The first one is to make an interface remotely available, but before doing this we first need to identify the right interface. The solution we considered is to add an attribute, servantIterfaceName, to the MTL Copier class as a placeholder for the name of the interface to be distributed. This attribute is transmitted to the MTL Copier class by means of the new method initDI defined in the MTL1-D-Aspect. The second modification is to display on the console the UML elements from the in model for which a correspondence in the out model has been requested. A thorough analysis of the complete MTL Copy transformation would clarify that such correspondences are only requested when invoking methods whose names start with "getTarget", and which belong to a class whose name ends with "Copier". These modifications are prescribed in the MTL1-D-Aspect that was partly presented in Figure 4, where part ① corresponded to the first modification, and part ② to the second one.

The result of weaving the MTL1-D-Aspect in the MTL Copy transformation is shown in Figure 7. Even though we have clearly stated in section 4 that the results of the MTL weaving process are just MTL binaries and Java source files, Figure 7 represents what a pretty printer would produce for the MTL binary. Changes introduced by the MTL-aspect are highlighted by change bars. Since the output MTL library is different from the original MTL Copy library, renaming has occurred according to the rename tag that was specified on the library definition inside the MTL1-D-Aspect, as shown in Figure 4.

Part ① of the MTL1-D-Aspect in Figure 4 states that an MTL class named Copier must appear with a servantIterfaceName attribute and an initDI operation in the output library. Even though such an MTL Copier class already exists in the input library, no name conflicts have been found, and therefore member definitions from both the MTL-aspect and the input class are directly added to the MTL Copier output class, as shown by Figure 7 ①.

The MTL-aspect method defined in part ② of the MTL1-D-Aspect in Figure 4 matches the input methods Copier::getTarget and UML14CreatorCopier::getTargetClass. One may note that the presence of the refactorParameters tag set to true in the MTL-aspect has forced the method matching mechanism to check that only one parameter is defined for these input methods, a parameter that will further on be used as the variable theSource inside the body of the MTL-aspect method. The tag merge set to Append defined on the MTL-aspect method indicates how possible conflicts should be solved. Since conflicts have indeed been found, the instructions defined in the MTL-aspect have to be inserted in the output class in such a way that they are executed just before returning from the corresponding reproductions of the input methods in the output class, as part of the output library. To achieve this, we rely on the MTL try-catch-finally statement: instructions of the input method are reproduced in the try part, and instructions from the MTL-aspect method are reproduced in the finally part, as shown in Figure 7 ②. In this way, we enforce that instructions from the MTL-aspect method are executed just before

```
①library Distribution;
model in  : RepositoryModel;   // should be a UML1.4 MetaModel
model out : RepositoryModel;   // should be a UML1.4 MetaModel
class Copier {

servantIterfaceName : Standard::String;

initDI(sin : Standard::String) : Copier {
     self.servantIterfaceName := sin;
     return self;

}

     getTarget(srcElt : in::Core::Element) : out::Core::Element {

          r : out::Core::Element;

          theSource : Standard::ModelElement;
        theSource := srcElt; // [*]
```

②

```
     try {

     ... // compute r
     return r;

     } finally {
     theSource.toOut(); // [*]
```

```
     try {

     ... // compute r
     return r;

     } finally {
     theSource.toOut(); // [*]
```

Fig. 7. Snippets of the `Distribution` Output Library

returning from the output method, wherever an MTL `return` instruction may appear in the input method. The `true` value for the `refactorParameters` tag also instructs the MTL weaver to produce new variables in the output methods according to the parameters defined in the MTL-aspect method that are supposed to match parameters from the input methods. These new variables represent placeholders for the values of the parameters of the input methods that were intercepted by the corresponding MTL-aspect method. Applying this rule to the two input methods matching the MTL-aspect method `{^getTarget(.*)}`, new `theSource` variables will be added in the corresponding output methods for storing the very input parameters that were previously matched (see Figure 7 [*]).

5 Conclusions and Future Work

All model transformation languages that we know of provide transformation developers with the facility to define "reflective" model transformations, i.e., model transformations that transform other model transformations. However, writing such model transformations is generally beyond the ability of transformation developers since it requires the developer to be familiar with the metamodel of the transformation language itself. In order to overcome this frustrating impediment for the INRIA MTL transformation language, we presented in this paper an MTL *weaver* that modifies MTL transformations according to some *weaving behavior* that is specified as a special kind of MTL transformations, called *MTL-aspects*. Inspired from the AOP world in general, and from AspectJ in particular, the syntax defining the weaving behavior in MTL-aspects is a small AOP-like extension to the concrete syntax of the MTL language itself. In this way, relying on a few high-level AOP-like but MTL-based constructs for defining the weaving behavior, average MTL transformation developers should not have any problems using this MTL extension straightforwardly in order to define their "reflective" model transformations.

The support provided by the MTL weaver through the MTL extension syntax was illustrated on a concrete example, namely modularizing the distribution concern in stand-alone units of encapsulation represented by MTL-aspects. We have shown in this way that transformation developers are given not only the possibility, but also the means to rely on the well-proven power of separation of concerns even at the model transformation level.

Even though our research was carried out for the INRIA MTL transformation language, most of the concepts presented in this paper are MTL independent and could easily be applied to the future QVT specification language by providing higher level constructs for specifying the weaving behavior. For example, we can very well imagine the `MTL1-D-Aspect` be written at the QVT specification level, and then automatically refine it for the MTL language when applying it in the context of MTL-based projects. Although the constructs introduced in this paper are very suitable for imperative model transformation languages (e.g., "`before method return`" or "`after call`"), we believe that similar counterparts may be identified in declarative model transformation languages as well (e.g., "`after rule match`"), and thus a common ground could be found at the QVT specification level.

References

[1] Object Management Group, Inc.: *Model Driven Architecture*. http://www.omg.org/mda/, September 2004.
[2] Miller, J.; Mukerji, J.: *Model Driven Architecture (MDA)*. Object Management Group, Document ormsc/2001-07-01, July 2001.
[3] Object Management Group, Inc., http://www.omg.org/, September 2004.
[4] Sendall, S.; Kozaczynski, W.: *Model Transformation – the Heart and Soul of Model-Driven Soft ware Development*. IEEE Software, **20**(5), Special Issue on Model-Driven Development, 2003, pp. 42 – 45. An extended version is available as Technical Report, EPFL-IC-LGL N° IC/2003/52, July 2003.
[5] Object Management Group, Inc.: *MOF 2.0 Query/Views/Transformations RFP*. Document ad/02-04-10, April 2002.
[6] French National Institute for Research in Computer Science and Control (INRIA): *Model Transfor mation Language (MTL)*. http://modelware.inria.fr/, September 2004.

[7]   Kiczales, G.; Lamping, J.; Mendhekar, A.; Maeda, C.; Lopes, C. V.; Loingtier, J.-M.;
      Irwin, J.: *As- pect-Oriented Programming*. Proceedings of the 11th European Conference
      on Object-Oriented Programming, ECOOP, Jyväskylä, Finland, June 9-13, 1997. LNCS
      Vol. **1241**, Springer-Verlag, 1997, pp. 220 – 242.

[8]   Kiczales, G.; Hilsdale, E.; Hugunin, J.; Kersten, M.; Palm, J.; Griswold, W. G.: *An
      Overview of AspectJ*. Proceedings of the 15th European Conference on Object-Oriented
      Programming, ECOOP, Budapest, Hungary, June 18-22, 2001. LNCS Vol. **2072**,
      Springer-Verlag, 2001, pp. 327 – 353.

[9]   Eclipse Project: *AspectJ*. http://www.eclipse.org/aspectj/, September 2004.

[10] Parnas, D. L.: *On the Criteria to be used in Decomposing Systems into Modules*.
      Communications of the ACM, **15**(12), December 1972, pp. 1053 – 1058.

[11] Rouvellou, I.; Sutton, S. M. Jr.; Tai, S.: *Multidimensional Separation of Concerns in
      Middleware*. Second Workshop on Multi-Dimensional Separation of Concerns in
      Software Engineering, held at the International Conference on Software Engineering,
      ICSE, Limerick, Ireland, June 4-11, 2000. http://www.research.ibm.com/
      hyperspace/workshops/icse2000/.

[12] Silaghi, R.; Strohmeier, A.: *Integrating CBSE, SoC, MDA, and AOP in a Software
      Development Method*. Proceedings of the 7th IEEE International Enterprise Distributed
      Object Computing Con ference, EDOC, Brisbane, Queensland, Australia, September 16-
      19, 2003. IEEE Computer Society, 2003, pp. 136 – 146. Also available as Technical
      Report, N° IC/2003/57, Swiss Federal Institute of Technology in Lausanne, Switzerland,
      September 2003.

[13] Silaghi, R.; Fondement, F.; Strohmeier, A.: *Towards an MDA-Oriented UML Profile for
      Distribution*. Proceedings of the 8th IEEE International Enterprise Distributed Object
      Computing Conference, EDOC, Monterey, CA, USA, September 20-24, 2004. IEEE
      Computer Society, 2004, pp. 227 – 239. Also available as Technical Report, N°
      IC/2004/49, Swiss Federal Institute of Technology in Lausanne, Switzerland, May 2004.

[14] Object Management Group, Inc.: *Common Object Request Broker Architecture: Core
      Specification*, v3.0.3, March 2004.

[15] Sun Microsystems, Inc.: *Java Remote Method Invocation Specification*. Revision 1.7,
      Java 2 SDK, Standard Edition, v1.3.0, December 1999. http://java.sun.com/j2se/
      1.3/docs/guide/rmi/, September 2004.

[16] Vojtisek, D.: *BasicMTL Realization Guide*. Inside the Carroll Research Program and part
      of the MOTOR project, Technical Report, February 2004. http://modelware.inria.
      fr/article.php3?id_article=45, September 2004.

[17] Bézivin, J.; Dupé, G.; Jouault, F.; Pitette, G.; Rougui, J. E.: *First Experiments with the
      ATL Model Transformation Language: Transforming XSLT into XQuery*. Second
      International Workshop on Generative Techniques in the Context of MDA, held at the
      ACM SIGPLAN Conference on Object-Oriented Programming, Systems, Languages, and
      Applications, OOPSLA, Anaheim, CA, USA, October 26-30, 2003.

MISTRAL: A Language for Model Transformations in the MOF Meta-modeling Architecture

Ivan Kurtev and Klaas van den Berg

Software Engineering Group, University of Twente, P.O. Box 217,
7500 AE, Enschede, The Netherlands
{kurtev, vdberg}@cs.utwente.nl

Abstract. In the Meta Object Facility (MOF) meta-modeling architecture a number of model transformation scenarios can be identified. It could be expected that a meta-modeling architecture will be accompanied by a transformation technology supporting the model transformation scenarios in a uniform way. Despite the fact that current transformation languages have similarities they are usually focused only on a particular scenario. In this paper we analyze the problems that prevent the usage of a single language for different transformation scenarios. The problems are rooted in the current organization of the MOF architecture and especially in its inability to define explicitly the mechanisms of instantiation and generalization found in different modeling languages. This causes a coupling between a transformation language and the instantiation mechanism specific for a given modeling language. We propose an organization of the MOF architecture based on a simple and uniform representation of all model elements no matter at which level they are defined. In this framework, different instantiation and generalization mechanisms are represented as a set of functions. We present a transformation language named MISTRAL[1] acting in this framework. Transformation language is separated from the instantiation and generalization mechanisms specific for a given modeling language.

1 Introduction

A key element of the MDA (Model Driven Architecture) [11] is the notion of model transformation. A model transformation is a process of generation of a target model from a source model. A number of model transformation scenarios can be identified in current OMG standards and other publications [14][12][16][10]. Fig. 1 shows four transformation scenarios in the context of the MOF (Meta Object Facility) meta-modeling architecture [13].

Fig. 1a shows a scenario with a transformation specified between two MOF meta-models (UML and Java meta-models). This is the context of the Query/Views/Transformation (QVT) Request for Proposals issued by OMG [14]. In this context transformations are specified between models at level M2 and executed on models at level M1. Fig. 1b shows similar scenario shifted one level down. It involves transfor-

---

[1] MISTRAL stands for *Multiple IntenSion TRAnsformation Language*. The notion of intension is regarded as a model of models and is elaborated in [9].

U. Aßmann, M. Aksit, and A. Rensink (Eds.): MDAFA 2003/2004, LNCS 3599, pp. 139–158, 2005.

mation execution on data at level M0. The diagram shows a transformation specified between a concrete DTD (Document Type Definition) and a concrete relational schema. The execution of the transformation converts an XML document to a relational database. This scenario is common in data warehousing and is addressed in the Common Warehouse Metamodel (CWM) [12]. Fig. 1c shows the Data Binding approach for XML processing [10] from the perspective of the MOF meta-modeling architecture. In this scenario a transformation is specified at level M2 and executed at the two lower levels. The execution at level M1 is known as *schema compilation*. The correspondence derived between the constructs in the models at level M1 serves as a specification of the transformation executed at level M0 known as *unmarshaling*. In current data binding tools transformation rules applied during unmarshaling are usually not powerful enough to express the correspondence between an arbitrary schema and an arbitrary set of application classes. In this respect XML processing can benefit from the ability of model transformation languages to express complex transformations [7].

The three scenarios may be regarded as intra-level transformations where input and output models reside at the same level. In contrast, we regard the scenario in Fig. 1d as inter-level transformation. Fig. 1d shows two standard mappings in MOF: XML Metadata Interchange (XMI) [16] and Java Meta-data Interchange (JMI). Both map the MOF Model (at M3) to a meta-model at M2 (e.g. DTD and Java meta-models). These transformations are executed on models at level M2 (e.g. the UML metamodel) and the result is a model at level M1. Furthermore, a UML model at level M1 may be transformed to an XML document or to a set of Java objects residing at level M0.

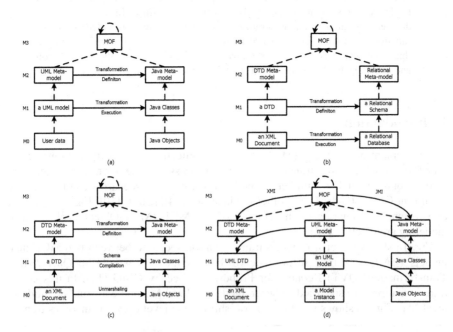

Fig. 1. Model transformation scenarios

How do the current model transformation techniques support these scenarios? The QVT initiative aims at defining a standard transformation language for the first scenario. CWM solves problems in the second scenario for a number of commonly used data sources. The third scenario is supported by proprietary data binding tools that do not consider transformations in the context of the MOF architecture. The mappings in the fourth scenario are described in a semi-formal notation using grammars, templates and textual descriptions. Although the transformation approaches taken in QVT and CWM share a number of similar concepts it is not possible to use a single transformation language for the first two scenarios. In the scenario in Fig. 1c the result of a transformation at level M1 is used to derive a new transformation executed at the lower level M0. Current model transformation languages do not address the problem of transformation execution over more than two consecutive levels. Finally, both QVT and CWM do not consider inter-level transformations.

One would expect that the outlined scenarios are addressed in a uniform way, that is, the organization of the MOF architecture allows a transformation language to operate on models at any level. The analysis of the current transformation techniques reveals that the reality is different. In this paper we analyze the problems that prevent the usage of a single language for all the scenarios. In our opinion the problems are rooted in the current organization of the MOF architecture and especially its inability to define explicitly the mechanisms of model instantiation. This causes a coupling between a transformation language and the instantiation mechanism specific to the models it operates upon. Apart from the instantiation mechanism, generalization relations also have an impact on the transformation language concerning selection of source model elements and the substitutability among values. Different modeling languages have similar but different semantics of the generalization relation. The same coupling is observed between a transformation language and a given generalization relation.

We propose a framework for the MOF architecture based on a simple and uniform representation of all the model elements no matter at which level they are defined. The framework does not introduce changes to any MOF-related standard. MOF, UML and other languages may be imported in it. In this framework the instantiation and generalization mechanisms are defined explicitly. We present a transformation language separated from the instantiation and generalization mechanisms specific for a given model. If a transformation is defined between two models the transformation engine is configured with the definitions of the corresponding instantiation and generalization relations. Thus, the language is decoupled from these relations and is able to express transformations between models at arbitrary level.

The paper is organized as follows. Section 2 gives detailed description of the problems we want to tackle. Section 3 describes our approach for representing model elements in the MOF architecture and how models are extended with additional information and used in the context of our transformation language. Section 4 presents the transformation language. Section 5 shows an example specification of an instantiation mechanism for the relational model. Section 6 analyses related work and section 7 gives the conclusions.

2 Problem Statement

The languages proposed as an answer to the QVT RFP are based on the instantiation mechanism used to create MOF meta-models and models (at level M2 and M1 respectively). A transformation selects instances of MOF classes in a source model at level M1 and produces instances in a target model at the same level. The definition of a transformation language that transforms models at level M1 is possible because all model elements conform to the MOF semantics. It defines which constructs at level M2 may be instantiated (instances of MOF *Classifier* that are not abstract) and the structure of these instances (having identity, slots and links). The specification also defines the meaning of the generalization relation: how features from a super-class are inherited in a sub-class and the rules for type substitutability based on the class hierarchy. Since the constructs at levels M3, M2 and M1 conform to a common structure and the models share the same instantiation and generalization mechanism it is possible to define a language that works on any model at level M1.

The MOF specification, however, does not specify the structure of the instances at M0 level and how they are related to their meta-constructs at level M1. The *instanceOf* relation between a construct in M1 and its instances in level M0 may differ from the *instanceOf* relation between constructs in M2 and its instances in M1. This observation has been made in [4] where it is argued that the actual number of levels is 3 instead of the widely accepted view of 4 levels. In fact, a model at level M2 defines a new language (e.g. UML, CWM, and Java) and that language brings its own definitions of the instantiation and generalization relations. If a transformation is defined between two user models in M1 then the transformation engine has to identify which model elements are instantiatable and how the instance values are set. The lack of a standard way to describe the instantiation mechanism for the model elements at level M1 prevents the usage of QVT languages for the M0 level.

How does the CWM solve that problem in dealing with a variety of data sources such as XML, relational, and record-based? It reuses the concepts of classes and instances defined in UML meta-model. A meta-model that would be separately defined at level M2 is defined as a specialization of the CWM meta-model. Constructs that specialize *Class* construct can be instantiated and their instances conform to constructs that specialize *Object*. The problem here is the inability to handle models conforming to meta-models at level M2 if the latter are not defined as specializations of the CWM meta-model.

If a transformation language is capable of transforming models residing at arbitrary level then it will require a common representation of the model constructs no matter the level they reside in and a uniform way of treating the different *instanceOf* and generalization relations. The discussion above showed that the MOF architecture does not provide these mechanisms. As a result current transformation languages are coupled with a particular instantiation and a generalization mechanism.

3 Approach

The approach for solving the problems explained in the previous sections is based on two ideas. First, we represent the model elements in the MOF architecture according to a simple generic model no matter the level they reside in. We define a transformation language that operates on instances of that generic model. Second, we consider four operations that occur in transformations: *instantiation* of an element from a meta-construct, *querying* the structural features of elements for their values, *setting* values to the features and *selection* of source elements on the base of their meta-constructs. We show how these operations are affected by the instantiation and generalization mechanisms. The specifics of the mechanisms are encapsulated in the implementation of a set of functions used by the transformation engine to execute the four operations. The transformation engine is configured with the implementations of the functions before executing a transformation. In this way we achieve separation between the transformation language and the instantiation and generalization mechanisms specific for a given modeling language.

3.1 Representation of Model Elements

The MOF architecture is viewed as a homogeneous modeling space populated with model elements. The level at which a model element resides does not affect its representation. Every model from the MOF architecture is represented as a set of model elements instances of a generic model (Fig. 2a).

The generic model is shown in Fig.2b. Every model element has an identity and a number of named slots. Simple values (strings, numbers, etc.) are instances of *Literal*. The concept of slot used here is similar to the concepts with the same name defined in MOF and UML but we do not require that slots are instantiated from attributes. In our modeling space slots are used to connect model elements or to hold values represented by literals. The model in Fig.2b is represented in UML notation only for the purpose of readability. It is defined outside of the MOF modeling space and can also be described in some other notation.

In the next sections two examples are given. Section 3.2 shows how the MOF Model itself is represented as an instance of the generic model. Section 3.3 shows a relational meta-model that defines the *instanceOf* relation explicitly.

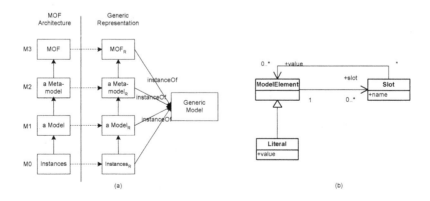

Fig. 2. Relation of the MOF architecture with the generic model of model elements

3.1 Representation of the MOF Model

As first example we represent a subset of the MOF Model shown in Fig. 3. Primitive data types and the multiplicity of attributes and association ends are omitted for simplicity. We assume that all the associations are unidirectional.

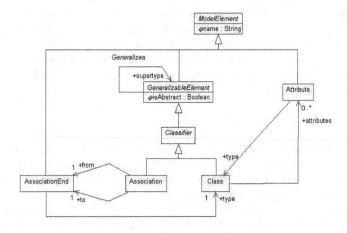

Fig. 3. Simplified MOF Model

The MOF Model can be represented as an instance of the generic model in Fig. 2b.

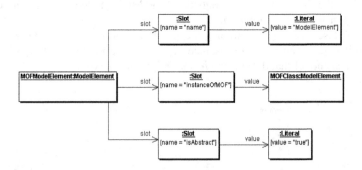

Fig. 4. Object diagram for the MOF class *ModelElement* as instance of the generic model

An object diagram for a part of the representation of the MOF abstract class *ModelElement* is shown in Fig. 4. The slot named "InstanceOfMOF" indicates the instantiation relation to the MOF *Class* construct. The following rule is used to represent the MOF Model: all instances of MOF *Class* construct and also their instances are represented as model elements. Instances of attributes and associations are represented as slots that connect the model elements. For simplicity, instances of associations are also represented as slots. The concept of *Link* is not used.

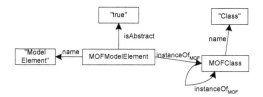

Fig. 5. Concise notation of the MOF Model (Fig. 4) as a graph of generic model elements

In this paper a more concise notation will be used for showing model instances of the generic model in Fig. 2b. Fig. 5 shows the object diagram in Fig. 4 represented as a graph of generic model elements. Model elements are shown as rectangles that contain an identifier of the element. Usually this identifier is the value of the slot 'name'. Literals are also shown as rectangles containing the value enclosed by quotes. Slots are represented as arrows labeled with the name of the slot and pointing to the slot value. A more detailed representation of the MOF Model can be found in [8].

In the MOF Model there is no construct that defines instantiation relations. In our framework this relation is explicitly represented by a slot. From now on we will refer to that relation as *instanceOf$_{MOF}$*.

3.3   The *instanceOf* Relation for the Relational Model

As second example we represent a relational model as an instance of the generic model. Some approaches [2][4] reduce the number of levels in the MOF architecture to 3 by defining a given meta-model and the model of the M0 instances at the same level M2. Therefore the models and their instances are situated at level M1 and instantiated with the standard MOF mechanism. The reduction of the levels, however, does not remove the presence of the second *instanceOf* relation defined within the meta-model. The authors of [2] identify the existence of these distinct *instanceOf* relations and distinguish between *linguistic* and *ontological* instantiations. In our examples *instanceOf$_{MOF}$* relation is the linguistic instantiation whereas the instantiation relation defined for a given modeling language is the ontological instantiation.

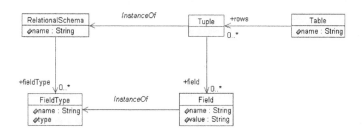

Fig. 6. Relational model and its instance model both defined at level M2

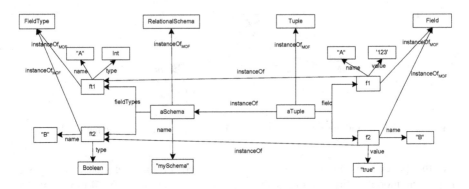

Fig. 7. A particular relational schema and relational data both at level M1 represented as generic model elements

We illustrate how this approach is represented in our framework by modeling relational databases. A relational model shown in Fig. 6 contains both the model of relational schemas (classes *RelationalSchema*, and *FieldType*) and the model of its instances (classes *Table*, *Tuple* and *Field*). The model is instantiated through the *instanceOf$_{MOF}$* mechanism and one example instance is shown in Fig. 7 following the notation used for the MOF Model.

The data (the model elements *aTuple*, *f1* and *f2*) that would reside at level M0 are now at level M1 and may be queried on the base of the constructs *Tuple* and *Field*. For instance, to access the value of field *B* one has to write the expression *aTuple.field→select(name="B").value*[2] that returns 'true'. A more natural way, however, is to use the relational schema of the tuple (represented by *aSchema* model element) that defines the fields *A* and *B* and to write the expression *aTuple.B* that reflects the ontological instantiation relation between *aTuple* and *aSchema*. This direct querying is not possible because *aTuple* does not have slot with name "B" created by the linguistic *instanceOf$_{MOF}$*. Therefore, some navigation over the graph should be specified to access the values of slots implied by the ontological instantiation. The ontological *instanceOf* relation is represented by the slots named 'InstanceOf' in Fig. 7. They are created by the linguistic MOF instantiation.

This example illustrates the need that both instantiation mechanisms should be available. A single model element may conform to more than one meta-construct through different *instanceOf* relations that are defined differently and these relations may be used to query the slots of the model elements. Our framework allows an explicit representation of more than one *instanceOf* relation for a given model element, which lacks in the MOF architecture.

3.4 Operations in Model Transformations

In the introduction we described several transformation scenarios. We assume that a transformation is executed on an input model and results in an output model. Both models have meta-models. In this section, we describe four operations observed in

---

[2] Object Constraint Language (OCL) [15] is used to specify the expression.

model transformations: *selection* of model elements on the base of their meta-constructs from which the elements are instantiated, *instantiating* model elements from a meta-construct, *reading* a slot value of an element, and *setting* the value of a slot. This list is not exhaustive, for instance, deletion of an element and operation invocation are not included in it. This paper focuses on the four operations mentioned above. Every operation is affected by the instantiation and generalization mechanisms specific for a modeling language. For every operation functions are identified and used to perform each operation. Different languages use different implementations of these functions.

Selection of Model Elements on the Base of Their Meta-construct. *instanceOf* relations are explicitly represented in our framework. They are represented either by a slot that does not have a defining construct as in the example of the MOF Model or by a slot instantiated from a construct in a meta-model as in the example of the relational model. Moreover, because multiple *instanceOf* relations are possible for a model element we may select on the base of more than one meta-construct. This helps in dealing with both linguistic and ontological instantiations.

With every meta-model we associate a function called *meta* defined over model elements in the input model. The function returns an element from the meta-model from which its argument is instantiated:

   meta(me: ModelElement): ModelElement

An implementation of that function in the context of the MOF Model will return the value of the slot *instanceOf$_{MOF}$*. In the context of the ontological instantiation in the relational model the function will return the value of the slot *instanceOf* (see Fig. 7). It should be noted that the function is defined only for model elements. We assume that the information about the meta-constructs used to create slots can be derived from the instantiation mechanism.

Apart from selection on the base of the meta-construct another form of selection is possible. In many cases not only the instances of a given meta-construct are selected but also the instances of its specializations. This selection uses the generalization-specialization hierarchy in the meta-model. Sometimes there are more than one hierarchy (e.g. derivation by restriction and extension in XML Schema, extension among classes and extension among interfaces in Java). To model this situation and to enable the transformation language to deal with different generalization hierarchies we associate every meta-model with a set of named relations representing its generalization relations. Every relation is associated with a function that for a given element in the meta-model returns all the specialized elements (direct and indirect):

   getSpecializedConstructs(me: ModelElement) : Set of ModelElement

Instantiation of Model Elements from a Meta-construct. Instantiation mechanism is modeled as a function that takes a construct from a meta-model and produces a model element with empty slots:

   instantiate(meta-construct: ModelElement) : ModelElement

The implementation of that function is influenced by the generalization mechanism defined for a given meta-model since the generalization mechanism specifies how features are inherited from a more general construct.

Accessing Slot Values of an Element. The slots of a model element are derived from its meta-construct based on the instantiation mechanism.

Slots implied by one instantiation mechanism may differ from the slots implied by other mechanism as in the example of the relational model. The model element, however, has a single representation conforming to the generic model. Different instantiations would create different representations.

This raises two questions: first, what is the instantiation mechanism used to generate the representation of a model element and second, if the slots implied by an instantiation are not directly presented how their values are obtained. The answer of the first question is that one instantiation mechanism is always chosen as default. In our approach we choose $instanceOf_{MOF}$ as default mechanism (or linguistic instantiation). To answer the second question we define a translation mechanism that obtains the slot values of slots implied by a given instantiation different from the default instantiation. This translation is implemented as a function that takes a model element and the name of a slot and returns the value of the slot, which is a set of model elements:

getSlotValue(me: ModelElement, slotName: String) : Set of ModelElement

Setting Values of a Slot. This operation is similar to the operation of accessing values of slots. The same two cases are presented here.

If the slot exists in the representation of the element the value is set directly on the slot. If the slot comes from an instantiation different from the default instantiation a translation mechanism is required. Setting the slot value is treated as an in-place transformation over the model element whose slot is being set. Generalization mechanism affects this operation in respect to the compatibility of the type of the value being set and the expected type of the value. The rules for type substitutability must be known when the transformation engine performs type checking of the value.

Two functions are defined to perform this operation. The first function sets the value of the slot by taking into account how the slot is represented. The second function checks if two model elements represent compatible types:

setValue(me: ModelElement, slotName: String, slotValue: Set of ModelElement)

isCompatible(expectedType: ModelElement, actualtype: ModelElement): Boolean

In summary, the four operations in model transformations are highly dependent on the instantiation and generalization mechanisms for a particular modeling language. We model the information required by the transformation engine to perform these four operations as a set of functions. Every meta-model provides its own implementation of these functions. We call the set of these functions a *configuration*.

Functions in a configuration may be implemented in any language and may be linked to the transformation engine as an external library. For illustrative purposes we will show how these functions can be implemented as transformation rules written in our transformation language. During the execution of a transformation the engine will invoke these rules. Before giving an example of the implementation of the configuration of the MOF Model and the relational model we will introduce the transformation language MISTRAL in the next section.

4 Transformation Language MISTRAL

In this section, we describe a transformation language based on the idea of separation between the transformation language and the instantiation and generalization mechanisms. The language is an extension of the one applied to XML processing described in [7].

4.1 Overview of the Language

Fig. 8 shows the basic concepts in the transformation environment in which the language is used.

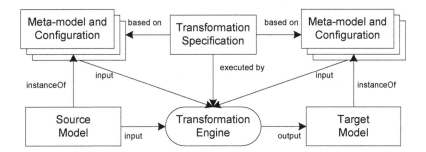

Fig. 8. Overall design of the transformation environment

A transformation engine transforms a source model to a target model by executing a transformation specification. A transformation specification is written in the transformation language being described here and is based on the meta-models of the source and the target models and the configurations of these meta-models. Source and target models must be associated to at least one meta-model. This requirement is always fulfilled since all models conform implicitly to the generic model of the modeling space. The meta-models and their configurations are passed as input to the transformation engine. The engine can only create instances of the constructs in the generic model, i.e. model elements and slots. The transformation designer, however, can specify the transformation against the meta-constructs in the meta-models. Based on the configurations of the meta-models the engine performs the operations analyzed in the previous section that ultimately result in creating model element and slot instances in the target.

A transformation specification is a set of rules. There are two types of rules: model element rules and slot rules. Model element rules create elements in the target model. Slot rules are used to relate the elements by setting their slot values. Both types of rules have rule source that selects elements in the source model.

4.2 Example: The Configuration of the MOF Model

The language is presented on the base of an example that implements the configuration functions for the MOF Model. Only two functions are implemented here: *instan-*

tiate and *getSpecializedConstructs*. The following 4 model element rules implement the instantiation mechanism in the MOF Model. The keywords of the language are shown in bold.

The *instantiate* model element rule implements the instantiation mechanism for the MOF Model. It creates a model element from a non-abstract class. Slots are obtained from the derived sets of attributes and outgoing associations of the class. These sets contain the attributes and outgoing associations defined in the class and also the inherited ones from its parent. Derived sets are created by the rule *DerivedConstructsFor-Class*. We assume that name collisions do not occur. Slots are created by the rules *MOFAttributeToSlot* and *MOFAssociationToSlot* respectively.

```
instantiate ModelElementRule{
  source [c:Class, condition {c.isAbstract=false}]
  target [instance: ModelElement {slots=slotRulesValue->union(instSlot)},
          instSlot: Slot {name='instanceOf_MOF', value=c}]
  SlotRules {
   attributeSlots
   source [a:Attribute=target (c, derivedAttributes)]
   target  [slots=MOFAttributeToSlot(a)]

   associationSlots
   source [assoc:Association=target(c, derivedAssociations)]
   target  [slots=MOFAssociationToSlot(assoc)]
  }
}
```

```
DerivedConstructsForClass ModelElementRule{
  source [c: Class link-to(derivedAttributes, derivedAssociations)]
  target [derivedAttributes: Set{elements},
          derivedAssociations: Set{elements}]
  SlotRules {
   ownAttributes
   source [a: Attributes=c.attributes]
   target [derivedAttributes.elements=a]

   attributesFromParent
   target [derivedAttributes.elements]
   alt { source [parent:Class=c.supertype]
       target [derivedAttributes.elements=target(parent, derivedAttributes)] }
   alt { target [derivedAttributes.elements=Set[]] }

   ownAssociations
   source [assoc:Association, condition{assoc.from.type=c}]
   target [derivedAssociations.elements=assoc]

   associationsFromParent
   target [derivedAssociations.elements]
   alt {source [parent:Class=c.supertype]
       target [derivedAssociations.elements=target(parent, derivedAssociations)] }
   alt { target [derivedAssociations.elements=Set[]] }
  }
}
```

```
MOFAttributeToSlot ModelElementRule{
  source [a:Attribute]
  target  [Slot {name=a.name}]
}

MOFAssociationToSlot ModelElementRule{
  source [assoc:Association]
  target [Slot {name=assoc.to.name}]
}
```

Fig. 9 illustrates the dependencies among the rules. Rules are shown as ovals and relations among them are shown as labeled arrows. A rule with an outgoing arrow obtains values for the variables denoted by the label of the arrow from the rule at which the arrow is pointing.

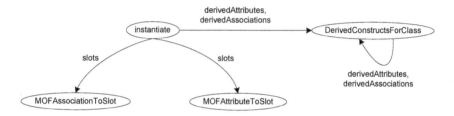

Fig. 9. Dependencies among the transformation rules

The following rule creates a set of all the classes that directly or indirectly inherit from a given class passed as a source of the rule and therefore implements the function *getSpecializedConstructs*.

```
getSpecializedConstructs ModelElementRule{
  source [c: Class]
  target [result: Set{elements=slotRulesValue->union(c)}]

  SlotRules{
   Elements
   source [s: Class, condition{s.supertype=c}]
   target [result.elements=getSpecializedConstructs(s)]
  }
}
```

This rule is an example of a recursive rule that for a given class determines all direct specializations and makes a union of their specialized constructs.

4.3 Transformation Language Syntax

In this section, we describe the syntax of some important constructs in the transformation language that were used in the previous example.

Model Element Rules. Model element rules create new elements in the target model or modify existing ones in the source model.

The creation of new elements is done in two ways: by instantiating the constructs from the generic model in Fig. 2 and by instantiating some meta-constructs from the target meta-model. Only the constructs in the generic model can be directly instantiated. When a meta-construct from the target meta-model has to be instantiated the function *instantiate* that implements that instantiation is invoked and results in instantiations of the constructs in the generic model.

The syntax of model element rules is specified below in a pseudo EBNF notation. Non-terminals are in italic.

```
ruleName ModelElementRule InputParameters? {
  RuleSource
  target [Action +]
  SlotRule*
}
```

Every model element rule has a name, a source, a target, an optional list of input parameters and is associated with a number of slot rules. Model element rules specify a correspondence between elements in the rule source and elements in the rule target. When a rule is executed elements in the rule target are instantiated for every tuple that matches the rule source.

The target of a model element rule contains a set of actions. Two types of actions are supported: instantiation and update. Every instantiation specifies a meta-construct in the target meta-model or a type from OCL. The element created by an instantiation might be assigned to an identifier. Instantiations enumerate the names of the slots that will be assigned with value after the instantiation. Slot values are determined from an optional expression specified in the slot list and an optional set of slot rules.

In the example, the rule *instantiate* specifies two instantiation actions based on *ModelElement* and *Slot* constructs respectively. The second instantiation is assigned to the identifier *instSlot*. All slots are assigned with expressions. Expressions may contain variables defined in the source of the rule (e.g. *value=c*) or assigned to the other instantiations in the same rule.

The second type of action that can be used in the rule target is the update action. It modifies the slot values of model elements selected by the rule source.

The transformation language supports single inheritance among model element rules. The inheriting rule inherits from the parent rule its source, target and the associated slot rules.

Rule Source. Rule source specifies the characteristics of the elements in the source model that will be selected by a transformation rule. Rule source is evaluated to a set of tuples containing elements in the source model. The syntax of the rule source is given below.

```
source [ Component +, (condition {BooleanExpressionInOCL})? ]
```

A rule source enumerates at least one component. An optional condition may be imposed on the components. The components are two kinds: an identifier that uniquely identifies an element in the source model or a variable that can be bound to more than one source element. Variables have a type which can be a model element from the meta-model (i.e. a meta-construct) or one of the primitive and collection types available in Object Constraints Language (OCL). If the type is a meta-construct then the variable matches its instances in the source model. The Cartesian product of the matches for all the variables forms a set of tuples filtered out by the condition of the source.

The source expression of *instantiate* model element rule contains a variable *c* that will be bound to instances of *Class*. The condition constrains the set of model elements that will be bound to *c* to those classes that are not abstract:

source [c: Class, **condition**{c.isAbstract=`false`}]

It is also possible to select elements instances of the specializations of a given meta-construct. In general, more than one generalization hierarchy may exist in a given meta-model. The names of the hierarchies must be defined in the configuration of the meta-model. These names may be used to specify a selection. A source rule that selects instances of a given class *aClass* and also instances of all its subclasses is specified below. The keyword *select* is used in combination with the name of the relation:

source [c: aClass **select** sub-classes]

Slot Rules. Slot rules are always associated to a model element rule and specify how to obtain the values of the slots of its instantiations. The syntax of the slot rules is given below:

ruleName RuleSource **target**[(*slotName*=*Expression*)+]

Every slot rule has a name, a source and a target. Rule target enumerates the slots to be set up with a value. Rule source specifies the elements in the source model that will be used to obtain the value of the slots. A given slot may have more than one slot rule for the calculation of the value.

There are two forms of slot rules: single form and form with alternatives. Slot rules in single form have only one source expression. It is evaluated in the context of the current matching of the model element rule that owns the slot rule. The source of the slot rule may refer to the variables defined in the owning model element rule. It is often the case that the values of variables in the slot rule source are determined relatively to the model elements that match the owner rule. The values of the slots are determined by evaluating expressions over the variables in the rule source.

In *instantiate* model element rule the value of the slot named *slots* in the *ModelElement* instantiation is calculated by two slot rules named *attributeSlots* and *associationSlots*. This is indicated by including the slot name in the target of a slot rule.

Slot rules in the form with alternatives specify multiple alternative sources. They are evaluated in the order of their appearance and the first source that results in a non-empty set is used to determine the values of the slots in the target. It is possible to specify an alternative without a source in the end of the list with alternatives. It is used if none of the preceding alternatives is applied. The slot rule *attributesFromParent* belonging to *DerivedConstructsForClass* rule is an example of a slot rule in form with alternatives.

To determine the value of a slot the transformation engine first evaluates the expression assigned to the slot in the instantiation. If there is no expression then the value is obtained by executing the associated slot rules. For every match of the source of a slot rule the expression assigned to the slot is evaluated. Results obtained from the matches are united in a set. The sets obtained from the slot rules are united and the result is used as value of the slot. Multiplicity and type constraints are checked. Expressions used in the instantiations may use the special variable *slotRulesValue* that contains the result of the execution of the slot rules.

Linking Source and Target Elements. Whenever a model element rule is executed the execution engine establishes an association link between the elements matched by the source and the elements instantiated by the target of the rule.

The created target model elements may be used as slot values of other model elements created by other rules. They are accessed by querying the source elements for the associated elements in the target model. The linking is done by the *link-to* construct that instructs the transformation engine to establish a link between an element of the source and the instantiations in the target of the rule.

In *DerivedConstructsForClass* rule the classes selected by the source are linked to the sets *derivedAttributes* and *derivedAssociations*. The built-in function *target* may be used to query a source element for the elements linked to it. An example usage of that function can be seen in the slot rules of *instantiate*.

Invoking Rules. By default, model element rules are executed exactly once on every match of their source. It is also possible to invoke a model element rule explicitly by name over a given source element and to use the result in expressions.

To create new slots every time when a model element is instantiated from a class we explicitly invoke *MOFAttributeToSlot* rule in the expression *slots = MOFAttributeToSlot(a)* in the *attributeSlots* slot rule. The same approach is used in *associationSlots* slot rule.

4.4 Transformation Engine Prototype

This section describes a prototype of a transformation engine developed for a previous version of the transformation language MISTRAL. The previous version of the language is designed for XML processing. A description of the approach for XML processing based on model transformations can be found in [7]. The approach reflects the scenario shown in Fig. 1c. The language is coupled with XML Schema Metamodel and Java Meta-model. This is the main difference with the current version of language MISTRAL. The two languages employ the same constructs presented in this paper: model element rules and slot rules.

The implementation of the transformation engine for the language applied for XML processing served as a proof of concept for the algorithms of rule execution. We give a short description of the architecture of the transformation engine. More detailed description of the architecture and implementation of the engine accompanied by several case studies are given in [17].

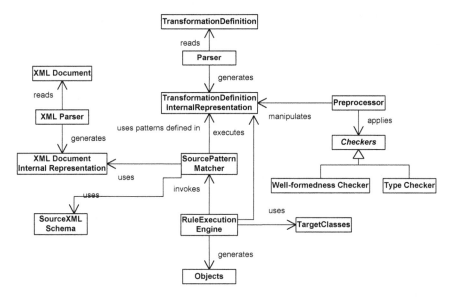

Fig. 10. Architecture of the prototype of the transformation engine

Fig. 10 shows the components in the architecture of the transformation engine prototype. An input *XML Document* is parsed by *XML Parser*, which generates *XML Document Internal Representation* used by other components in the engine. *TransformationDefinition* is parsed by *Parser*, which generates *Transformation Definition Internal Representation*. This representation is checked by *Preprocessor*. *Preprocessor* applies *Well-formedness Checker* and *Type Checker* to perform the checking. Transformation is executed by *Rule Execution Engine* that invokes *Source Pattern Matcher* to extract nodes from *XML Document Internal Representation*. Pattern matcher uses information from *Source XML Schema*. *Rule Execution Engine* uses *Target Classes* to generate the output *Objects*.

5   Defining the Configuration of the Relational Model

In this section, we present an example implementation of some of the functions identified in section 3.4. For illustrative purposes functions are implemented as transformation rules written in the transformation language presented in section 4. The instantiation mechanism of the relational model (function *instantiate*) is defined below.

In this transformation the targets are not the generic classes *ModelElement* and *Slot* as in the definition of the instantiation for the MOF Model. Instead *Tuple* and *Field* are used and these classes are instantiated through the MOF instantiation defined in the previous section. The transformation engine will use the rule *instantiate* defined for the MOF Model to instantiate *Tuple* and *Field* and will build the underlying representation.

```
instantiate ModelElementRule{
  source [s:RelationalSchema]
  target [Tuple{field, instanceOf =s}]

  SlotRules{
    Fields
    source [f:FieldType=s.fieldTypes]
    target [field=FieldTypeInstantiation(f)]
  }
}

FieldTypeInstantiation ModelElementRule{
  source [ft:FieldType]
  target [Field{name=ft.name, instanceOf=ft}]
}
```

The next rule implements the function *meta* that returns the meta-construct for a given tuple or field. Note that it does not distinguish between instances of *Tuple* and *Field* since the generic class *ModelElement* is used.

```
meta ModelElementRule {
  source [me: ModelElement, slot=me.slots, condition{slot.name='instanceOf'}]
  target [meta-construct: ModelElement=slot.value]
}
```

We also specify a transformation rule used for slot value access that implements the function *getSlotValue*:

```
getSlotValue ModelElementRule inputParameters [slotName: String]{
  source [context: Tuple, f:Field=context.field, condition {f.name=slotName}]
  target [result: Set=f.value]
}
```

This rule is executed on a tuple supplied by the transformation engine and bound to the variable *context*. The rule navigates over the fields and selects a field with name equal to the input parameter *slotName*. Selection and slot value access is based on the functions defined for the MOF Model.

Setting slot values is implemented as an in-place transformation over tuples. The rule takes as input parameters the slot name and the value to be assigned. The source of the rule (the variable *context*) is supplied by the transformation engine. Then the slot *f* with name 'value' will be set.

```
setSlotValue ModelElementRule
inputParameters [slotName:String, newValue:Set]{
  source [context:Tuple, f:Field=context.field, condition {f.name=slotName}]
  target [update f {value=newValue}]
}
```

With this example we have shown how to use the transformation language for the specification of transformation rules that implement some of the functions in the configuration of relational model.

6 Related Work

Meta-modeling architectures based on a common representation of the elements in different levels can be found in other domains of computer science. RDF Schema [6] defines a three level architecture where all constructs are represented as triples according to the RDF data model [3]. The approach for meta-modeling described in [5] also has three levels and 5 types of instantiation mechanisms called conformance relationships. The framework uses a transformation language based on logical formulas. Transformations between any levels are possible. The authors of [18] propose a multilevel meta-modeling framework where instantiation and generalization are treated in a uniform way. In [1] the instantiation mechanism is explicitly defined as a function that can be applied on a model at any level. That function resembles the MOF instantiation mechanism and is reused also in the UML meta-model. The paper does not study how other instantiation mechanisms would be defined in that framework.

7 Conclusions

We presented an approach for defining a model transformation language that allows specifying transformations between models residing at arbitrary level in the MOF architecture. Our language treats the MOF architecture as a homogeneous modeling space consisting of model elements all represented by the same generic structure. Different *instanceOf* and generalization relations may be defined within that space. These relations have a significant impact on the transformation language. The primary design goal for our transformation language is separation between the language and specific instantiation and generalization mechanisms. The latter are implemented as functions linked to the transformation engine. We showed examples of how these functions themselves can be implemented in the transformation language.

Our approach illustrates the need for a systematic definition of modeling languages within the MOF architecture and one particular example how transformation technology can benefit from that.

As a next step for research we plan to study the representation of various UML profiles within the framework presented in the paper.

References

1. Álvarez, J., Evans, A., Sammut, P.: Mapping between Levels in the Metamodel Architecture, In Proceedings of UML2001, Springer-Verlag Heidelberg, Toronto, Canada, 2001
2. Atkinson, C., Kühne, T.: Model-Driven Development: A Metamodeling Foundation, IEEE Software 20(5), 2003, pp. 36-41
3. Beckett, D.: RDF/XML Syntax Specification, W3C Document, 2003
4. Bézivin, J., Lemesle, R.: Ontology-Based Layered Semantics for Precise OA&D Modeling, ECOOP'97 Workshop Reader, Finland, 1997
5. Bowers, S., Delcambre, L.: On Modeling Conformance for Flexible Transformation over Data Models, In Proc. of the Workshop on Knowledge Transformation for the Semantic Web at the 15th European Conference on Artificial Intelligence (KTSW-2002), Lyon, France, 2002

6. Brickley, D., Guha, R. V.: RDF Vocabulary Description Language 1.0: RDF Schema, W3C Document, 2003
7. Kurtev, I., van den Berg, K.: Model Driven Architecture based XML Processing, Proceedings of ACM Symposium on Document Engineering, Grenoble, France, 2003
8. Kurtev, I., van den Berg, K.: Unifying Approach for Model Transformations in the MOF Metamodeling Architecture. In M. van Sinderen and L. Pires (Eds.), 1st European MDA Workshop on Industrial Applications (MDA-IA), CTIT Technical report TR-CTIT-04-12, Enschede, the Netherlands, 2004
9. Kurtev, I.: Adaptability of Model Transformations. PhD Thesis. University of Twente. ISBN 90-365-2184-x. 2005
10. McLaughlin, B.: Java & XML Data Binding. O'Reilly. 2002
11. OMG. MDA Guide version 1.0.1. OMG document omg/2003-06-01, 2003
12. OMG. Common Warehouse Metamodel (CWM) Specification. OMG document formal/03-03-02, 2003
13. OMG. Meta Object Facility (MOF) Specification. OMG document formal/02-04-03, 2002
14. OMG. MOF 2.0 Query/Views/Transformations RFP. OMG document ad/2002-04-10, 2002
15. OMG. Object Constraint Language (OCL). OMG document ptc/03-10-14
16. OMG. XML Metadata Interchange (XMI) Specification. OMG document formal/03-05-02, 2003
17. Rosheuvel, A.: XML processing based on model transformations: design, implementation, and testing of unmarshaler. MSc Thesis. University of Twente. 2003
18. Varró, D., Pataricza, A.: VPM: A visual, precise and multilevel metamodeling framework for describing mathematical domains and UML, Software and System Modeling 2(3), Springer-Verlag, 2003, pp. 187-210. 2003

Integrating Platform Selection Rules in the Model Driven Architecture Approach

Bedir Tekinerdoğan[1], Sevcan Bilir[2] and Cem Abatlevi[2]

[1] TRESE Software Engineering Group, Faculty of Computer Science,
University of Twente, P.O. Box 217, 7500 AE, Enschede, The Netherlands
bedir@cs.utwente.nl
[2] Department of Computer Engineering, Bilkent University,
06800 Bilkent Ankara, Turkey
{sbilirm, abatlevi}@cs.bilkent.edu.tr

Abstract. A key issue in the MDA approach is the transformation of platform independent models to platform specific models. Before transforming to a platform specific model, however, it is necessary to select the appropriate platform. Various platforms exist with different properties and the selection of the appropriate platform for the given application requirements is not trivial. An inappropriate selection of a platform, though, may easily lead to unnecessary loss of resources and lower the efficiency of the application development. Unfortunately, the selection of platforms in MDA is currently implicit and lacks systematic support. We propose to integrate so-called platform selection rules in the MDA approach for systematic selection of platforms. The platform selection rules are based on platform domain models that are derived through domain analysis techniques. We show that the selection of platforms is important throughout the whole MDA process and discuss the integration of the platform selection rules in the MDA approach. The platform selection rules have been implemented in the prototypical tool *MDA Selector* that provides automated support for the selection of a platform. The presented ideas are illustrated for a stock trading system.

1 Introduction

One of the key motivations for Model Driven Architecture (MDA) is the existence of too many platforms, and too many conflicting implementation requirements, reducing the interoperability, portability and reuse of the applications [13]. To this end, MDA explicitly separates the functionality from platform specific concerns and provides Computation Independent Models (CIMs), Platform Independent Models (PIMs), Platform Specific Models (PSMs) and the code (model). One of the key issues is then the transformation among these models. In general, the transformations concern the mapping from PIM to PSM, from PSM to PSM, and from PSM to code. Several transformation techniques have been proposed between the various models and this is actually one of the active research topics.

As such, the development of a system in MDA starts with defining the computation independent model, which is mapped to a platform independent model, and by a series of transformations gradually the platform specific properties are included through the platform specific models, eventually resulting in the final code.

U. Aßmann, M. Aksit, and A. Rensink (Eds.): MDAFA 2003/2004, LNCS 3599, pp. 159 – 173, 2005.
© Springer-Verlag Berlin Heidelberg 2005

Although, the mapping to different models and the related transformations have gained more interest, the selection of particular platform is not explicitly addressed. During the last years, different platforms have been proposed such as CORBA, .NET and J2EE. Each project may have its own requirements and constraints and depending on the project parameters, different types of platforms may be required. It is important that the right platform is selected to meet the project requirements and to avoid unnecessary loss of resources because of maintenance problems later on. Selecting an inappropriate platform will require redoing the whole transformation process between the different models including PIM to PSM, PSM to PSM and PSM to code.

Selecting a platform, however, is not a trivial process. Each platform usually addresses different properties and selecting a platform requires a broad understanding of the available platforms. Currently, in MDA the selection of platforms is basically implicit, and no systematic support is provided to guide the software engineer in selecting the right platforms.

We propose to integrate so-called *platform selection rules* for selecting an appropriate platform in the MDA approach. Platform selection rules are derived from the *platform domain model*. The *platform domain model* defines the commonality and variability of a set of platforms and is derived using domain analysis techniques. The platform selection rules help to determine to which extent the platform is suitable or not.

The approach is generic, yet as an example we define the rules for selecting .NET and J2EE platforms. We illustrate our ideas for a stock trading system and describe a prototypical tool *MDA Selector,* which implements the platform selection rules.

The remainder of this paper is organized as follows: Section 2 introduces the example case stock trading system that is used throughout the paper to discuss the problems and the solutions. Section 3 provides the background on transformation rules and additionally introduces the notion of platform selection rules. Section 4 discusses the approach for extracting and specifying the platform selection rules. Section 5 discusses how platform selection rules can be integrated in the MDA approach. Section 6 presents the prototypical tool that implements the platform selection rules for J2EE and .NET. Section 7 provides the related work and finally section 8 presents the conclusions.

2 Example: Stock Trading System

Development of a system in MDA proceeds from CIM to PIM, from PIM to PSM, and from PSM to code. In the following, we will show the CIM and the PIM for a stock trading system and then discuss the motivation for systematic selection of platforms.

2.1 Computation Independent Model

In the stock trading system, the client requests the stockbroker to enter a buy or sell order for a certain number of stocks. An order results in a deal when a matching bid of the opposite type is present. The system automatically performs the possible deals and entails several bookkeeping actions.

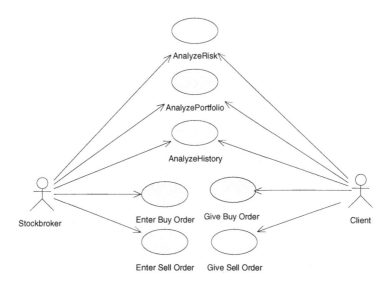

Fig. 1. Computation Independent Model for Trading System (Business Model)

Figure 1 represents (part of the) computation independent (business) model of the stock trading system. In the use case, there are three two actors: *StockBroker* and *Client*. The actor *StockBroker* performs the use cases *Analyze Risk, Analyze History, Analyze Portfolio, Enter Buy Order, Enter Sell Order*. The actor *Client* can apply the use cases *Analyze Risk, Analyze Portfolio*, *Analyze History*, *Give Sell Order* and *Give Buy Order*.

2.2 Platform Independent Model

The CIM does not include any computational issues and defines the solution from a requirements and business perspective. The PIM provides a model of the application including the computational aspects but refraining from the platform specific aspects. Fig. 2 shows the (simplified) PIM for the stock trading system.

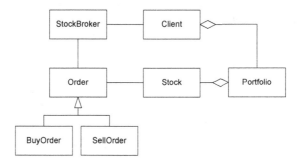

Fig. 2. (Simplified) PIM for stock trading system

2.3 Selection of Platforms

The representation of the platform independent model is important to support the quality factors of reuse, interoperability and portability to different platforms. However, for the more concrete implementation it is necessary that a platform is selected after which the PIM is mapped to a PSM including the specific properties of the selected platform.

For the stock trading system, the first important question is then which platform to select. There are various platforms and it is not trivial to select a platform that best fits the needs of the stock trading system. All of the existing platforms have different properties and in principle can be selected to realize the PSM. Albeit any changes to the platform will not influence the PIM in the MDA perspective, the selection of a given platform will have a serious impact on the platform specific model. If a non-optimal platform is selected this will directly impact the PSMs which need to be generated again. If the right transformation rules exist, and if these are automated then the generation of PSMs might be better supported. Nevertheless, it is not efficient to continuously rely on a trial-and-error approach until the right platform has been selected, and likewise it is worthwhile to provide a systematic approach, which supports the decision on a platform. Unfortunately, this is not explicit in MDA yet. The following sections elaborate on this issue.

3 Transformation Rules and Platform Selection Rules

Several approaches have been proposed for mapping PIM to PSM, such as use of templates, marks, and patterns. We can categorize all these approaches as *transformations*. Within this context, Kleppe et. al. provide the following definitions [10]:

Transformation is the automatic generation of a target model from a source model, according to a transformation definition.

A **Transformation Definition** is a set of transformation rules that together describe how a model in the source language can be transformed into a model in the target language.

A **Transformation Rule** is a description of how one or more constructs in the source language can be transformed into one or more constructs in the target language.

All these definitions and tools are primarily focused on *transformation* of the models down to code. Although MDA improves the interoperability and portability of the systems, it does not explicitly define which platform to choose for a given set of project requirements, though. In fact, this is actually the strength of MDA; it does not commit to a particular platform.

Nevertheless, sooner or later a platform must be selected to realize the system. Since the selection of the platform is not explicit this is usually done in an informal and less systematic manner.

Complementary and in alignment to the above definitions we introduce the definitions that are required for selecting platforms:

Platform Selection is the automatic selection of a platform according to the input from the application requirements.

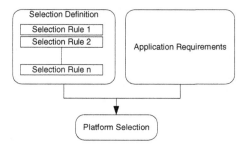

Fig. 3. Platform selection inputs

Platform Selection Definition is a set of selection rules that together describe the selection of platforms,

Platform Selection Rule is a description on the selection of a particular platform based on a given property.

The idea of selecting platforms is given in Fig. 3.

The rules for selecting platforms are different from existing transformation rules in two perspectives. First, the rules are defined before the transformation rules. Second, the rules do not transform any model but only support the system designer in the selection of the platform. Altogether, we think that these platform selection rules are complementary to the existing transformation rules.

4   Approach for Defining Platform Selection Rules

Intuitively, it seems sound to support the software engineer in selecting a platform based on a given set of rules. The question of course is how to define these rules. For this, we propose to apply domain analysis techniques. In section 4.1, we will discuss the approach for defining a *platform domain model* using domain analysis techniques. Based on this platform domain model, the approach for deriving *platform selection rules* will be explained in section 4.2. Finally, section 4.3 discusses the selection of platforms based on the defined rules and the project constraints.

4.1   Defining a Platform Domain Model

Domain analysis can be defined as the process of identifying, capturing and organizing domain knowledge about the problem domain with the purpose of making it reusable when creating new systems [1]. Domain analysis focuses on a given domain and aims to represent this domain in a reusable format. The UML glossary provides the following definition of the term domain [8]:

Domain: An area of knowledge or activity characterized by a set of concepts and terminology understood by practitioners in that area.

Conventional domain analysis methods consist generally of the activities *Domain Scoping* and *Domain Modeling* [1]. *Domain Scoping* identifies the domains of interest, the stakeholders, and their goals, and defines the scope of the domain. *Domain Modeling* is the activity for representing the domain, or the *domain model*.

The domain model can be represented in different forms such as object-oriented language, algebraic specifications, rules, conceptual models etc. Typically a domain model is formed through a commonality and variability analysis to concepts in the domain.

Our focus in this paper is on modeling platforms for reuse. The MDA Guide provides the following definition for platform [13]:

Platform: a set of subsystems and technologies that provide a coherent set of functionality through interfaces and specified usage patterns, which any application supported by that platform can use without concern for the details of how the functionality provided by the platform is implemented.

The MDA guide further classifies platforms into *generic platform types, technology specific platform types* and *vendor specific platform types*. The discussion of our study is independent of these classifications.

A domain for our purposes represents the area of knowledge on the set of platforms that we are interested in. We term this as the **platform domain model.** Related to this, in the MDA Guide the notion of platform model is defined [13]:

Platform model provides a set of technical concepts, representing the different kinds of parts that make up a platform and the services provided by that platform.

This definition focuses implicitly on the modeling of a single platform. With *platform domain model,* we define a model that represents one or more platforms. For this, it is required to model the common properties and the variant properties of the corresponding alternative platforms. To this end, we apply *feature modeling,* which is a well-known technique in domain analysis [6]. Feature modeling results in a *feature model*, which consists of a feature diagram and additional semantic information such as descriptions of features, rationale of features, etc. A feature diagram represents a hierarchical representation of the features of a system. The root of a feature diagram represents a concept.

Fig. 4 presents the approach for modeling platforms. In the first step, it is decided which platforms one is interested in and the corresponding domains are identified. This is actually the domain scoping for platforms. As an example, one might decide to focus on *Corba, .NET* and *J2EE*. Once the platforms are known, the corresponding platform domain model will be developed. An appropriate platform domain model that meets the application requirements might already exist in the literature. If no suitable platform model exists then this is defined using commonality and variability analysis to the knowledge sources on the corresponding platforms. The knowledge sources might include textbooks, technical papers, human experts or systems, which implement the corresponding pattern. Once the platform domain model is developed it will be evaluated based on the application requirements and the platform information. If the evaluation is passed then the platform domain model can be utilized.

Fig. 5 presents, for example, a feature diagram for platforms as a result of domain analysis to J2EE and .NET platforms. It describes a platform as consisting of *Vendor, Operating System, Architecture, Language* and *Services* features. This feature model has been derived after a commonality and variability analysis to knowledge sources on .NET and J2EE [14][15] [16].

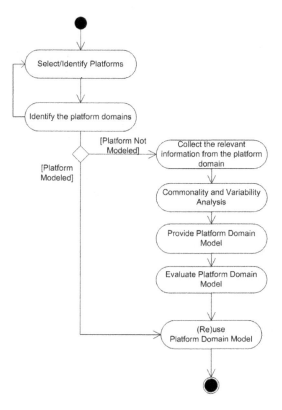

Fig. 4. Process for deriving platform domain model

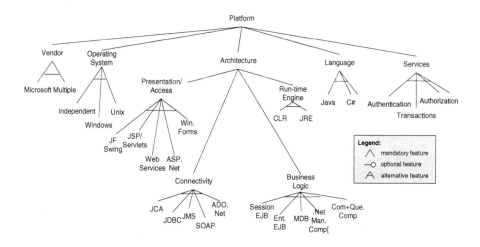

Fig. 5. Feature Diagram for Platform Domain

Table 1. Properties for .NET Platform

P1. Vendor is Microsoft
P2. Operating System is Windows
P3. Presentation Access is ASP.Net, Windows Forms, Web Services
P4. For Database Connectivity ADO.Net and SOAP is used.
P5. Business logic is provided through .NET Managed components and COM Queued components
P6. Requires Common Language Runtime (CLR) run-time engine.
P7. Source code is written in C#.
P8. Supports transaction and authentication services
P9. ....

Table 2. Properties of J2EE Platform

P1. Vendor is independent (more than 30)
P2. Operating System is independent
P3. Presentation Access is JSP, JFC, Web Services
P4. For Database connectivity Java Database Connectivity (JDBC) protocol, Java Connector Architecture (JCA), Java Messaging Service (JMS) and SOAP is used.
P5. Business logic is provided through Session Enterprise JavaBeans, Entity Enterprise JavaBeans and Message Driven Beans.
P6. Requires Java Runtime Engine (JRE)
P7. Source Code is written in Java
P8. ....

For deriving *platform selection rules*, we represent the platform domain model as a set of *platform properties*. A platform property is defined as a description of the feature of a platform and as such, is directly derived from the feature diagram. For example, Table 1 and Table 2 represent (a set of) properties for .NET and J2EE platforms, which have been derived from the feature diagram in Fig. 5.

4.2   Extracting the Rules from Platform Domain Model

Once the platform domain model has been derived it can already be manually utilized in selecting the appropriate platform. For automating the rules a further formalization is required. We do this by mapping the properties to the platform selection rules. The platform selection rules are expressed using conditional statements in the form IF <condition> THEN <consequent>. For example property P1 in Table 1 and Table 2 lead to the rules R1 and R2, respectively in Table 3. Note that the list is not comprehensive due to space limitations.

4.3   Selecting Platforms Using Application Constraints

The platform selection rules represent the general cases for selecting platforms. For selecting a platform we need to define the corresponding application constraints as it was discussed in section 3 and illustrated in Fig. 3. Each constraint can trigger a rule in the rule definition. As such, for a given set of constraints, a set of rules will be triggered. The triggering of a rule means that the condition requested by the constraints matches the condition of the platform selection rule. Assume that, for example, the constraints as defined in Table 4 are specified for the stock trading system.

Table 3. Heuristic Rules for Platform Selection for J2EE and .NET

R1.	IF the vendor should be independent THEN select the platform J2EE
R2.	IF the vendor should be Microsoft THEN select the platform .NET
R3.	IF the platform should be independent from the operating system THEN select the platform J2EE
R4.	IF the platform should have Windows operating system THEN select platform .NET
R5.	IF JVM run-time engine is installed/required THEN select the platform J2EE
R6.	IF CLR run-time engine is installed/required THEN select the platform .NET
R7.	IF the application will be implemented in Java THEN select the platform J2EE
R8.	IF the application will be implemented in C# THEN select the platform .NET
R9.	IF transaction and authentication support is required THEN select the platform J2EE
R10.	IF database access with JDBC is required THEN select the platform J2EE
R11.	IF database access with ADO.NET is required THEN select the platform J2EE
R12.	IF ASP.NET is required as a web-tier component THEN select the platform .NET
R13.	....

These constraints trigger five rules R3, R6, R7 and R9 in Table 3. This leads to an indecisive result to select J2EE (for R3, R7 and R9) and .NET (for R6). As in this case, very often the application requirements do not lead to a single possible platform. The reason for this is, firstly that the corresponding platforms share some common properties, and secondly, the application requirements might be conflicting itself. To support the decision process in case of conflicts, we apply the prioritization of the constraints by assigning each of these a value between 1 and 9. Hereby the value 1 is defined as a supportive but least important constraint, whereas 9 represent a very strong decisive constraint. Note that the constraints C1 to C4 in Table 4 correspond to the elements in the feature diagram as defined in Fig. 5. In principle, it would be possible to annotate the priorities to the feature diagram as well. On the other hand, the priorities for each project might change and in that sense, it is more appropriate to separate the priorities from the feature diagram.

The priority values are assigned to the triggered rules. The decision for each platform depends then on the number of fired rules and the values of the constraints. Therefore, for the constraints in Table 4 this means that the total score for J2EE is 9+8+8=27 and the score for .NET is 5. This information could be used for the final decision or for a closer look at the conflicting requirements. In fact, the prioritization and the policy for selecting platforms based on these scores might be refined. What is important here is that this decision is made explicit.

Table 4. Constraints and Priorities for Stock Trading Application

Constraint	*Priority*
C1. The application should work in all environments so the platform must be operating system independent.	*9*
C2. The language which will be used for implementation must be in Java	*5*
C3. The run time engine should be CLR.	*8*
C4. Transactions and authentication are required.	*8*

5   Integrating Selection of Platforms in the MDA Pattern

Fig. 6a illustrates the integration of the platform selection rules in the MDA pattern. The drawing builds on the pattern as defined in the MDA Guide [13]. The rectangles represent either the platform independent models or the platform specific models, the arrows represent transformations and selections. In fact, the selection of platforms appears to be complementary to the MDA pattern. In the current MDA pattern the selection is implicit. Fig. 6a makes this explicit by adding an operation which selects (and models) the platform. Similar to the initial MDA pattern the drawing is intended to be suggestive and generic. The platform independent model together with the selection of platform and the corresponding information on the platforms are combined to produce a platform specific model. There can be many ways in which transformations may be done. The selection is based on the approach as defined in the previous sections.

It should be noted that the terms PIM and PSM are just relative terms and it is difficult to draw a strict line between platform independent and platform specific model. In fact, a platform specific model can function as a platform independent model for a next stage. For example, the upper PIM that is independent of many platform choices, could be mapped to a PSM which is specific to middleware platforms. However, the transformation could be carried out so that the PSM is independent of the particular component platforms.

This can also be derived from the given example case. The original platform independent model is first mapped to a J2EE platform specific model, which remains independent of the choice of a particular component platform in J2EE. In the given example case, the J2EE-specific model can thus be considered as a PIM as well. There are three basic component platforms in J2EE: JSP (Java Servlet Pages), Servlet and EJB (Enterprise Java Beans). Before transforming the J2EE specific platform independent model, we have to select the specific component platform in J2EE. This process is illustrated in Fig. 6b. Note that the extended MDA pattern as defined in Fig. 6a is applied twice in Fig. 6b.

Selecting the component platforms of the J2EE platform requires defining the corresponding platform selection rules. In principle, this is the same process as defined in the previous sections, and we do not elaborate further on this.

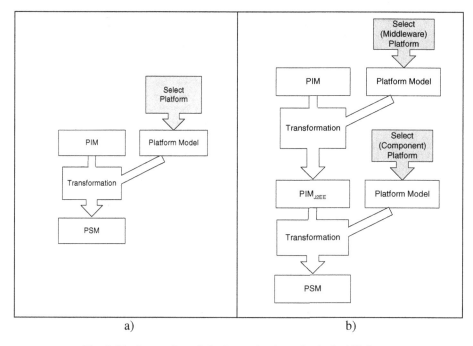

a)   b)

Fig. 6. The integration of platform selection rules in the MDA pattern

6   Platform Selection Tool

Since the platform selection rules have been formalized, they can be easily implemented in a tool to provide automated support for the decision of a platform. We have implemented a prototypical tool environment for selecting a platform for a given PIM. The tool environment is called *MDA Selector*. A snapshot of this tool is given in Fig. 7. *MDA Selector* simply implements the rules that have been derived from the platform domain model. The tool starts by prompting the user in order to determine the middleware platform by using the check boxes, which represents the properties for different platforms. In addition, each property can be assigned a number between 1 and 9. If all the required properties are checked and the numbers to these properties have been assigned, then the user of the tool can click the action button *Decide*, to get the decision on the platform. The decision is shown in the right corner using colored rectangles. The size of the rectangle indicates the degree of preference for the given platform. The rules themselves have been implemented as objects with the attributes *condition, platform* and *value*. The attribute *condition* represents the condition of the rule, the attribute *platform* refers to the selected platform for the condition, and the attribute *value* represents the number assigned to the rule. Upon pressing the *Decide* button the algorithm for selecting the platform is executed. Hereby, the selected properties are matched against the implemented rules. In case a selected property matches the condition of a rule, the rule will be triggered, that is the value for the rule

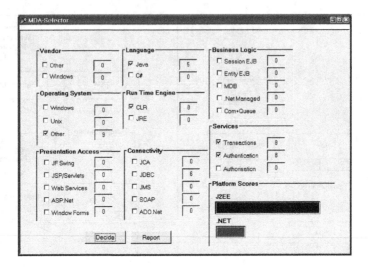

Fig. 7. Platform Selection Tool

is set to the entered value for the property and the degree for the corresponding platform is updated. The action button *Report* provides additional information on the result of the selection. The tool is implemented in Visualworks 3.0 and currently includes a simple, though, effective implementation.

7   Related Work

The MDA guide [13] provides a definition of platform model but no explicit process for deriving the platform model is given. We adopt domain analysis techniques for systematically defining platform models. In [3] and [19], the notion of Platform Description Model is presented, which is similar to our notion of platform model since both are representations of the corresponding platform. In [4] the Platform Model is expressed at a conceptual level and does not specifically represent a formal model. In all of these approaches, the term platform model is utilized in transforming a PIM to a PSM. In our approach, the platform model is used to derive the rules for selecting the platforms. Later on, the platform model can still be used as an input to the transformation process.

In [12] exploration and selection of alternative transformation models using algebraic techniques is presented. Hereby the possible set of transformation models is represented as *transformation spaces*. In our approach, we focus on modeling the heuristic rules for selecting platform models. As such, both approaches seem to be complementary to each other.

In [7] the authors discuss the relation between MDA and a configurable software product line family. Similar to our understanding, the authors state that platform models are at best derived using domain engineering techniques. A PIM in MDA represents the model for a family of platform specific models and as such, seems to perfectly align with the idea of developing domain models in domain engineering. We have shown how we can derive platform properties from feature diagrams, and platform selection rules from these properties. It would be interesting to investigate the relation between MDA and domain engineering further.

In our previous work, we have modeled heuristic rules for automating software development methods [17] [18]. In these approaches, the rules represented selection, elimination and transformation actions. In this paper, we have utilized rules merely to select a platform. A useful further step would be to integrate both selection and transformation rules in a common tool environment.

The tool that we developed can be considered as an initial expert system that codifies the rules for selecting platforms. An expert system usually consists of a knowledge base (facts), rule base including production rules, and an inference engine for triggering these rules [11]. Expert systems have also been applied for the hardware configuration problem. Hereby, the expert system determines the best hardware configuration based on the rules in the expert system knowledge base as well as the customer requirements.

8 Conclusions

It appears that current research on MDA primarily focuses on transformation of models. Before transforming to a particular platform specific model, however, it is necessary that the appropriate target platform is selected. Currently, the selection of platforms is generally considered an ad hoc issue and largely remains implicit. However, given the currently relatively broad set of platforms, which is despite MDA still expected to grow in the future, it is certainly not a trivial task to select the platform that optimally meets the application requirements. As such, we argue that besides of transformation process in MDA also the selection of platforms should be integrated in the MDA development pattern.

In section 3 we have given the definitions of *platform selection*, *platform selection definition*, and *platform selection rule* as a complementary set of definitions on *transformation*, *transformation definition* and *transformation rule*.

To extract the platform selection rules we have proposed to adopt domain analysis techniques. In this context, we have primarily focused on defining properties of platforms and derived the rules based on these properties. Further, a first prototypical tool environment which indicates the use of the selection of platforms is provided. We have illustrated the approach for selecting a platform for stock trading system.

Since PIM and PSM are just relative terms and a PSM can also function as a PIM the platform specific transformations can be applied at different levels in MDA. Similarly, in section 6 we have shown that this counts for selecting platforms as well. Hereby, first the middleware platform was selected and then the particular component platform in the given middleware.

Although the standard use of MDA assumes that products are built for all platforms, and the transformation is considered as automatic, we have highlighted the selection of platforms to determine whether it is suitable or not. From our study, we can also conclude that the selection of platforms is complementary to the transformation process. We have primarily focused on the platforms J2EE and .NET. Although the presented example application is rather small, we think that the presented ideas can scale easily for larger applications. This is because the basic complexity for selecting the platforms is mostly defined by the platform domain model itself, rather than the size of the application. In fact, the presented rules are directly derived from the platform model and are more or less fixed for a given platform. The only difficulty for larger applications is that the decision for each rule could be more difficult, but still manageable. In our future work, we will provide the domain models for other platforms as well and derive the rules to support the software engineer in selecting the appropriate platforms.

Acknowledgements

We would like to thank the anonymous reviewers, Klaas van den Berg, and Ivan Kurtev for their valuable feedback on earlier versions of this paper. This research has been carried out in the *Aspect-Oriented Software Architecture Design project*, which is funded by the Dutch Scientific Organisation in the *Jacquard Software Engineering Program*.

References

[1] G. Arrango. Domain Analysis Methods. In Software Reusability, Schäfer, R. Prieto-Díaz, and M. Matsumoto (Eds.), Ellis Horwood, New York, New York, pp. 17-49, 1994.

[2] U. Assmann, Automatic roundtrip engineering, Electronic Notes in Theoretical Computer Science Vol. 82, Issue 5.

[3] J. Bézivin and N. Ploquin, Combining the Power of Meta-Programming and Meta-Modeling in the OMG/MDA Framework, OMG's 2nd Workshop on UML for Enterprise Applications, San Francisco, USA, December, 2001

[4] S. Bilir & C. Abatlevi. Model-Driven Architecture Based on Design Space Modeling. Technical Report, Department of Computer Engineering, Bilkent University, Ankara, Turkey, June, 2003.

[5] S.E. Borch, J.W. Jespersen, J. Linvald, Kasper Østerbye. A Model Driven Architecture for REA based systems. In Proc. of Model Driven Architecture: Foundations and Applications, pp. 103-108, University of Twente, Enschede, The Netherlands, 2003.

[6] K. Czarnecki & U. Eisenecker. Generative Programming: Methods, Tools, and Applications, Addison-Wesley, 2000.

[7] S. Deelstra, M. Sinnema, J. van Gurp & J. Bosch. Model Driven Architecture as Approach to Manage Variability in Software Product Families. In Proc. of Model Driven Architecture: Foundations and Applications, pp. 109-114, University of Twente, Enschede, The Netherlands, 2003.

[8] G. Booch, J. Rumbaugh & I. Jacobson. The Unified Modeling Language User Guide, Addison-Wesley, 1999.

[9] K. Kang, S. Cohen, J. Hess, W. Nowak, & S. Peterson. Feature-Oriented Domain Analysis (FODA) Feasibility Study. Technical Report, CMU/SEI-90-TR-21, Software Engineering Institute, Carnegie Mellon University, Pittsburgh, Pennsylvania, November 1990.

[10] A. Kleppe, J. Warmer, W. Bast. MDA Explained, The Model-Driven Architecture: Practice and Promise, Addision-Wesley, 2003.

[11] M.R Klein & L.B. Methlie, Knowledge-based Decision Support Systems, 2nd Ed., Wiley, 1995.

[12] I. Kurtev & K. van den Berg. A Synthesis-Based Approach to Transformations in an MDA Software Development Process. In Proc. of Model Driven Architecture: Foundations and Applications, pp. 121-126, University of Twente, Enschede, The Netherlands, 2003.

[13] MDA Guide Version 1.0. Edited by Joaquin Miller and Jishnu Mukerji. http://www.omg.org/mda/mda_files/MDA_Guide_Version1-0.pdf, June, 2003.

[14] J2EE and Microsoft .NET, Oracle White Paper, April 2002.

[15] P. Perrone, S.R. & T. Schwenk J2EE Developer's Handbook, SAMS, 2003.

[16] C. Szypersky. Component Software: Beyond Object-Oriented Programming, Addison-Wesley, 2002.

[17] B. Tekinerdogan & M. Aksit. Providing automatic support for heuristic rules of methods. In: Demeyer, S., & Bosch, J. (eds.), Object-Oriented Technology, ECOOP '98 Workshop Reader, LNCS 1543, Springer-Verlag, pp. 496-499, 1999.

[18] B. Tekinerdogan. Formalizing heuristic rules of Extreme Programming. Dept. of Computer Science, University of Twente, 2003.

[19] E.D. Willink. UMLX: A graphical transformation language for MDA. In Proc. of Model Driven Architecture: Foundations and Applications, pp. 13-24, University of Twente, Enschede, The Netherlands, 2003.

Platform-Independent Modelling in MDA: Supporting Abstract Platforms

João Paulo Almeida, Remco Dijkman, Marten van Sinderen,
and Luís Ferreira Pires

Centre for Telematics and Information Technology, University of Twente,
PO Box 217, 7500AE, Enschede, The Netherlands
{almeida, dijkman, sinderen, pires}@cs.utwente.nl

Abstract. An MDA-based design approach should be able to accommodate designs at different levels of platform-independence. We have previously proposed a design approach [2], which allows these levels to be identified. An important feature of this approach is the notion of abstract platform. An abstract platform is determined by considering the platform characteristics that are relevant for applications at a certain level of platform-independence as well as the various design goals. In this paper, we discuss how our design approach can be supported using the MDA standards UML 2.0 and MOF 2.0. Since our methodological framework is based on the notion of abstract platform, we pay particular attention to the representation of abstract platforms and the language requirements to specify abstract platforms.

1 Introduction

A current trend in the development of distributed applications is to separate their technology-independent and technology-specific aspects, by describing them in separate models. The most prominent example of this trend is the Model-Driven Architecture (MDA) [15], [18]. A common pattern in MDA development is to define a platform-independent model (PIM) of a distributed application, and to apply (parameterised) transformations to this PIM to obtain one or more platform-specific models (PSMs). The main benefit of this approach stems from the possibility to derive different alternative PSMs from the same PIM depending on the target platform, and to partially automate the model transformation process and the realization of the distributed application on specific target platforms.

The concept of platform-independence plays a central role in MDA development. We believe that platform-independence can only be defined once a set of target platforms is known, such that their general capabilities and their irrelevant technological and engineering details can be established. This leads to the observation that there can be several PIMs, possibly at different abstraction levels, depending on whether one wants to consider different sets of target platforms. Another observation is that different application characteristics or different sets of target platforms generally lead to different types of (intermediate) models, design structures or patterns, and model transformations. These observations have motivated our investigations into what types of models can be useful in the MDA development

U. Aßmann, M. Aksit, and A. Rensink (Eds.): MDAFA 2003/2004, LNCS 3599, pp. 174–188, 2005.

trajectory, how these models are related, and which criteria should be used for their application. Some of the results of these investigations have been presented earlier in [2], where we have proposed an MDA design trajectory that accommodates designs at different levels of platform-independence.

An architectural concept that plays an important role in this approach is that of *abstract platform*. An abstract platform defines an acceptable or, to some extent, ideal platform from an application developer's point of view; it represents the platform support that is assumed by the application developer at some point of (the platform-independent phase of) the design trajectory. Alternatively, an abstract platform defines characteristics that must have proper mappings onto the set of concrete target platforms that are considered for an MDA design process, thereby defining the level of platform-independence for this particular process. Defining an abstract platform forces a designer to address two conflicting goals: (i) to achieve platform-independence, and (ii) to reduce the size of the design space explored for platform-specific realization.

Any design approach that is intended to be successfully applied in practice should be supported by suitable design concepts in suitable design languages. In this paper, we present some methodological guidelines for platform-independent design and define requirements for design languages intended to support platform-independent design. Since our methodological framework is based on the notion of abstract platform, we pay particular attention to the representation of abstract platforms and the language requirements to specify them. We discuss how the architectural concept of abstract platform can be supported in UML 2.0 [23] and MOF 2.0 [19].

This paper is further structured as follows: Section 2 provides some background on the concept of abstract platform; Section 3 discusses how abstract platforms relate to design languages; Section 4 discusses how abstract platforms can be represented in UML 2.0 and MOF 2.0; Section 5 presents examples of abstract platforms and their representations; Section 6 discusses limitations of UML 2.0 with respect to the representation of abstract platforms; Section 7 positions our work with respect to related work. Finally, Section 8 presents our conclusions and outlines future work.

2 Abstract Platforms

Platform-independence is a quality of a model that relates to the extent to which the model abstracts from the characteristics of particular technology platforms. In order to refer to platform-independent or platform-specific models, one must define what a platform is. The following rather general definition of platform can be found in [18] (page 2-3): "a platform is a set of subsystems and technologies that provide a coherent set of functionality through interfaces and specified usage patterns". This paper concentrates on platforms that correspond to some middleware technology supporting operation invocation and asynchronous message exchange, such as CORBA/CCM [16], .NET [13] and Web Services [28], [29].

When pursuing platform-independence, one could strive for PIMs that are neutral with respect to all different classes of middleware platforms. This is possible for models in which the characteristics of the supporting technological infrastructure are irrelevant, such as, e.g., conceptual domain models [4] and RM-ODP Enterprise

Viewpoint models [9], which can be considered as Computation Independent Models [18]. However, along a development trajectory, when system architecture is captured, some platform characteristics become relevant, and different sets of platform-independent modelling concepts may be used, each of which being adequate only with respect to specific classes of target middleware platforms. This leads to the observation that platform-independence is not a binary quality of models; instead, a distributed application can be described at several levels of platform-independence. The level of platform-independence of a model must be carefully identified. We propose to make this identification an explicit step in MDA development. The notion of abstract platform, as proposed initially in [2], supports a designer in this step.

An abstract platform is determined by the platform characteristics that are relevant for applications at a certain platform-independent level. For example, if a platform-independent design contains application parts that interact through operation invocations, then operation invocation is a characteristic of the abstract platform. Capabilities of a concrete platform are used during platform-specific realization to support this characteristic of the abstract platform. For example, if CORBA is selected as a target platform, this characteristic can be mapped onto CORBA operation invocations.

The PIM of a distributed application depends on an abstract platform model, in the same way as the PSM depends on a (concrete) platform model (see Figure 1). Given the PIM of an application and an abstract platform model, we distinguish two contrasting extreme approaches to proceed with platform-specific realization:

1. *Adjust the concrete platform*, so that it corresponds directly to the abstract platform.
2. *Adjust the (scope of the) application during platform-specific realization*, such that the requirements specified at platform-independent level are preserved and the platform-specific application model can be composed with the target platform model.

In approach 1, the boundary between abstract platform and platform-independent application model is preserved during platform-specific realization. This implies the introduction of some platform-specific *abstract platform logic* to be composed with the concrete target platform. The nature of this composition depends on the particular requirements for the abstract platform. It may be possible to implement abstract platform logic on top of the concrete platform. Nevertheless, this composition may also imply the introduction of platform-specific (e.g., QoS) mechanisms, possibly defined in terms of internal components of the concrete platform. Extension in a non-intrusive manner is often the preferred way to adjust the concrete platform. Techniques that can be used for non-intrusive extension include interceptors [16], aspect-oriented programming and composition filters [5].

Approach 2 may imply the introduction of (e.g., QoS) mechanisms in the platform-specific design of the application. This approach may be suitable in case it is impossible to adjust the concrete target platform, e.g., due to the lack of extension mechanisms or the cost implications of these adjustments. Figure 1 illustrates these approaches to platform-specific realization.

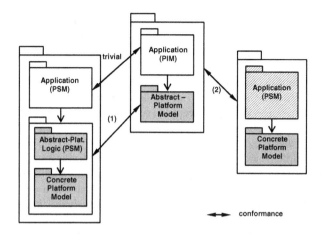

Fig. 1. Alternative approaches to platform-specific realization

Both approaches allow us to target different concrete platforms from the same platform-independent model, with different quality characteristics [2]. Approach 1 can be generalized as a recursive application of service definition (external perspective) and the service's internal design, resulting in a hierarchy of abstract platforms and a concrete target platform. At each step of the recursion, both approaches to realization can be chosen.

3   Design Languages

Designs must be supported by suitable design concepts and represented using suitable design languages. In an MDA design trajectory, several design languages may be used, e.g., to produce models at different levels of abstraction. Alternatively, a single "broad spectrum" design language [6] may be used. The design language adopted for a design has an important role in defining characteristics of an abstract platform assumed for the design.

In an MDA-based development trajectory, we may apply the *implicit abstract platform definition* approach, in which the characteristics of an abstract platform are implied by the set of design concepts used for describing the platform-independent model of a distributed application. These concepts are often inherited from the adopted modelling language. For example, the exchange of "signals" between "agents" in SDL [10] may be considered to define an abstract platform that supports reliable asynchronous message exchange. The restricted use of particular constructs in a design language or the use of certain modelling styles can serve as a means to select subsets of a language's design concepts.

Instead of implying an abstract platform definition from the adopted set of design concepts for platform-independent modelling, it may be useful or even necessary to define the characteristics of an abstract platform explicitly, resulting in one or more separate and reusable design artefacts. We call this approach *explicit abstract platform definition*. During platform-independent modelling, parts of a pre-defined abstract platform model may be composed with the model of the distributed application. For example, although group communication is not a primitive design concept of UML 2.0, it is possible to specify the behaviour of a group communication sub-system using UML 2.0. This sub-system is then re-used in the design of a distributed application. Other examples of pre-defined artefacts that may be included in abstract platforms are the ODP trader [8] and the OMG pervasive services [18] (yet to be defined). The set of design concepts of a design language is still relevant in this approach, since the distributed application and the abstract platform model are described in the language.

In both the implicit and explicit abstract platform definition approaches, there is some overlap between language characteristics and abstract platform characteristics. This leads to the formulation of an important requirement for a design language to support platform-independent design: *the concepts underlying the design language should be precisely defined, so that the characteristics of the abstract platform can be unambiguously derived from these concepts.* This is important for at least two reasons: (1) designers need to know the characteristics of the abstract platform when defining platform-independent models of an application; and (2) abstract platforms are a starting point for platform-specific realization.

Furthermore, a comprehensive MDA design approach should allow designers to select or define suitable abstract platforms for their platform-independent designs. This leads to the formulation of a second requirement for design languages suitable for MDA: *a design language should enable the definition of appropriate levels of platform-independence.*

4 Abstract Platform Definition with MDA Standards

In this section, we pay particular attention to the definition of abstract platforms using MDA standards, namely UML 2.0 [23] and MOF 2.0 [19]. We discuss the fulfilment of the design language requirements presented in Section 3, with both the implicit and explicit abstract platform definition approaches.

4.1 Implicit Abstract Platform Definition

The concepts that plain UML prescribes for specifying communication between application parts (objects or components) imply an abstract platform that is based on request-response invocations and on message passing. In the UML 2.0 meta-model, *BehavioredClassifiers* may offer *operations* and *receptions*. *Operations* represent the capability of a classifier to receive and to respond to requests. Requests are sent when objects execute *CallOperationActions*. *Receptions* represent the capability of a classifier to receive *Signal* instances, which are sent asynchronously by other objects when these execute *SendSignalActions* and *BroadcastSignalActions*. For plain UML, the usefulness of the implicit abstract platform definition approach is restricted to abstract platforms based on request-response invocations and on point-to-point message passing.

UML has been developed as a general purpose language that is expected to be customized for a wide variety of domains, platforms and methods [25]. A certain degree of customization may be obtained in UML through semantic variation points and profiles. This choice in the definition of UML has two implications for implicit abstract platform definition: the UML specification ("plain" UML) is not conclusive with respect to the abstract platform implied, and, the customization mechanisms have to be applied in order to precisely define specific abstract platforms.

Semantic variation points provide an intentional degree of freedom for the interpretation of the UML's metamodel semantics. Some semantic variation points defined in the UML specification should be resolved for plain UML to be conclusive with respect to the abstract platform implied by the language. An example of such a semantic variation point is described in the UML 2.0 specification [23] (page 381): "The means by which requests are transported to their target depend on the type of requesting action, the target, the properties of the communication medium, and numerous other factors. In some cases, this is instantaneous and completely reliable while in others it may involve transmission delays of variable duration, loss of requests, reordering, or duplication." Without resolving this semantic variation point, a designer would be forced to assume worst-case interpretations, e.g., that the implied abstract platform provides an unreliable request/response mechanism. If this is undesirable, e.g., because the abstract platform should provide a reliable request/response mechanism, a designer should resolve the semantic variation point, by defining that requests and response signals are transported reliably. Semantic variation points may be partially resolved, i.e., only for the relevant aspects. For example, a designer may consider the reliability characteristics of requests relevant, but may consider the timing characteristics irrelevant. In this case, any interpretation of the timing characteristics of requests would be acceptable. One could resolve these semantic variation points by relating the UML metamodel with a formal semantics, or to a basic set of design concepts with a formal semantics.

The specialization of UML for defining abstract platform characteristics can be made more manageable and clearly defined through the use of UML profiles. Profiles are language extensions consisting of metamodel elements that specialise elements of a reference metamodel. The specialized elements can be given specific semantics, in this way resolving semantic variation points. Furthermore, constraints expressed in a language like OCL [22] can be added to profiles to restrict the use of specific concepts or combinations of concepts. This use of profiling for implicit abstract platform definition is restricted to constraining or specialising the abstract platform implicitly defined by plain UML. In this approach, the referenced metamodel (UML 2.0's metamodel) in combination with the UML profile assumes the role of abstract platform model.

In case the relevant abstract platform characteristics cannot be represented by resolving semantic variation points through the definition of profiles, one should define new languages in terms of MOF metamodels. The design concepts of these languages are not constrained by UML, and can be arbitrarily defined through mappings from the metamodel elements to any suitable semantic domain. In this approach, the MOF metamodel assumes the role of abstract platform model. Profiling is more suited to the abstract platforms that require concepts that can be represented as specialisations of UML concepts. MOF metamodelling is suited in case the required concepts differ too much from the UML concepts, so that a new independent metamodel has to be defined. When used systematically, profiling has the advantage that UML tools can be used for model validation and verification, since the resulting models still comply with the UML rules and constraints. MOF metamodelling has a potential drawback that available validation and verification tools may be impossible to reuse, so that new tools may have to be built for the new metamodel.

4.2 Explicit Abstract Platform Definition

As an alternative to changing the design concepts of plain UML by means of profiling and thereby changing the implicit abstract platform, we can define the abstract platform explicitly. The abstract platform is then composed with the design of the application. This can be accommodated in UML 2.0 by using model library packages [23] to define the abstract platform model. Model library packages are packages stereotyped with the standard <<*modelLibrary*>> stereotype. The abstract platform model library package can be imported by the PIM of the application. This is represented by creating a dependency between the package where the PIM is defined and the model library package where the abstract platform is defined.

An abstract platform can have an arbitrarily complex behaviour and structure, varying from a simple one-way message passing mechanism to a communication system that maintains transactional integrity and time order of messages. To make the design of complex abstract platforms manageable, we can use UML 2.0's composite structures to break up a complex design into smaller pieces. State-machine and activity diagrams may be associated with encapsulated classifiers to define their behaviour.

Since the behaviour of the abstract platform is also described in UML, it may be necessary to combine the explicit and the implicit abstract platform definition approaches, e.g., by resolving semantic variation points that are relevant for the composition of the abstract platform (explicitly defined) and the platform-independent model of the application.

5 Examples

In order to illustrate both approaches to abstract platform definition in UML, we specify the platform-independent model of a simple chatting application. This application allows users residing in different hosts to exchange text messages.

Initially, the application is described in terms of an abstract platform that supports the interaction of objects through a conference binding object. We call this abstract platform the *ConferenceAbstractPlatform*. In order to define the composition of the conference binding object with the application, we use reliable exchange of asynchronous signals. For this purpose, we define an abstract platform that supports reliable signal exchange with the implicit approach, by defining a UML profile. Later, we consider two possible realizations of the *ConferenceAbstractPlatform*, one of these relies on an event-based platform we define explicitly, and the other relies solely on the exchange of reliable signals. The relations between the different models are depicted in Figure 2 (the *EventAbstractPlatform* is only necessary for the realization presented in section 5.4).

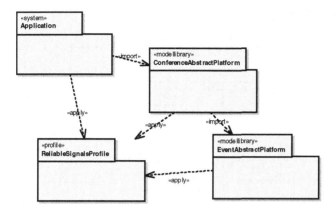

Fig. 2. Relations between the PIM of the application and the abstract platforms defined with the implicit and explicit approaches

5.1 Reliable Signal Exchange

Figure 3 depicts the *ReliableSignalsProfile* that specializes the exchange of asynchronous messages in UML 2.0. A stereotype $<<reliable>>$ is defined that can be applied to instances of *SendSignalAction* (defined in the package *IntermediateActions* of the UML 2.0 meta-model). Signals created by executing a *SendSignalAction* with this stereotype are exchanged reliably, in that they cannot be lost or duplicated. The *SendSignalAction* meta-class is the only meta-class specialized in the profile. It is not necessary to specialise the meta-classes *Signal* and *Reception*, since these represent respectively, the type of signal instances exchanged and the ability to receive signal instances. The semantics of these meta-classes are independent of the manner of transmitting signal instances.

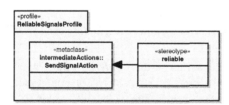

Fig. 3. A UML profile specializing the exchange of asynchronous messages

5.2 The *ConferenceAbstractPlatform*

The *ConferenceBinding* component provides the *ConferenceInterface* and requires the *ParticipantInterface*. An application part that uses the *ConferenceBinding* should provide the *ParticipantInterface*. The signals exchanged between application parts and the abstract platform are defined explicitly. A class diagram showing the *ConferenceAbstractPlatform*'s component, signals and interfaces is depicted in Figure 4.

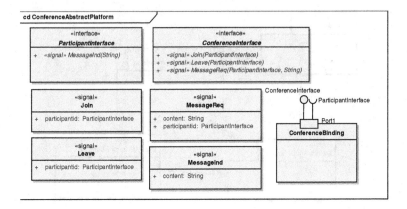

Fig. 4. The ConferenceAbstractPlatform

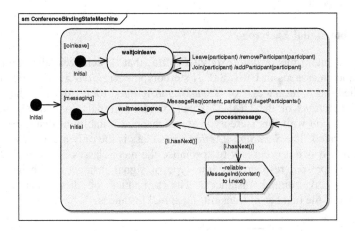

Fig. 5. The *ConferenceBinding* state-machine

Figure 5 shows the behaviour of the *ConferenceBinding* component specified as a state-machine. *ComponentBinding* keeps a list of conference participants, which is updated whenever a *Join* or *Leave* signal is handled. Upon reception of a *MessageReq* signal, the *ConferenceBinding* sends out *MessageInd* signals to all participants of the conference. In order to simplify the behaviour we have assumed that the *MessageInd* signals are sent sequentially based on the order imposed by the list of participants (result of *i.next()*). This illustrates the use of the <<*reliable*>> stereotype.

The application that uses the *ConferenceAbstractPlatform* may be defined at a high-level of platform-independence, communicating with the conference binding through signal exchange. Many alternative implementations for signal exchange are possible, depending on the target platform. Further, there is a large freedom of implementation for the conference abstract platform itself. Since the application is shielded from the internal design of the conference abstract platform, it does not depend on the interaction support eventually used by the conference binding object.

5.3   Realization of the ConferenceAbstractPlatform

Figure 6 depicts a realization of the *ConferenceBinding*. This realization relies on the abstract platform that provides reliable signals.

The interaction point that corresponds to *port1* is of type *ConferencePort*. The *ConferencePort* handles the signals *Join* and *Leave* and delegates the handling of signals *MessageReq* to the appropriate *ConferenceComponent*. There is a *Conference Component* instance for each participant in the conference. *ConferenceComponent* instances exchange *message* signals among each other and *messageInd* with the interaction point of *port1*. The definition of these signals is omitted. An OCL [22] constraint is used to define that *ConferenceComponent* instances are fully connected, and that there are no links between an instance and itself. Figure 7 shows the behaviour associated with the *ConferenceComponent*. The behaviour of *ConferencePort* is omitted due to space limitations. The signals are exchanged reliably, and therefore, the stereotype *<<reliable>>* is applied to all *SendSignal Action* instances.

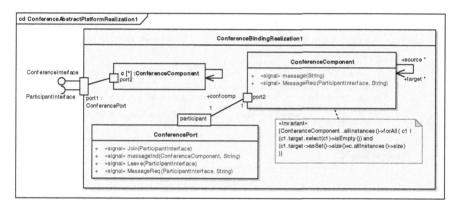

Fig. 6. A realization of the *ConferenceAbstractPlatform*

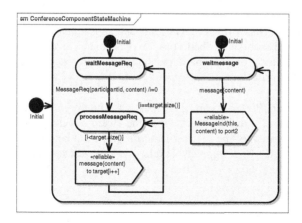

Fig. 7. Behaviour of the *ConferenceComponent* represented as a state-machine

5.4 ConferenceAbstractPlatform Realized in Terms of EventAbstractPlatform

Figure 8 depicts an alternative realization of the *ConferenceBinding*. This realization illustrates the recursive use of an explicitly defined abstract platform. The *EventAbstractPlatform* is used as part *eap* in *ConferenceBindingRealization2*. The dashed line around part *eap* is used to denote that this part is contained by reference. The multiplicity of *eap* is one, i.e., only one instance of the *EventAbstractPlatform* is used in this decomposition of the *ConferenceBinding*.

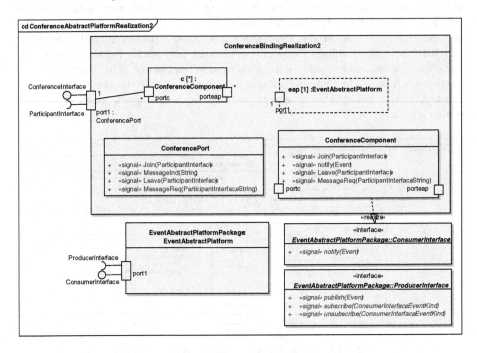

Fig. 8. Alternative realization of the *ConferenceAbstractPlatform*

The *EventAbstractPlatform* accepts events and subsequently forwards these events to objects that have subscribed to the particular event type. There is a *ConferenceComponent* for each participant in the conference. The definition of the behaviour of the *EventAbstractPlatform* is omitted here, as well as the classes *Event* and *EventKind*.

The *EventAbstractPlatform* can be realized on a number of event-based platforms, such as, e.g., JMS [27] and CORBA (with the Event Service) [16]. Alternatively, a recursive decomposition of the *EventAbstractPlatform* can be done, resulting, e.g., in a design of the *EventAbstractPlatform* that relies on a request-response abstract platform.

6 Discussion

The example from the previous section illustrates two kinds of problems that can arise when defining abstract platforms with a particular modelling language.

Firstly, a language's design concepts may force decisions about desired platform properties to be taken too early in the design process, because they do not permit abstraction of these properties. The example in the previous section illustrates this for the case of UML state machines. The state machine in Figure 5 determines that message requests are processed one at a time. Therefore, a strict interpretation of this model would exclude realizations of this abstract platform that accept multiple message requests simultaneously. Alternatively, we could have specified that a number of concurrent threads process multiple message requests at the same time. However, this alternative commits to a particular concurrency model. Ideally, we would have stated only that message requests are independent of each other, which is appropriate at the level of abstraction considered. The decision on a particular concurrency model would be delayed, and different alternative implementations would be deemed acceptable. A designer may try to mitigate the limitation of the UML representation by interpreting the behavioural specification loosely, e.g., informally defining that message requests can also be treated simultaneously despite the state machine model. However, this limits the usability of models for model transformation, automated testing, validation and simulation.

Secondly, a language's design concepts may indirectly favour some platforms over others, due to similarities in the structure of models and realizations in a particular platform. Although an implementer could try to ignore the structure and choose to adhere only to the model's semantics, he or she will be inclined to use the platform with the matching structure. The example from the previous section illustrates this for UML composite structures. In composite structures, interaction points that correspond to ports can only be created and destroyed along with the component to which they are attached. This implies that, if we want to model that an unbound number of distinct users may use the component through ports, we have to use a multiplexing scheme like the one used in Figures 6 and 8. Although the specification gives the impression that the multiplexing scheme has to be implemented, it is wiser for the implementer to ignore this scheme in case the target platform allows the dynamic creation and destruction of a component's interaction points.

7 Related Work

The MDA Guide [18] provides some examples of "generic platform types" and mentions briefly the need for a "generic platform model", which "can amount to a specification of a particular architectural style." Nevertheless, the introduction of these concepts is superficial: for example, the term "generic platform" is not even defined explicitly. In our interpretation of that documentation, we position our notion of abstract platform as subsuming that of generic platform. Abstract platforms can have other relevant characteristics in addition to defining a "particular architectural style". We have identified models that may serve as abstract platform models, in two different approaches to abstract platform definition that can be incorporated in MDA using OMG core technologies, namely UML, profiles and MOF.

The UML profile for EDOC Component Collaboration Architecture (CCA) [24] defines implicitly an abstract platform in which application part interactions are always decomposed into asynchronous messages that are exchanged through "Flow

Ports". This profile also introduces the notion of recursive component collaboration (not present in UML 1.5 [26]), which can be explored to define abstract platforms explicitly, similarly to what we have obtained by using UML 2.0's composite structures.

Explicit abstract platform definition is comparable to the definition of (the behaviour of) connectors in Architecture Description Languages (ADLs), such as Rapide [11], [12] and Wright [1], when considering exclusively the characteristics of interaction support. While the role of middleware platform characteristics in ADLs have been recognized in [14], mechanisms to systematically separate and relate platform-independent and platform-specific descriptions have not been proposed in the scope of the work on Software Architecture.

8 Concluding Remarks

We have argued previously [2] that the architectural concept of abstract platform should have a prominent role in MDA development. An abstract platform defines platform characteristics that are considered at the particular level of platform-independence, and may also serve as starting point for platform-specific realization.

Design language concepts and characteristics of abstract platforms are interrelated. Therefore, careful selection of a design language is indispensable for the beneficial exploitation of the PIM/PSM separation and the definition of abstract platforms.

Often, some platform characteristics are assumed implicitly in platform-independent designs. This may lead to PIMs that cannot be reused for different platforms or it may lead to PIMs that cannot be directly compared and integrated. It may also lead to transformations that cannot be reused. Platform characteristics assumed in platform-independent designs are better understood and controlled by designers if the characteristics of the abstract platform are explicitly represented in abstract platform definitions. Furthermore, explicitly identifying an abstract platform brings attention to *balancing* between two conflicting goals: (i) platform-independent modelling, and (ii) platform-specific realization.

We have discussed how to support the concept of abstract platform in standard UML, through both the implicit and the explicit abstract platform definition approaches. In the implicit definition approach, the semantic variation points of UML should either be resolved or should be considered irrelevant for deriving intended abstract platform characteristics. UML Profiles can be useful in this approach to specialise design concepts, and manage and package abstract platforms. In the explicit definition approach, UML 2.0's composite structures are useful both for defining abstract platforms from an external and from an internal perspective. Composite structures have been a useful addition to UML 2.0. Nevertheless, we have identified some limitations with respect to the level of abstraction that can be obtained in the representation of abstract platforms with composite structures. In addition, UML 2.0 still lacks some notion of behaviour conformance in order to relate behaviours defined at a high-level of abstraction and the refined realizations of these behaviours. Consequently, we cannot formally assess the correctness of abstract platform realizations.

We have presented an example in UML in which a number of abstract platforms can be combined, both in the implicit and the explicit abstract platform definition approaches. We intend to investigate further modularisation criteria for abstract platform definitions, aiming at obtaining a reference architecture for abstract platform definition. A designer should then be able to compose an abstract platform from abstract platform definition modules. This modularisation would ideally be preserved in transformation specifications and ultimately at platform-specific level.

Acknowledgements

This work is part of the Freeband A-MUSE project. Freeband (http://www. freeband.nl) is sponsored by the Dutch government under contract BSIK 03025. This work has also been partly supported by the European Commission within the MODA-TEL IST project (http://www.modatel.org).

References

1. Allen, R. J., Garlan, D.: A Formal Basis for Architectural Connection. ACM Transactions on Software Engineering and Methodology, Vol. 6, No. 3 (1997) 213–219
2. Almeida, J. P. A., van Sinderen, M., Ferreira Pires, L., Quartel, D.: A systematic approach to platform-independent design based on the service concept. In: Proceedings 7th IEEE Intl. Enterprise Distributed Object Computing Conference (EDOC 2003). IEEE Computer Society, Los Alamitos, CA (2003) 112–123
3. Almeida, J. P. A., van Sinderen, M., Ferreira Pires L.: The role of the RM-ODP Computational Viewpoint Concepts in the MDA approach. In: Proceedings of the 1st European Workshop on Model-Driven Architecture with Emphasis on Industrial Applications (MDA-IA 2004). CTIT Technical Report TR-CTIT-04-12. University of Twente, the Netherlands (2004) 43–51
4. Arango, G.: Domain Analysis: from Art Form to Engineering Discipline. ACM SIGSOFT Software Engineering Notes, Vol. 14, No. 3 (1989) 152–159
5. Elrad, T., Filman, R. E., Bader, A. (eds.), Communications of the ACM, Special Section on Aspect-Oriented Programming, Vol. 44, No.10 (2001) 29–97
6. Ferreira Pires, L.: Architectural Notes: a framework for distributed systems development, Ph.D. Thesis. University of Twente, Enschede, the Netherlands (1994)
7. ITU-T / ISO: Open Distributed Processing - Reference Model - Part 2: Foundations, ITU-T X.902 | ISO/IEC 10746-2 (1995)
8. ITU-T / ISO: Open Distributed Processing - Reference Model - Part 3: Architecture, ITU-T X.903 | ISO/IEC 10746-3 (1995)
9. ITU-T / ISO: Open Distributed Processing - Reference Model - Enterprise Language, ITU-T X.901 | ISO/IEC 15414:2002 (2001)
10. ITU-T: Recommendation Z.100 - CCITT Specification and Description Language. International Telecommunications Union (2002)
11. Luckham, D., Kenney, J., Augustin, L., Vera, J., Bryan, D., Mann, W.: Specification and Analysis of System Architecture Using Rapide. IEEE Transactions on Software Engineering, Vol. 21, No. 4 (1995) 336–355
12. Luckham D., Vera, J.: An Event-Based Architecture Definition Language. IEEE Transactions on Software Engineering Vol. 21, No. 9 (1995) 717–734

13. Microsoft Corporation: Microsoft .NET Remoting: A Technical Overview (2001), available at http://msdn.microsoft.com/library/en-us/dndotnet/html/hawkremoting.asp
14. Di Nitto, E., Rosenblum D.: Exploiting ADLs to Specify Architectural Styles Induced by Middleware Infrastructures. In: Proceedings of the 21st International Conference on Software Engineering (ICSE'99). Los Angeles, CA (1999)
15. Object Management Group: Model driven architecture (MDA), ormsc/01-07-01 (2001)
16. Object Management Group: Common Object Request Broker Architecture: Core Specification, Version 3.0, formal/02-12-06 (2002)
17. Object Management Group: CORBA Component Model, Version 3.0, formal/02-06-65 (2002)
18. Object Management Group: MDA-Guide, Version 1.0.1, omg/03-06-01 (2003)
19. Object Management Group: Meta Object Facility (MOF) 2.0 Core Specification, ptc/03-10-04 (2003)
20. Object Management Group: Meta Object Facility (MOF) Specification, Version 1.4, formal/02-04-03 (2002)
21. Object Management Group: MOF 2.0 Query / Views / Transformations RFP, ad/2002-04-10 (2002)
22. Object Management Group: Unified Modelling Language: Object Constraint Language Version 2.0, Draft Adopted Specification, ptc/03-08-08 (2003)
23. Object Management Group: UML 2.0 Superstructure, ptc/03-08-02 (2003)
24. Object Management Group: UML Profile for Enterprise Distributed Object Computing Specification, ptc/02-02-05 (2002)
25. Object Management Group: Unified Modelling Language (UML) Specification: Infrastructure, Version 2.0, ptc/03-09-15 (2003)
26. Object Management Group: Unified Modelling Language (UML) Specification, Version 1.5, formal/03-03-01 (2001)
27. Sun Microsystems: Java(TM) Message Service Specification Final Release 1.1 (2002), available at http://java.sun.com/products/jms/docs.html
28. World Wide Web Consortium: SOAP Version 1.2 Part 1: Messaging Framework, W3C Proposed Recommendation (2003), available at http://www.w3.org/TR/soap12-part1
29. World Wide Web Consortium: Web Services Description Language (WSDL) 1.1, W3C Note (2001), available at http://www.w3.org/TR/wsdl

Context-Driven Model Refinement

Dennis Wagelaar*

Vrije Universiteit Brussel, Pleinlaan 2,
1050 Brussels, Belgium
dennis.wagelaar@vub.ac.be

Abstract. An important drive for Model-Driven Architecture is that many software applications have to be deployed on a variety of platforms and within a variety of contexts in general. Using software models, e.g. described in the Unified Modeling Language (UML), one can abstract from specific platforms. A software model can then be transformed to a refined model, given the context in which it should run. Currently, each target context requires its own model transformation. Only a limited number of contexts can be supported in this way. We propose a context-driven modelling framework that models each target context in a context model, described in the Web Ontology Language (OWL). Multiple reusable transformation rules are used, which are annotated with context constraints, based on the OWL context model. The framework can automatically select the transformation rules that are applicable for a concrete context.

1 Introduction

The Model-Driven Architecture (MDA) allows for mapping a high-level software design to a specific implementation platform. Model transformations are used to refine a Platform-Independent Model (PIM) to a Platform-Specific Model (PSM). Several layered PSMs can be used to gradually refine the design.

An important drive for MDA is that a lot of software has to run within a variety of computing contexts. The vision of Ambient Intelligence only increases this variety, with many portable and embedded devices such as personal digital assistants (PDAs), smartphones and embedded computers in cars and houses. For our purposes, context includes the software/hardware platform on which the software must run, but also other factors, such as required run-time qualities (e.g. adaptability, performance, security, etc.) and user preferences (e.g. chosen software features).

In current MDA approaches [1], each target platform requires its own (set of) model transformation(s). This means that for each new target platform, at least one new model transformation is needed, even if that platform is only a variant

---

* The author's work is part of the CoDAMoS project, which is funded by the Institute for the Promotion of Innovation by Science and Technology in Flanders (IWT-Flanders).

U. Aßmann, M. Aksit, and A. Rensink (Eds.): MDAFA 2003/2004, LNCS 3599, pp. 189–203, 2005.

of another, already supported platform (e.g. J2ME Personal Profile[1] is a variant of Java). In practice, this means that only a relatively small number of general platforms can be targeted, e.g. Java or C++. Targeting very specific platforms, e.g. the previously mentioned J2ME Personal Profile 1.0, is not feasible because of the maintenance overhead, even though such precise targeting can result in PSM that is better optimised for the given context.

Looking into the model transformations themselves, it appears that they can often be made reusable over multiple platforms and it is only how they are configured that makes them applicable to only one platform. For example, one model transformation could target all Java 2 platforms by transforming "to-many" association ends in the Unified Modeling Language (UML) to attributes using the Java 2 Collections framework. If this transformation is configured to be applied in combination with a transformation that targets the Java Swing framework, the target platform is already limited to J2SE for the desktop computer[2]. The fact that each configuration of model transformations is also maintained by hand, makes that the problem of limited platform support remains.

We propose a context-driven modelling framework that can automatically select appropriate transformation rules for a concrete context and configure them into a context-optimised transformation. The developer can define a number of alternative refinement transformation rules. These transformation rules are annotated with context constraints within which the transformation will work. These context constraints, as well as the concrete context description, are based upon an explicit context model. This context model is expressed in the Web Ontology Language (OWL) [2], which is an extensible language for describing ontologies. Furthermore, we use the OWL-DL variant, which corresponds to description logics [3], such that computational completeness can be guaranteed. The context model forms a basis for describing contexts in general and can be extended to include the specific context information that is relevant for a particular application domain. An automatic reasoner, such as RACER [4], can be used to verify whether a concrete context satisfies the constraints of a model transformation. Subsequently, one transformation rule is selected for each group of remaining transformation alternatives, based on how close its constraint lies to the actual context.

Section 2 discusses how computing context can be modelled and section 3 explains how model transformations can be augmented with context constraints. In section 4 the mechanism for selecting model transformations is explained. Section 5 discusses related work and section 6 states the conclusions for this paper.

2   Context Modelling

In order to reason about context and context constraints, an ontology of computing context is used. Ontologies can serve as a common vocabulary for a domain [5]. The relationships between the ontology elements can be used to rea-

---

[1] http://java.sun.com/j2me/

[2] http://java.sun.com/j2se/

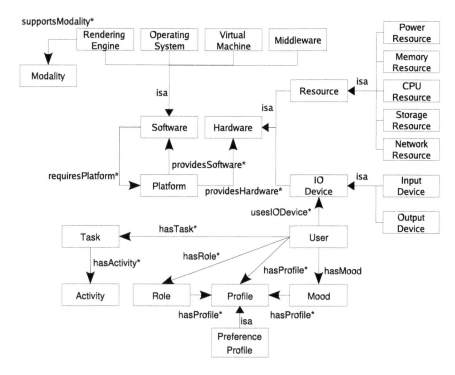

Fig. 1. Part of the context ontology for describing platforms and users

son about elements based on that ontology. A context ontology allows one to base expressions about a concrete context on the vocabulary expressed by the ontology. By using a shared model of context, we can reason about the relationship between a context description and a context constraint, even if the two do not have a direct relationship. An example context constraint is that the Java 2 Collections framework needs to be present. An example of a context description includes a Sharp Zaurus PDA. Since both the context constraint and the context description refer to the context ontology to explain what the Java 2 Collections framework resp. the Zaurus PDA is, one can derive whether the Zaurus PDA satisfies the Java 2 Collections framework constraint.

2.1   A Context Vocabulary

Before modelling any specific context or context properties, a basic context structure needs to be defined. In this paper, the context ontology described in [6] is used for this purpose[3]. This ontology is in turn inspired by the User Agent Profile specification (UAProf) [7] and Composite Capability/Preference Profiles (CC/PP) [8], both of which are standards intended to describe target platforms.

---

[3] Other ontologies can be used, but it is necessary to use the same ontology for describing context and constraints on that context.

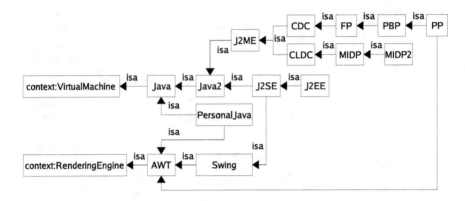

Fig. 2. An ontology describing Java virtual machines

The ontology is expressed in OWL, an extensible standard for describing ontologies. OWL has a variant, called OWL-DL, that corresponds to description logics, allowing for automated reasoning about the ontology. The ontology used complies to this OWL-DL variant. The part of the ontology that models platforms and users is shown in Fig. 1.

The platform concept in this ontology can provide software and hardware. The '*' next to the "providesSoftware" relationship denotes a one-to-many relationship. Software and hardware are broken down into different sub-concepts. This is denoted by the special "isa" subsumption relationship, e.g. the set of operating systems subsumes the set of software in general. The software can impose requirements on the platform, e.g. the need for a network resource, a particular virtual machine or a user interface rendering engine that supports voice communication. This is denoted by the "requiresPlatform" relationship, which points to a description of the required platform. The user concept has profile elements, amongst others, which describes the user. A special case of a profile is a preference profile, which describes user preferences only.

The ontology can be extended for particular domains of platforms, such as Java virtual machines. Fig. 2 shows such an ontology. The "VirtualMachine" concept starts with "context:" to indicate it refers to the "VirtualMachine" concept from the main context ontology. The "Java" virtual machine can be subdivided in many different configurations. "Java2" refers to the virtual machines that run Java 1.2 or up. "Java2" is split up into "J2ME", "J2SE" and "J2EE", which is based on "J2SE". In the ontology, two other concepts are introduced: "AWT" and "Swing". These refer to the Java Abstract Window Toolkit (AWT) resp. Swing rendering engines. Since some Java virtual machine configurations already include these, instances of such virtual machines also serve as instances of the AWT and/or Swing rendering engine. This is represented in the ontology by defining additional "isa" relationships to the AWT or Swing rendering engine from the virtual machines.

In order to discriminate on user profile data as well, an ontology extension for user profiles can be defined. For the purpose of this paper, we will use a very

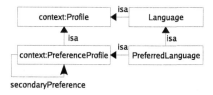

Fig. 3. An example ontology for describing user profiles

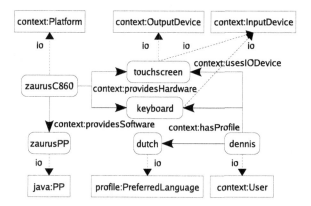

Fig. 4. Example context description for the author using the Sharp Zaurus PDA

simple profile ontology, describing only the languages that a user can use and/or prefers to use. This ontology extension is depicted in Fig. 3.

2.2 Modelling Concrete Contexts

The actual context for the PSM can now be described by instances of the context concepts. Fig. 4 shows an example context description for a Sharp Zaurus PDA. This PDA has a Personal Profile (PP) J2ME virtual machine installed.

The concepts "Platform" and "PP" are taken from the context resp. Java ontologies. The instances, "zaurusC860" and "zaurusPP", are depicted as rounded rectangles and are instances of the "Platform" and "PP" classes. This is depicted by the "io" relationships. The "zaurusC860" platform has a "providesSoftware" relationship with the "zaurusPP" Java Personal Profile virtual machine. The "zaurusC860" platform provides a "touchscreen" and a "keyboard" I/O device, through which the user "dennis" interacts with the platform. Finally, "dennis" prefers to communicate in "dutch".

3   Modelling Context Dependencies

Model transformations can now define constraints on instances of the ontology concepts. This is done by defining new, *completely specified* concepts. Such concepts have *necessary and sufficient* conditions in addition to any *necessary* conditions. For example, whereas it is *necessary* that each "J2ME" instance is also an instance of "Java2" (depicted by the "isa" relationship in Fig. 2), being a "Java2" instance is not *sufficient* for also being a "J2ME" instance. The notation for describing conditions as used in the Protégé tool [9] is also used here.

In order to check if the current platform has a "Java2" class virtual machine, a concept "Java2Platform" can be defined, which is a sub-concept of "Platform" (*necessary*) and provides a "Java2" virtual machine (*necessary and sufficient*):

$$Java2Platform \sqsubseteq context : Platform$$
$$\equiv \exists\ context : providesSoftware\ platform : Java2$$

Whenever a "Platform" instance fulfils the condition of providing a "Java2" virtual machine, it can be classified as an instance of "Java2Platform". This classification can be performed by automatic reasoners. This way, concrete platform instances can be matched against a completely defined constraint concept. If the platform instance classifies as an instance of the constraint concept, then the constraint holds for that instance. For example, the "zaurusC860" platform from Fig. 4 classifies as an instance of "Java2Platform", since "zaurusPP" is an instance of "PP", which is a sub-class of "Java2".

3.1   Example PIM

Fig. 5 shows part of a PIM for a simple Breakout game, expressed in UML 1.5 [10]. The objective of the game is to remove all the bricks from the screen by hitting them with the ball. The ball must be bounced back with the paddle, which is controlled by the player. If the ball falls down the screen (paddle has missed), the game is over. In the design, the "Field" class represents the screen, which has composition associations with a "Ball", a "Paddle" and multiple "Bricks". A separate "view" package has been modelled to separate the graphical user interface from the game model itself. AWT and Swing implementations of the "view" package have also been modelled, but are not shown in the diagram. Note that our example PIM contains platform-specific elements that rely on the AWT and Swing rendering engine. Our notion of PIM includes all models that have not (yet) committed to a specific platform.

The example PIM contains several elements that are not available in the programming environment that is needed for the target platform[4]. These elements are the "process", "Observer", "Observable", "subscribe" and "thread" stereotypes, the "Integer" and "Boolean" Object Constraint Language (OCL) data types, association relationships and specifications of operations (e.g. in OCL, a dynamic diagram or an Action Language). Model transformations can be defined to translate each of these elements to one or more elements that are available in the target programming environment. In addition, the PIM contains several platform-specific elements, such as the view implementations relying on Java AWT and Swing. The selection of relevant platform-specific elements can

---

[4] The programming environment comprises the programming language and available libraries.

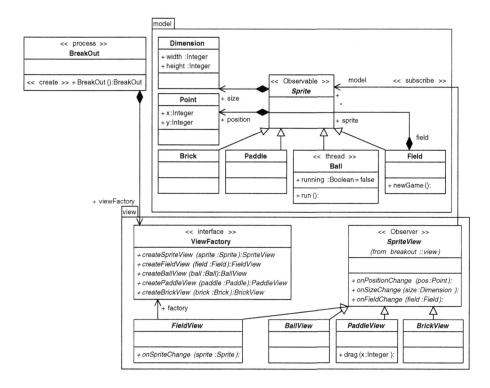

Fig. 5. Example PIM class diagram for a breakout game

also be performed by model transformations. Examples of some of these model transformations will be discussed below. The Atlas Transformation Language (ATL) [11], which has a simple, rule-based syntax, will be used to express these examples.

3.2   Example Model Transformations

A model transformation for translating UML 1.5 associations to corresponding attributes for Java could use the Java 2 Collections framework to implement a one-to-many association. The following transformation rules use the `java.util.List` interface and the implementing `java.util.ArrayList` class to achieve a one-to-many relationship[5]:

```
rule AssociationEndSingleAttribute {
  from s : INMODEL! AssociationEnd (s.isNavigable and s.isSingle ())
  to t : OUTMODEL! Attribute (
    name <- s.name,
    owner <- s.navigableFrom(),
    type <- s.participant,
    visibility <- s.visibility,
```

---

[5] Note that, in ATL, additional headers are needed and rules are necessary for each model element that needs to be copied/transformed. Only the rules that perform actual transformation are shown here for brevity.

```
      ownerScope <- s.targetScope,
      changeability <- s.changeability)
  }

rule AssociationEndArrayList {
  from s : INMODEL!AssociationEnd (s.isNavigable and not s.isSingle())
  using { collection: INMODEL!Interface = INMODEL!Interface.allInstances()
    ->select(c|c.name='Collection')->first(); }
  to t : OUTMODEL!Attribute (
    name <- s.name,
    owner <- s.navigableFrom(),
    type <- collection,
    visibility <- s.visibility,
    ownerScope <- s.targetScope,
    changeability <- s.changeability,
    initialValue <- v),
  v : OUTMODEL!Expression (
    language <- 'java',
    body <- 'new java.util.ArrayList()')
}

helper context INMODEL!AssociationEnd def : navigableFrom() :
INMODEL!Classifier =
    self.association.connection->select(x|x<>self)->first().participant;

helper context INMODEL!AssociationEnd def : isSingle() : Boolean =
    self.multiplicity.range->select(r|r.upper<>1)->isEmpty();
```

The transformation rules translate only the navigable association ends to attributes. The first rule translates all association ends with an upper multiplicity range of "1" to simple attributes. The second rule translates all association ends with an upper range other than "1" to Java Lists. The **from** keyword indicates the element to read from the source model, whereas the **to** keyword indicates the element to be created in the target model. The **INMODEL** and **OUTMODEL** in the transformation refer to the meta-models used, which is the UML 1.5 meta-model in both cases. Two **helper** functions have been defined to reuse the OCL expressions for determining the class from which the association end can be navigated (**navigableFrom()**)[6] and whether an association end only points to a single target (**isSingle()**). The second rule has a **using** clause, which locates the Java Collection interface. This Collection interface is then used as the type of the attribute that is created. The ArrayList class is used for the initial value of this attribute.

The **AssociationEndSingleAttribute** transformation rule does not use any Java-related elements, and has no platform dependencies. The **AssociationEnd-ArrayList** rule uses the Java 2 Collections framework and therefore needs at least a "Java2" virtual machine (see Fig. 2). This corresponds with the "Java2-Platform" constraint given at the beginning of this section. An alternative for the **AssociationEndArrayList** rule could use the **java.util.Vector** class to implement the one-to-many association:

```
rule AssociationEndVector {
  from s : INMODEL!AssociationEnd (s.isNavigable and not s.isSingle())
  using { vector : INMODEL!Class = INMODEL!Class.allInstances()
    ->select(c|c.name='Vector')->first(); }
  to t : OUTMODEL!Attribute (
    name <- s.name,
```

---

[6] Only binary associations are considered.

```
    owner <- s.navigableFrom(),
    type <- vector,
    visibility <- s.visibility,
    ownerScope <- s.targetScope,
    changeability <- s.changeability,
    initialValue <- v),
  v : OUTMODEL! Expression (
    language <- 'java',
    body <- 'new java.util.Vector()')
}
```

Because the Java Vector class was already available in Java 1.0, the platform constraint can be relaxed to only requiring a Java virtual machine:

$$JavaPlatform \sqsubseteq context : Platform$$
$$\equiv \exists \, context : providesSoftware \, java : Java$$

4   Context-Driven Refinement

The mechanism that selects the appropriate model transformations is based on Synthesis-Based Design [12] and its version for MDA transformations [13]. Synthesis-Based Design uses a *design space* of possible combinations of alternative design choices. The design choices are represented by model transformations in this case. The transformations are grouped into sets of alternatives that represent the same functionality. This grouping can be done automatically, based on a heuristic that checks the input specification of the transformation rules. If certain transformation rules have the same input specification, they are considered to be alternatives. The transformation rules `AssociationEndArrayList` and `AssociationEndVector`, given in subsection 3.2, have the same input specification (represented by the `from` part). Hence, they are considered to be alternatives belonging to one group. The groups that are formed in this way only have to be created once for a set of transformation rules and can be adapted manually afterwards. Each time a PSM has to be generated for a specific platform, the existing transformation rules are considered, using the existing grouping information. An example grouping for the model transformations needed for our example PIM is shown in Table 1.

The `English`, `French`, `German` and `Dutch` transformations are simple selection transformations that select their corresponding language package to be included in the deployment. They form one group, since they take all language package deployment information as input and differ only in which language packages are copied back out. Similarly, the `AWTView` and `SwingView` transformations select the AWT resp. Swing view implementation from all view implementations. The `AssociationEndArrayList` and `AssociationEndVector` transformations have already been discussed and form one group. The `Accessors` transformation creates accessor operations (getters and setters) for each public attribute. The `Process` transformation augments all classes with the "process" stereotype with a "main" operation. The `Thread` transformation adds a realization relationship to the `java.lang.Runnable` class to each class with the

Table 1. Example model transformations grouping

English | French | German | Dutch
AWTView | SwingView
Accessors
AssociationEndArrayList | AssociationEndVector
Process
Thread
Observer | PropertyChangeListener
DataTypes

"Thread" stereotype. The `Observer` and `PropertyChangeListener` transformations both implement the "Observer", "Observable" and "subscribe" stereotypes. The first transformation uses the Java 1.0 `java.util.Observer` interface and the `java.util.Observable` class to accomplish this, while the latter uses the `java.beans.PropertyChangeListener` interface and corresponding classes. Finally, the `DataTypes` transformation translates the OCL data types into Java data types.

From each group, one model transformation is selected. First, all transformation constraints are checked against the platform, after which the non-matching transformations are discarded. Note that, if no transformations are left for a particular group after this step, no PSM can be generated for the given context. Each group of remaining alternative transformations is sorted by context relevance, such that the most relevant transformation alternative appears at the top of the list. The context relevance is determined by subsumption of constraint concepts. If a constraint concept defines a subset of another constraint concept, then that constraint is considered more context-specific. Consider the following context constraint:

$$Java2Personal \sqsubseteq context : Platform$$
$$\equiv (\exists\ context : providesSoftware\ \ java : Java2)\ \sqcup$$
$$(\exists\ context : providesSoftware\ \ java : PersonalJava)$$

This constraint demands either a "Java2" or a "PersonalJava" VM, whereas the "JavaPlatform" constraint (see before) demands a "Java" class VM. Both "Java2" and "PersonalJava" are subconcepts of "Java". The set defined by the union of "Java2" and "PersonalJava" is still a subset of "Java", so the "Java2-Personal" concept can be classified as a subconcept of "JavaPlatform". Again, existing automatic reasoners can be used to classify the subsumption taxonomy of concepts as they are defined by the constraints.

It is possible that the context constraints of alternative transformations do not contain enough information to determine whether one constraint subsumes another. Consider the following example constraint:

$$AWTPlatform \sqsubseteq context : Platform$$
$$\equiv \exists\ context : providesSoftware\ \ java : AWT$$

Table 2. Example model transformations selected and sorted

Dutch
AWTView
AssociationEndArrayList
Accessors
Process
Thread
PropertyChangeListener
DataTypes

Compared to the "Java2Platform" constraint mentioned earlier, one cannot classify either as a subset of the other. In such a case, the group of transformation alternatives (see Table 1) will first be reduced to those alternatives of which the constraints are leafs in the constraint concept taxonomy. From these alternatives, the alternative specified left-most in the initial group will be chosen. Consider three transformation alternatives, A, B and C, which have the "JavaPlatform", "Java2Platform" and "AWTPlatform" constraint respectively. If a taxonomy is created for these constraints, "Java2Platform" and "AWTPlatform" are both direct subconcepts of "JavaPlatform". The group of alternatives is reduced to B and C, since their constraints are the leafs in the taxonomy. If alternative B is listed before alternative C in the initial group of alternatives, then alternative B will be chosen.

Since some model transformations may depend on the result of other model transformations, they need to be ordered. The transformation dependencies can also be checked automatically by a heuristic that checks if the input specification of a transformation may overlap with the output specification of another (represented by the **to** part). The output specification of the `AssociationEnd-ArrayList` transformation states that it creates new attributes. If another model transformation, `Accessors`, creates accessor operations for each public attribute, then its input specification could match elements generated by `Association-EndArrayList`. Hence, `AssociationEndArrayList` is placed before `Accessors`. If no decision can be made on whether to put one transformation before another, the order is left unchanged. This way, the developer can already pre-sort the groups of transformations manually and no manual intervention is needed for each context. The sorted list of chosen transformations for the example platform from Fig. 4 is shown in Table 2.

The `AssociationEndArrayList` transformation was chosen over the `Asso-ciationEndVector` transformation, because it requires a "Java2" VM instead of any "Java" VM. For the same reason, the `PropertyChangeListener` transformation is chosen over the `Observer` transformation. Also, the transformations have been sorted according to input-output dependencies: the `Accessors` transformation has been placed after `AssociationEndArrayList`. The `Dutch` selection transformation takes in all kinds of elements and can also output all kinds of elements, so the sorting heuristic could not determine what to do with it. In this case, the developer knows that this rule does not depend on any transformation output, so it remains pre-sorted as the first transformation to execute. The other transformations don't generate any elements that may be matched by the input specification of another transformation, so their order is also not adapted.

5   Related Work

In Generative Programming [14] and Step-Wise Refinement [15], *features* and *feature models* are used to model a family of software systems instead of a single system. Features can be optional or mandatory for a software system, depending on the presence of other features. In our framework, features are implicitly generated or selected by model transformations, which are chosen based on context constraints. Feature models can be used to verify if the chosen transformations represent a valid set of features.

The lack of explicit platform models is discussed in [16]. The notion of *abstract platform* is introduced, which describes a set of elements to model a PIM against. This set of elements includes design artifacts that are available in a target platform (classes, interfaces) and design constructs that can be mapped to that platform (stereotypes, profiles), e.g. with model transformations. The goal of abstract platforms is to ease platform-independent modelling, whereas our context models are meant to decouple context information, which includes the platform, from model transformations.

In [17], platform selection rules are discussed, which allow for pre-selecting a number of target platforms. In that way, less platforms need to be supported. In our case, platform selection rules can be used to narrow down the amount of platform domain aspects (e.g. Java virtual machines) that need to be modelled for a particular application domain (e.g. instant messaging). This does not conflict with the envisioned ambient intelligence scenario that targets an open-ended infrastructure of unanticipated devices, since this is supported by in-depth modelling of platform domain aspects, not the amount of aspects that are modelled.

In [18], an infrastructure for combining UML models and ontologies is introduced. Such as infrastructure can be useful for a better integration of platform constraints into model transformation languages.

The KobrA method [19] is an approach for component-based product line engineering with UML. It uses pattern-based refinements for design elements. OO-Method [20] also introduces a pattern-based approach for design refinement and code generation. PRISMA [21] is a modelling approach that can be used to model context data. Our approach differs in that it uses refinement alternatives, such that context-based optimisation is possible.

The Catalysis approach [22] is a UML-based development method for component-based systems. An important part of this method consists of refinement of the model elements. As such, our context-driven modelling framework can be used as a means to refine the model elements in a context-optimised way.

The Context Ontology Language (CoOL) [23] is an ontology-based context modelling approach, which uses the Aspect-Scale-Context (ASC) model where each aspect (e.g. spatial distance) can have several scales (e.g. kilometre scale or mile scale) to express some context information (e.g. 20). Chen et al. [24] propose a context broker architecture (CoBrA) using an ontology to describe persons, places and intentions. Gu et al. [25] present a service-oriented context-aware middleware (SOCAM) based on a context model with person, location, activity and computational entity (such as a device, network, application, service, etc.) as basic context concepts. Henricksen and Indulska [26] propose a context model that describes context based on several types of facts (e.g. sensed, static and profiled) subject to constraints and quality annotations. The context ontology used in this paper puts more focus on the platform description, which is central to MDA.

6   Conclusion and Future Work

This paper has introduced a context-driven modelling framework that can automatically choose the most context-specific model transformations from a set of alternatives. Instead of providing a set of alternative model transformations, multiple sets of alternative model transformations are provided, which together can form a complete model transformation. In this way, many more computing contexts can be supported with a similar design effort.

The proposed modelling framework fits within the MDA vision in that it also uses several layered refinement transformations. Based on a context model described in OWL, specific transformations are chosen to transform a PIM to a PSM.

The selection mechanism relies on the classification of a taxonomy of context constraints. This classification needs to be done only once for a set of available model transformations and can then be reused for each concrete context. Furthermore, the constraint checking mechanism implemented by RACER is highly optimised. It should scale no worse than the matching algorithm needed for the model transformations themselves.

In the future, a configuration language will be introduced to support the transformation selection and sorting mechanism. This configuration language will express the inter-dependencies of the model transformations and will discriminate between mandatory (e.g. an accessor method generator) and non-mandatory transformations (e.g. a language support selection transformation). This configuration language will probably be based upon feature models. MOF can be used for the description of the abstract syntax, such that the same repository that is used for storing the various MDA models can also be used for storing the configuration model.

Acknowledgement

The author would like to thank Ragnhild van der Straeten and the anonymous review committee for reviewing this paper. Many improvements have been made based on their comments. In addition, the author would like to thank Willem Hajenius and Wouter Heyse for their work on the breakout game example case used in this paper.

References

1. Czarnecki, K., Helsen, S.: Classification of Model Transformation Approaches. In: OOPSLA 2003 Workshop on Generative Techniques in the context of Model Driven Architecture. (2003)
2. Smith, M.K., Welty, C., McGuinness, D.L.: OWL Web Ontology Language Guide. World Wide Web Consortium. (2004) W3C Recommendation 10 February 2004.
3. Baader, F., Calvanese, D., McGuinness, D.L., Nardi, D., Patel-Schneider, P.F.: The Description Logic Handbook: Theory, Implementation and Applications. Cambridge University Press, Cambridge, UK (2003)
4. Möller, R., Haarslev, V.: Description Logics for the Semantic Web: Racer as a Basis for Building Agent Systems. Künstliche Intelligenz (2003) 10–15
5. Gruber, T.R.: A Translation Approach to Portable Ontology Specifications. Knowledge Acquisition **5** (1993) 199–220
6. Preuveneers, D., den Bergh, J.V., Wagelaar, D., Georges, A., Rigole, P., Clerckx, T., Berbers, Y., Coninx, K., Jonckers, V., Bosschere, K.D.: Towards an extensible context ontology for Ambient Intelligence. In: Proceedings of the Second European Symposium on Ambient Intelligence, Eindhoven, The Netherlands, Springer-Verlag (2004) 148–159
7. Open Mobile Alliance: User Agent Profile 2.0 Specification. (2003) Version 20-May-2003.
8. Klyne, G., Reynolds, F., Woodrow, C., Ohto, H., Hjelm, J., Butler, M.H., Tran, L.: Composite Capability/Preference Profiles (CC/PP): Structure and Vocabularies 1.0. World Wide Web Consortium. (2004)
9. Noy, N.F., Sintek, M., Decker, S., Crubézy, M., Fergerson, R.W., Musen, M.A.: Creating Semantic Web Contents with Protege-2000. IEEE Intelligent Systems **16** (2001) 60–71
10. Object Management Group, Inc.: Unified Modeling Language Specification. (2003) Version 1.5 (formal/03-03-01).
11. Bézivin, J., Dupé, G., Jouault, F., Pitette, G., Rougui, J.E.: First experiments with the ATL model transformation language: Transforming XSLT into XQuery. In: OOPSLA 2003 Workshop on Generative Techniques in the context of Model Driven Architecture. (2003)
12. Tekinerdoğan, B., Akşit, M.: Synthesis Based Software Architecture Design. In Akşit, M., ed.: Software Architectures and Component Technology, Dordrecht, The Netherlands, Kluwer Academic Publishers (2001) 143–173
13. Kurtev, I., van den Berg, K.: A Synthesis-Based Approach to Transformations in an MDA Software Development Process. In Rensink, A., ed.: CTIT Technical Report TR-CTIT-03-27, Enschede, The Netherlands, University of Twente (2003) 121–126
14. Czarnecki, K., Eisenecker, U.: Generative Programming: Methods, Tools, and Applications. 1st edn. Addison Wesley, Reading, Massachusetts, USA (2000)
15. Batory, D., Sarvela, J.N., Rauschmayer, A.: Scaling Step-Wise Refinement. In: Proceedings of the 25th International Conference on Software Engineering (ICSE 2003), Portland, Oregon, USA, IEEE Computer Society (2003) 187–197
16. Almeida, J.P., Dijkman, R., van Sinderen, M., Pires, L.F.: On the Notion of Abstract Platform in MDA Development. In: The 8th International IEEE Enterprise Distributed Object Computing Conference, Monterey, California, USA, IEEE Computer Society (2004) 253–263

17. Tekinerdoğan, B., Bilir, S., Abatlevi, C.: Integrating Platform Selection Rules in the Model-Driven Architecture Approach. In Aßmann, U., ed.: Proceedings of Model Driven Architecture: Foundations and Applications (MDAFA 2004), Linköping, Sweden, Research Center for Integrational Software Engineering, Linköping University (2004) 184–200
18. Bézivin, J., Devedžić, V., Djurić, D., Favreau, J., Gašević, D., Jouault, F.: An M3-Neutral infrastructure for bridging model engineering and ontology engineering. In: First International Conference on Interoperability of Enterprise Software and Applications (INTEROP-ESA'05), Geneva, Switzerland, Springer-Verlag (2005)
19. Atkinson, C., Bayer, J., Bunse, C., Kamsties, E., Laitenberger, O., Laqua, R., Müthig, D., Paech, B., Wüst, J., Zettel, J.: Component-Based Product Line Engineering with UML. 1st edn. Addison Wesley, Reading, Massachusetts, USA (2001)
20. Pelechano, V., Pastor, O., Insfrán, E.: Automated code generation of dynamic specializations: an approach based on design patterns and formal techniques. Data and Knowledge Engineering **40** (2002) 315–353
21. Martinez, J.J., Salavert, I.R.: A Conceptual Model for Context-Aware Dynamic Architectures. In: Proceedings of the 23rd International Conference on Distributed Computing Systems Workshops (ICDCSW'03), Providence, Rhode Island, USA, IEEE Computer Society (2003) 138–143
22. D'Souza, D.F., Wills, A.C.: Objects, Components, and Frameworks with UML: The Catalysis(SM) Approach. Addison Wesley, Reading, Massachusetts, USA (1998)
23. Strang, T., Linnhoff-Popien, C., Frank, K.: CoOL: A Context Ontology Language to enable Contextual Interoperability. In: Proceedings of 4th IFIP WG 6.1 International Conference on Distributed Applications and Interoperable Systems (DAIS2003), Paris, France, Springer-Verlag (2004) 236–247
24. Chen, H., Finin, T., Joshi, A.: An Ontology for Context-Aware Pervasive Computing Environments. Knowledge Engineering Review **18** (2004) 197–207 Special Issue on Ontologies for Distributed Systems.
25. Gu, T., Wang, X.H., Pung, H.K., Zhang, D.Q.: An Ontology-based Context Model in Intelligent Environments. In: Proceedings of Communication Networks and Distributed Systems Modeling and Simulation Conference (CNDS'04), San Diego, California, USA (2004) 270–275
26. Henricksen, K., Indulska, J.: A Software Engineering Framework for Context-Aware Pervasive Computing. In: Proceedings of the 2nd IEEE International Conference on Pervasive Computing and Communications (PerCom'04), Orlando, Florida, USA, IEEE Computer Society (2004) 77–86

A UML Profile for OWL Ontologies

Dragan Djurić[1], Dragan Gašević[1], Vladan Devedžić[1], and Violeta Damjanović[2]

[1] FON – School of Business Administration, University of Belgrade, POB 52,
Jove Ilića 154, 11000 Belgrade, Serbia and Montenegro
dragandj@gmail.com, gasevic@yahoo.com,
devedzic@galeb.etf.bg.ac.yu
[2] Postal Savings Bank, 27.marta 71, Belgrade, Serbia and Montenegro
vdamjanovic@gmail.com

Abstract. The paper presents Ontology UML Profile (OUP); which, together with Ontology Definition Metamodel (ODM), enables the usage of Model Driven Architecture (MDA) standards in ontological engineering. Other similar metamodels and UML profiles are based on ontology representation languages, such as RDF(S), DAML+OIL, etc. However, none of these other solutions uses the recent W3C effort – The Web Ontology Language (OWL). In our approach, we firstly define the place of ODM and OUP in the context of the MDA four-layer architecture and identify the main OWL concepts. Then, to support ODM, we define OUP and describe its details. The proposed UML profile enables usage of the well-known UML notation in ontological engineering more extensively. We implemented an XSLT that transforms OUP ontologies into OWL in order to provide a suitable tool support.

1 Introduction

The Semantic Web and its XML-based languages are the main directions of the future Web development. Domain ontologies [1] are the most important part of the Semantic Web applications. They are formal organization of domain knowledge, and in that way enable knowledge sharing between different knowledge-base applications. Artificial intelligence (AI) techniques are used for ontology creation, but those techniques are more related to research laboratories, and they are unknown to wider software engineering population.

In order to overcome the gap between software engineering practitioners and AI techniques, there are a few proposals for UML usage in ontology development [2]. But, UML itself does not satisfy needs for representation of ontology concepts that are borrowed from description logics, and that are included in Semantic Web ontology languages (e.g. RDF, RDF Schema, OWL, etc.). The OMG's Model Driven Architecture (MDA) concept has the ability to create (using metamodeling) a family of languages [3] that are defined in the similar way like the UML is. Accordingly, in this paper, the authors briefly show a metamodel for ontology modeling language – Ontology Definition Metamodel (ODM). This metamodel is defined using Meta-Object Facility (MOF), and is based on the Web Ontology Language (OWL). Since Unified Modeling Language (UML) is widely accepted as a modeling language, we define a profile that supports ontology design – Ontology UML Profile. It is a standard extension of UML, and is also based on MOF. Ontology UML Profile is

U. Aßmann, M. Aksit, and A. Rensink (Eds.): MDAFA 2003/2004, LNCS 3599, pp. 204–219, 2005.

intended to be used as a support to ODM, not as a stand-alone solution for Ontology modeling.

The overview of the Semantic Web languages and OWL is given in the next section, while the description of the MDA and MOF is in section three. In section four we give a framework for our approach of the ontology language metamodel in the MDA context and the overview of ontology metamodel definition. The details of Ontology UML Profile are shown in the section five. Section six contains an XSLT-based implementation example for transforming an ontology UML Profile into OWL, as well as our experiences in using this transformation. The last section contains final conclusions. This work is a part of the effort of the GOOD OLD AI research group (http://goodoldai.org.yu/) in developing AIR - a platform for building intelligent systems.

2   An Overview of the Semantic Web, Web Ontology Language, MDA and MOF

The step beyond the World Wide Web is the Semantic Web [4], which will enable machine-understandable data to be shared across the Net. The Semantic Web will be powered by metadata, described by ontologies that will give machine-understandable meaning to its data. Ontology is one of the most important concepts in knowledge representation. It can be generally defined as shared formal conceptualization of particular domain [1]. The World Wide Web and XML will provide the ontologies with interoperability, and these interoperable ontologies will, in return, facilitate Web that can "know" something.

Semantic Web architecture is a functional, non-fixed architecture [5]. Barnes-Lee defined three distinct levels that incrementally introduce expressive primitives: *metadata* layer, *schema* layer and *logical* layer [6]. Languages that support this architecture and the place of OWL are shown in Figure 1.

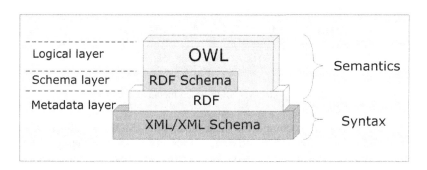

Fig. 1. OWL in the Semantic Web architecture

Common data interoperability in present applications is best achieved by using XML [7]. As shown in the Figure 1, XML supports syntax, while semantics is provided by RDF, RDF Schema and mainly by OWL [8]. In order to provide capabilities for unconstrained representation of the Web knowledge and, in the same time, to support calculations and reasoning in finite time with tools that can be built on the existing or soon available technologies, OWL introduces three increasingly expressive sublanguages for various purposes: OWL Full (maximal expressiveness), OWL DL (guaranties computational completeness) and OWL Lite (for starters).

Model Driven Architecture (MDA) [9] defines three viewpoints (levels of abstraction) from which some system can be seen. From a chosen viewpoint, a representation of a given system (viewpoint model) can be defined. These models are (each corresponding to the viewpoint with the same name): *Computation Independent Model* (CIM), *Platform Independent Model* (PIM) and *Platform Specific Model* (PSM).

OMG's MDA is based on the four-layer metamodeling architecture, and several OMG's complementary standards; which is shown in Figure 2. These standards are *Meta-Object Facility* (MOF) [10], *Unified Modeling Language* (UML) [11] and *XML Metadata Interchange* (XMI) [12]. Layers are: meta-metamodel (M3) layer, metamodel (M2) layer, model (M1) layer and instance (M0) layer.

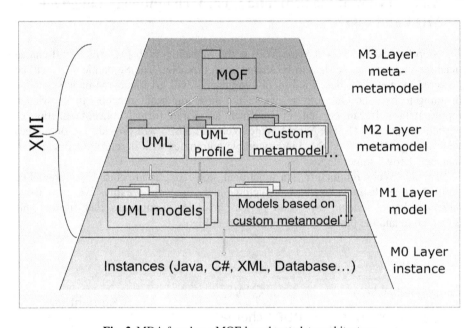

Fig. 2. MDA four-layer MOF-based metadata architecture

On the top of this architecture is the meta-metamodel (MOF). It defines an abstract language and framework for specifying, constructing and managing technology neutral metamodels. It is the foundation for defining any modeling language; such as UML or even MOF itself. MOF also defines a framework for implementing repositories that hold metadata (e.g. models) described by metamodels [10]. The main aim of having four layers with common meta-metamodel is to support multiple metamodels and models; to enable their extensibility, integration and generic model management and metamodel management. Present software tools support for MDA is concentrated primarily on UML as a graphical notation and MDA's M1 layer, with no concern of metamodeling layers [13].

3   The Ontology Modeling Architecture

To be widely adopted by users and to succeed in real-world applications, knowledge engineering and ontology modeling must catch up with mainstream software trends. It will provide a good support in software tools and ease the integration with existing or upcoming software tools and applications, which will add values to both sides. To be employed in common applications, software knowledge management must be taken out of laboratories and isolated high-tech applications and put closer to ordinary developers. This issue has been addressed in more details in Cranefield's papers [2].

MDA and its four-layer architecture provides a solid basis for defining metamodels of any modeling language, therefore it is the straight choice to define an ontology-modeling language in MOF. Such language can utilize MDA's support in modeling tools, model management and interoperability with other MOF-defined metamodels. Present software tools do not implement many of the concepts that are the basis of MDA. However, most of these applications, which are mostly oriented to the UML and M1 layer, are expected to be enhanced in the next few years to support MDA.

Currently, there is a RFP (Request for Proposal) within OMG that tries to define a suitable language for modeling Semantic Web ontology languages in the context of MDA [14]. According to this RFP we give our proposal of such architecture [15]. In our approach of ontology modeling in the scope of MDA, which is shown in Figure 3, several specifications should be defined:

- Ontology Definition Metamodel (ODM)
- Ontology UML Profile – a UML Profile that supports UML notation for ontology definition
- Two-way mappings between OWL and ODM, ODM and Ontology UML Profile and from Ontology UML Profile to other UML profiles.

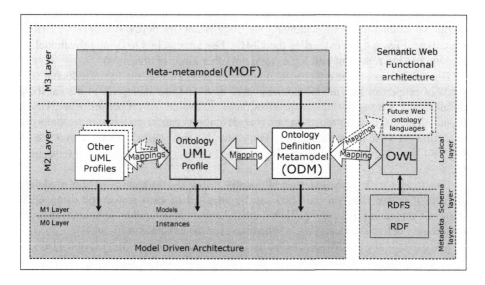

Fig. 3. Ontology modeling in the context of MDA and Semantic Web

We designed *Ontology Definition Metamodel* (ODM) to comprehend common ontology concepts. A good starting point for ODM construction was OWL since it is the result of the evolution of existing ontology representation languages and is a W3C recommendation [8]. It is at the Logical layer of the Semantic Web [8], on top of RDF Schema (Schema layer). In order to make use of graphical modeling capabilities of UML, an ODM should have a corresponding UML Profile [16]. This profile enables graphical editing of ontologies using UML diagrams as well as other benefits of using mature UML CASE tools. Both UML models and ODM models are serialized in XMI format so the two-way transformation between them can be done using XSL Transformation. OWL also has representation in the XML format, so another pair of XSL Transformations should be provided for two-way mapping between ODM and OWL. For mapping from the Ontology UML Profile into another, technology-specific UML Profiles, additional transformations can be added to support usage of ontologies in design of other domains and vice versa.

4 Ontology UML Profile Essentials

UML Profile is a concept used for adapting the basic UML constructs to some specific purpose. Essentially, this means introducing new kinds of modeling elements by extending the basic ones, and adding them to the modeler's tools repertoire. Also, free-form information can be attached to the new modeling elements.

4.1 UML Profile Basics

The basic UML constructs (model elements) can be customized and extended with new semantics by using four *UML extension mechanisms* defined in the UML Specification [17]: stereotypes, tag definitions, tagged values, and constraints. *Stereotypes* enable defining virtual subclasses of UML metaclasses, assigning them additional semantics. For example, we may want to define the «OntClass» stereotype, Figure 4, by extending the UML Class metaclass to denote the modeling element used to represent ontologies (and not other kinds of concepts).

Tag definitions can be attached to model elements. They allow for introducing new kinds of properties that model elements may have and are analogous to metaattribute definitions. Each tag definition specifies the actual values of properties of individual model elements, called *tagged values*. Tag definitions can be attached to a stereotype to define its virtual metaattributes. For example, the «OntClass» stereotype in Figure 4 has a tag definition specifying 4 tagged values (for enumeration, intersection, etc.).

Constraints make possible to additionally refine the semantics of the modeling element they are attached to. They can be attached to each stereotype using OCL (Object Constraint Language) [17] or English language (i.e. spoken language) in order to precisely define the stereotype's semantics (see the example in Figure 4).

More details about UML extension mechanisms can be found in [17] and [18].

A coherent set of extensions of the basic UML model elements, defined for specific purposes or for a specific modeling domain, constitutes a *UML profile*.

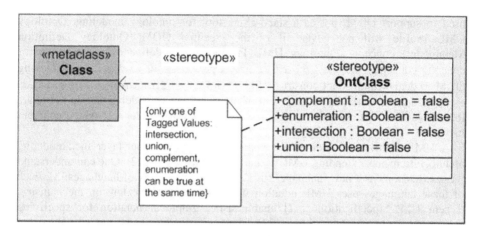

Fig. 4. New stereotype definition

4.2 Design Rationale for Ontology UML Profile

In order to customize UML for modeling ontologies, we define UML Profile for ontology representation, called *Ontology UML Profile*. In developing our Ontology UML Profile we used experiences of other UML Profile designers (e.g., see [19]). Applying such experiences to our case, we wanted our Ontology UML Profile to:

- offer stereotypes and tags for all recurring ontology design elements, such as classes, individuals, properties, complements, unions, and the like;
- make specific ontology modeling and design elements easy to represent on UML diagrams produced by standard CASE tools, thus keeping track of ontological information on UML models;
- enable encapsulating ontological knowledge in an easy-to-read format and offer it to software engineers;
- make possible to evaluate ontology UML diagrams and to indicate possible inconsistencies;
- support Ontology Definition Metamodel, hence be able to represent all ODM concepts.

Currently, several different approaches to ontology representation in UML have been proposed. We note two major trends among them:

- Extending UML with new constructs to support specific ontology concepts (Property for example) [20].
- Using standard UML and defining a UML Profile for ontology representation [21].

We believe that ontology representation in UML can be achieved without non-standard UML extensions, hence our approach belongs to the latter of the above two trends. In our Ontology UML profile, specific ontology concepts are annotated using the standard UML extension mechanisms described above. Models created with such a UML Profile will be supported by standard UML tools, since they do not add non-standard concepts to UML, thus they are UML models. Since in our approach UML is used to support ODM, not as a stand-alone tool for ontology modeling, Ontology UML Profile will not cover all of the essential ODM (Ontology Definition Metamodel) concepts. Ontology UML Profile should define only constructs for concrete concepts, such as `ObjectProperty`, `Class` or `Individual`, leaving ODM to deal with abstract constructs like `Resource`, `Instance`, `Classifier`, etc, which are not used in development of real ontologies (models), and do not relate to real-world things; they are only introduced to ODM in order to create a coherent hierarchy.

A UML Profile definition in the context of the MDA four-layer metamodeling architecture means extending UML at the metamodel layer (M2). One can understand these extensions as a new language, but also UML as a family of languages [3]. Each of these languages uses UML notation with the four UML extension mechanisms. Recent UML specifications [17] enable using graphical notation for specifying stereotypes and tagged definitions [22]. Thus, all stereotypes and tagged values that are defined in this paper can be shown in this way.

The notation used for stereotype creation of Ontology UML Profile («OntClass» stereotype) accomodetes UML's Class («metaclass»). Having this graphical notation for the UML extension mechanism can be useful for explaining certain relations between UML constructs and new stereotypes, but also between stereotypes themselves.

Since stereotypes are the principle UML extension mechanism, one might be tempted to think that defining Ontology UML Profile is a matter of specifying a couple of stereoptypes and using them carefully in a coherent manner. In reality, however, it is *much* more complicated than that. The reason is that there is a number of fine details to take care of, as well as the existence of some conceptual inconsistencies between MDA and UML that may call for alternative design decisions. The following subsections describe the most important Ontology UML Profile concepts in detail.

4.3 Ontology Classes

`Class` is one of the most fundamental concepts in ODM and Ontology UML Profile. As we noted in the discussion about the essential ODM concepts, there are some differences between traditional UML `Class` or OO programming language Class concept and ontology class as it is defined in OWL (`owl:Class`). Fortunately, we are not trying to adopt UML as stand-alone ontology language, since that might require changes to UML basic concepts (`Class` and other). We only need to customize UML as a support to ODM.

In ODM, Ontology Class concept is represented as an instance of MOF `Class`, and has several concrete species, according to the class description: `Class`, `Enumeration`, `Union`, `Intersection`, `Complement`, `Restriction`, and a special built-in OWL class `AllDifferent`. These constructs in the Ontology UML Profile are all inherited from the UML concept that is most similar to them, UML `Class`. But, we must explicitly specify that they are not the same as UML `Class`, which we can do using UML stereotypes. An example of `Classes` modeled in Ontology UML Profile is shown in Figure 5.

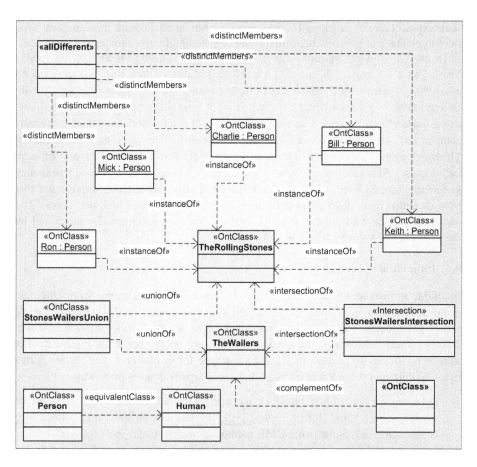

Fig. 5. Class Diagram showing relations between Ontology Classes and Individuals in the Ontology UML Profile

ODM `Class` identified by a class identifier will have the stereotype «OntClass», AllDifferent - «AllDifferent» and Restriction - «Restriction». In ODM, `Enumeration`, `Intersection`, `Union` and `Complement` are descendants of ODM `Class`; in Ontology UML Profile they have stereotypes «Enumeration», «Intersection», «Union» and «Complement». The «OntClass» stereotype would be extended by each of these new stereotypes. Additionally, enumeration, intersection, union and complement are defined by Boolean tagged values - enumeration, intersection, union and complement, which can be added to «OntClass» with the constraint that only one of them can be true. This would be similar to the solution used in other UML profiles. A good example is the XML Schema UML profile [23] that has stereotypes for modeling the content model of the XML Schema complex type: any, choice, and sequence. Complex type itself is a distinct stereotype as well. Also, in parallel with these stereotypes, there is a tagged value modelGroup attributed to the complex type stereotype that can take a value from the set consisting of: any, choice, and sequence.

Figure 5 shows various types of ontology classes modeled in UML. The Class Person is an example of an ontology Class that is identified by a class identifier, TheRollingStones and TheWailers are enumerations, StonesWailersIntersection is an intersection, and StonesWailersUnion is a union. There is one unnamed class that represents complement of TheWailers – all individuals that are not members of TheWailers. AllDifferent is an auxiliary class whose members are different individuals. Also shown is an «OntClass» Human and the Dependency «equivalentClass», which means that Person and Human are classes that have the same class description (i.e. all Persons are Humans and vice versa). The names of classes whose name is not important could be automatically generated by the tool, and not shown in the diagram.

4.4 Individuals

In ODM, an instance of an AbstractClass is called Individual. In UML, an instance of a Class is an Object. ODM Individual and UML Object have some differences, but they are similar enough, so in Ontology UML Profile, Individual is modeled as UML Object, which is shown in Figure 5. The stereotype for an object must match the stereotype for its class («OntClass» in this case). Stating that some Individual has some type is done in three ways:

1. by using an underlined name of an Individual followed by ":" and its «ontClass» name (for example, Mick:Person is an Individual whose type is Person. This is the usual UML method of stating an Object's type.
2. by using a UML Dependency's stereotype «instanceOf» between an Individual and its «ontClass». This method is also allowed in standard UML. For example, Mick is an instance of TheRollingStones.
3. indirectly – through logical operators on «OntClass». If some «OntClass» is a union, intersection or complement, it is a class of Individuals that are not explicitly defined as its instances. For example, Mick is not explicitly defined as a member of StonesWailersUnion, but it is its member since he is a member of TheRollingStones, which is connected with StonesWailersUnion through a «unionOf» connection.

Although there are some UML tools (Together, Visio) that allow relations between a UML Class and a UML Object in a UML Class Diagram, many popular UML tools (e.g. Rational Rose, Poseidon for UML) do not support this, even though the UML specification [17] clearly states that Objects and Links can be drawn on Class Diagrams. The authors believe that this is closely related to understanding UML as a graphical notation for modeling and using it with object-oriented programming languages. Another very important issue is related to the MDA metamodeling architecture. UML classes are usually thought of as belonging to the model layer (M1), whereas UML objects are believed to belong exclusively to the instance level

(M0). But, this is not quite correct: the UML class and object are defined at the same MDA layer (i.e. M2). Thus, their instances are at the same layer – the model layer (i.e. M1). Actually, a UML object models a thing from the real world [24]. But, objects only *model* real world things; they are not real things (e.g. in Figure 5 the object Mick only models an instance of Human). Then, how can we distinguish between the *instance-of* relation between objects and classes, and, on the other hand, between UML Class (metaclass) and some concrete class? We believe that Atkinson and Kühne [25] have adequately proposed the solution to this problem by introducing two kinds of *instance-of* relations: linguistic and ontological. The linguistic *instance-of* relation is the *instance-of* relation between concepts from different layers (UML Class definition and some concrete class, for instance TheWailers). The ontological *instance-of* relation is the *instance-of* relation between concepts that are at the same linguistic layer, but which are at different ontological layers (for instance, <<OntClass>> Person and object Keith are at different ontological layers since Human is the class (type) of Keith).

4.5 Ontology Properties

Property is one of the most unsuitable ontology concepts to model with object-oriented languages and UML. The problem arises from the major difference between Property and its similar UML concepts – Association and Attribute. Since Property is an independent, stand-alone concept, it can not be directly modeled with Association or Attribute, which can not exist on their own. Some authors [20] suggested extending UML with new constructs to support the stand-alone Property, introducing aspect-oriented programming concepts into UML. In our view, this solution is rather extreme, since it demands non-standard changes to UML. We try to introduce Property in UML in some other way instead.

Since Property is a stand-alone concept it can be modeled using a stand-alone concept from UML. That concept could be the UML Class' stereotype «Property». However, Property must be able to represent relations between Resources (Classes, Datatypes, etc. in the case of UML), which the UML Class alone is not able to do. If we look at the ODM Property definition more closely, we will see that it accomplishes relation representation through its range and domain. According to the ODM Model, we found that in the Ontology UML Profile, the representation of relations should be modeled with UML Association's or UML Attribute's stereotypes «domain» and «range». In order to increase the readability of diagrams, the «range» association is unidirectional (from a Property to a Class).

ODM defines two types (subclasses) of Property – ObjectProperty and DatatypeProperty. ObjectProperty, which can have only Individuals in its range and domain, is represented in Ontology UML Profile as the Class' stereotype «ObjectProperty». DatatypeProperty is modeled with the Class' stereotype «DatatypeProperty».

An example of a Class Diagram that shows ontology properties modeled in UML is shown in Figure 6. It contains four properties: two «DatatypeProperty»s (name and socialSecurityNumber) and two «ObjectProperty»s (nationality and colleague) UML Classes. In cooperation with «domain» and «range» UML Associations, or «domain» and «range» UML Attributes, they are used to model relationships between «OntClass» UML Classes. Tagged values describe additional characteristics, for example, «ObjectProperty» colleague is symmetric (if one Person is a colleague of another Person, the other Person is also a colleague of the first Person) and transitive (if the first Person is a colleague of the second Person, who is a colleague of the third Person, the first and third Person are colleagues). In ODM, these characteristics are added to an ODM Class applying the Decorator Design Pattern [26]. The transformation that maps an Ontology UML Profile model to an ODM model should create one decoration of an ODM Property per attribute of Ontology UML Profile «ObjectProperty» or «DatatypeProperty».

There is an important issue that must be clarified with this diagram. In UML, relations are represented by Associations (graphically represented as lines) or Attributes, which looks nice and simple. Ontology UML Profile diagrams may look overcrowded, since each relation requires a box and two lines to be properly represented. The solution shown in this paper uses standard graphical symbols, but UML allows custom graphical symbols for a UML Profile. For example, a custom graphical symbol for Property could be a tiny circle with lines, which reduces the space on diagrams. Also, additional custom settings, like distinct colors for «OntClass» (green), «ObjectProperty» (orange) or «DatatypeProperty» (orange) in this paper, can be used to increase the diagram readability. For the sake of readability, this UML Profile allows two styles of «DatatypeProperty» domain and range presentation. An example of the first style (a UML Class with two UML Associations) is socialSecurityNumber, and an example of the second one (a Class with Attributes as domain or range) is name. The second style is allowed only for «DatatypeProperty» whose range multiplicity is equal or less than one. So, if a «DatatypeProperty» has range multiplicity of 0..1 or 1, the style with Attributes can be used to reduce the clutter.

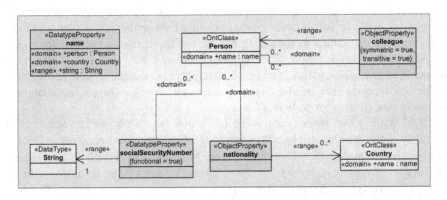

Fig. 6. Ontology Properties shown in UML Class Diagram

4.6 Statement

ODM Statement is a concept that represents concrete links between ODM instances – Individuals and DataValues. In UML, this is done through Link (an instance of an Association) or AttributeLink (an instance of an Attribute). Statement is some kind of instance of a Property, which is represented by the UML Class' stereotype («ObjectProperty» or «DatatypeProperty»). Since in UML a Class' instance is an Object, in Ontology UML Profile Statement is modeled with Object's stereotype «ObjectProperty» or «DatatypeProperty» (stereotype for Object in UML must match the stereotype for its Class' stereotype). UML Links are used to represent the subject and the object of a Statement. To indicate that a Link is the subject of a Statement, LinkEnd's stereotype «subject» is used, while the object of the Statement is indicated with LinkEnd's stereotype «object». LinkEnd's stereotype is used because in UML Link can not have a stereotype. These Links are actually instances of Property's «domain» and «range». In brief, in Ontology UML Profile Statement is represented as an Object with two Links – the subject Link and the object Link, which is shown in Figure 7. The represented Persons Mick and Keith are colleagues. They both have UK (Great Britain) nationality.

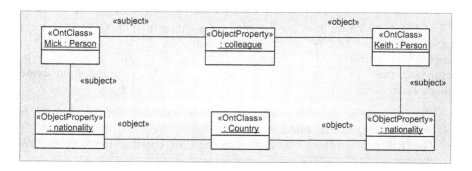

Fig. 7. Individuals and Statements shown in a UML Object Diagram

As with Ontology Properties, the diagram's readability can be further increased by using distinct colors and custom graphical symbols. A tiny circle can be used instead of the standard box for representing the Statement in order to reduce clutter on a diagram.

5 Tool Support

In this section we describe our XSLT-based implementation for transforming OUP into OWL [27]. A UML tool (e.g. Poseidon for UML) can export an XMI document that an XSLT processor can use as the input. An OWL document is produced as the output, and this format can be imported into a tool specialized for ontology development (e.g. Protégé), where it can be further refined. On the other hand, since we obtain an OWL described document, we do not need to use any ontology tool, instead we are able to use this ontology description as a final OWL ontology. Furthermore, when we use an approach based on XSLT (the XSLT principle) we do not need to change (i.e. recompile) a UML tool, but we just apply an XSLT on an output document of the UML tool. Accordingly, we can use well-defined XML/XSLT procedure that is shown in Figure 8.

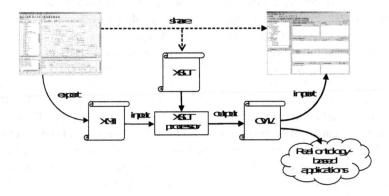

Fig. 8. Used XSLT principle: extensions of present UML tools for ontology development

The XSLT, which we have implemented for mapping from the OUP XML format (i.e. UML XMI) to the OWL description, contains a set of rules (i.e. templates) that match XMI constructs and transform them into equivalent OWL primitives. While developing these rules we faced some serious obstacles resulting from evident differences between source and target format. We note some of them:

– The structure of an XMI document is fairly awkward since it contains full description of an UML model.
– The OUP, in some cases, uses more than one UML construct to model one OWL element.
– UML tools can only draw UML models, but they do not have an ability to check the completeness of an OUP ontology. Thus, the XSLT is incurred to check XMI documents. This is the only way to avoid generation of erroneous OWL ontologies.
– The XSLT must make difference between classes that are defined in other classes (nested classes that can not be referenced from other classes using their ID) and classes that can be referenced using their ID. Accordingly, we included the *odm.anonymous* tagged value into OUP. This tagged value helps detect these two cases.

The developed solution acts as an extension for standard UML tools and thus enables us to create complete OWL ontologies without need to use ontology-specialized development tools. We have decided to use *Poseidon for UML* since it supports all requirements for OUP. We decide to generate OWL ontologies in the fashion similar to the Protégé's OWL plugin. Hence, we have managed to provide an additional way to import Poseidon's models into Protégé through the OWL. Of course, since Protégé has more advanced features for ontology development, an OUP-defined ontology can be further refined.

We have tested our solution on the well-known example of the Wine ontology. Firstly, we represented this ontology in Poseidon using OUP. Then we exported this extended UML into XMI, and after performing the XSLT, we obtained an OWL document. Finally we imported this document into Protégé using its OWL plugin.

The current XSLT version has a limitation since it does not support packages (i.e. the OUP multi-ontology development). Actually, OUP supports multiple ontologies within the same XMI project, but the XSLT standard and XSLT processors introduce this limitation.

So far, we have developed two ontologies using OUP that we later transformed in OWL using the XSLT. These two ontologies are: the ontology of saints and philosophers, and the Petri net ontology. The first ontology was developed using the Porphyry's tree method. The Petri net ontology was developed in order to provide the Semantic Web support for Petri nets [28].

6 Conclusions

The Ontology UML Profile defined in this paper and ODM are in accordance with the OMG's RFP initiative for ontology modeling. Accordingly, we borrowed the name ODM for our metamodel from the OMG's RFP. The proposed solution enables using ontologies in the way that is closer to software engineering practitioners. Also, since the UML and ODM are defined as MOF-compliant languages it is possible to store ontologies in MOF-based repositories, to store ontology diagrams in a standard way (UML2 XMI), as well as to share and interchange ontologies using XMI.

The proposed Ontology UML Profile can be considered as a part of the effort to specify standard ontology metamodel. Their important feature is that they are based on OWL. With the Ontology UML Profile, the ODM concepts can be used as stereotypes in the UML models (similar to UML CORBA Profile or other OMG's UML Profiles).

The possibilities of defining other AI metamodels in MOF should and will be explored in the future work. This means that MDA and MOF will be the integrating point for metamodels, both common and AI-related. Another important research direction is to examine the usability of the proposed OUP on real-world ontologies. Further plans also include using Java Metadata Interface (JMI) [29] to enable creation, storage, access, discovery, and exchange of ODM-defined ontologies using standard Java interfaces.

References

1. Gruber, T. R.: A translation approach to portable ontology specifications, Knowledge Acquisition, Vol. 5, No. 2 (1993) 199-220
2. Cranefield, S.: Networked Knowledge Representation and Exchange using UML and RDF, Journal of Digital information, Vol. 1, No.8 (2001) http://jodi.ecs.soton.ac.uk

3. Duddy, K.: UML2 Must Enable A Family of Languages, Communications of the ACM, Vol. 45, No. 11, (2002) 73-75
4. Berners-Lee, T: Weaving the Web, Orion Business Books, London (1999)
5. Brickley, D. and Guha, R. V. (eds.): RDF Vocabulary Description Language 1.0: RDF Schema, W3C Recom., http://www.w3.org/TR/2000/CR-rdf-schema-20000327 (2004)
6. Berners-Lee,   T.:   Semantic   Web   Road   Map,   W3C   Design   Issues, http://www.w3.org/DesignIssues/Semantic.html, (1998)
7. Bray, T., et al (eds.): Extensible Markup Language (XML) 1.0 (Second Edition), W3C Recommendation, http://www.w3.org/TR/2000/REC-xml-20001006 (2000)
8. Bechhofer, S. et al: OWL Web Ontology Language Reference, W3C Recommendation, http://www.w3.org/TR/2004/REC-owl-ref-20040210 (2004)
9. Miller, J., Mukerji, J. (eds.): MDA Guide Version 1.0, OMG Document: omg/2003-05-01, http://www.omg.org/mda/mda_files/MDA_Guide_Version1-0.pdf (2003)
10. Meta Object Facility (MOF) Specification v1.4, OMG Document formal/02-04-03, http://www.omg.org/cgi-bin/apps/doc?formal/02-04-03.pdf (2002)
11. Booch, G., Rumbaugh, J., Jacobson, I.: The Unified Modeling Language User Guide, Addison-Wesley, Massachusetts (1998)
12. OMG   XMI   Specification,   v1.2,   OMG   Document   formal/02-01-01, http://www.omg.org/cgi-bin/doc?formal/2002-01-01 (2002)
13. Gašević, D., Damjanović, V., Devedžić, V.: Analysis of the MDA Standards in Ontological Engineering, In Proceedings of the 6th International Conference of Information Technology, Bhubaneswar, India (2003) 193-196
14. Ontology Definition Metamodel Request for Proposal, OMG Document: ad/2003-03-40, http://www.omg.org/cgi-bin/doc?ad/2003-03-40 (2003)
15. Djurić, D. Gašević, D., Devedžić, V.: Ontology Modeling and MDA, Journal on Object Technology, Vol. 4, No. 1 (2005) forthcoming
16. Sigel, J.: Developing in OMG's Model-Driven Architecture, Revision 2.6, Object Management Group White Paper, ftp://ftp.omg.org/pub/docs/-omg/01-12-01.pdf (2001)
17. OMG Unified Modeling Language Specification, OMG Document formal/03-03-01, http://www.omg.org/cgi-bin/apps/doc?formal/03-03-01.zip (2003)
18. Rumbaugh, J., Jacobson, I., Booch, G.: The Unified Modeling Language Reference Manual, Addison-Wesley (1998)
19. Juerjens, J.: Secure Systems Development with UML. Springer-Verlag, Berlin (2003)
20. Baclawski, K. et al: Extending the Unified Modeling Language for ontology development, Journal on Software and Systems Modeling, Vol. 1, No. 2 (2002) 142-156
21. Baclawski, K. et al: UOL: Unified Ontology Language, Assorted papers discussed at the DC Ontology SIG meeting, http://www.omg.org/cgi-bin/doc?ontology/2002-11-02 (2002)
22. Kobryn, C.: The Road to UML 2.0: Fast track or Detour, Software Development Magazine,   http://www.sdmagazine.com/documents/s=732/sdm0104b/0104b.htm   (April 2001)
23. Carlson, D.: Modeling XML Applications whit UML: Practical E-Business Applications, Addison-Wesley, Boston, USA (2001)
24. Atkinson, C., Kühne, T.: Rearchitecting the UML Infrastructure, ACM Transactions on Modeling and Computer Simulation, Vol. 12, No. 4 (2002) 290–321
25. Atkinson, C., Kühne, T.: Model-Driven Development: A Metamodeling Foundation, IEEE Software, Vol. 20, No. 5 (2003) 36-41
26. Gamma, E., et al: Design Patterns: Elements of Reusable Object-Oriented Software, Addison-Wesley (1995)

27. Gašević, D. et al: Converting UML to OWL ontologies, In Proceedings of the 13th International WWW Conference, NY, USA (2004)
28. Gašević, D. and Devedžić, V.: Reusing Petri Nets Through the Semantic Web, In Proc. of the 1st European Semantic Web Symposium Heraklion, Greece (2004)
29. Dirckze, R. (spec. leader): Java Metadata Interface (JMI) Specification Version 1.0, http://jcp.org/aboutJava/communityprocess/final/jsr040/index.html (2002)

Developing a UML Profile for Modelling
Knowledge-Based Systems

Mohd Syazwan Abdullah[1,2], Chris Kimble[1], Richard Paige[1], Ian Benest[1],
and Andy Evans[1]

[1] Department of Computer Science, University of York,
Heslington, YO10 5DD, York, United Kingdom
{syazwan, kimble, paige, idb, andye}@cs.york.ac.uk
[2] Faculty of Information Technology, Universiti Utara Malaysia,
06010 Sintok, Kedah, Malaysia
pathma@webmail.uum.edu.my

Abstract. Knowledge engineers have favoured a diagrammatic approach for
developing knowledge-based systems and have adopted those used in software
engineering. However, these modelling techniques tend to be used in an *ad hoc*
way and are highly dependent on the modelling experience of the engineers involved. This paper focuses on the use of profiles for knowledge modelling that
are available in the Unified Modeling Language (UML). It identifies the shortcomings of current approaches to adopting UML and discusses the need for an
extension to UML using the profile mechanism. A profile based on the eXecutable Modelling Framework (XMF) is also presented as work-in-progress.

1   Introduction

The use and management of knowledge in enterprises has become a commercial ne-
cessity for many organisations, in order that they manage their corporate intellectual
assets and gain competitive advantage. Most knowledge resides in human memories
and managing it is seen as a human-oriented process rather than a technology-based
solution. Nevertheless, technology can be utilised as a knowledge management en-
abler by adopting software tools, including the internet and groupware systems. One
of the prominent tools in managing knowledge is the knowledge-based system (KBS).

Knowledge-based systems can be deployed as the technological means for capturing and managing both explicit and tacit knowledge as part of an organisation's
knowledge management initiative. But, before these can be built, the knowledge that
pervades the organisation must be identified and modelled using appropriate acquisition, representation and modelling techniques.

This paper is organised as follows: Section 2 generally describes knowledge-based
systems and the field of knowledge engineering. Section 3 gives an overview of the
rôle of knowledge modelling and the techniques that are currently used. Section 4
explains the need to have an extension to UML for modelling knowledge, while Section 5 describes what is a UML profile. Section 6 presents the initial knowledge modelling profile constructed using identified modelling concepts, while Section 7 concludes and indicates the direction for future work.

U. Aßmann, M. Aksit, and A. Rensink (Eds.): MDAFA 2003/2004, LNCS 3599, pp. 220–233, 2005.

2 Knowledge-Based System and Knowledge Engineering

A knowledge-based system (KBS) is a software application with an explicit, declarative description of knowledge for a certain application [1]. There is no single dividing line that differentiates a KBS and an information/software system as almost all contain knowledge elements within them [2]. An information system is a set of interrelated components that together collects, processes, stores, analyses, and disseminates data and information in an organization. In contrast, a KBS has knowledge represented in an explicit form, and hence the increased importance of knowledge modelling [2] compared with that required of an information system.

The development process of a KBS is similar to any general system development; stages such as requirements gathering, system analysis, system design, system development and implementation are common activities. The stages in KBS development are: business modelling, conceptual modelling, knowledge acquisition, knowledge system design and KBS implementation [1].

A KBS is developed using knowledge engineering (KE) techniques [3]. These are similar to software engineering (SE) techniques, but have an emphasis on knowledge rather than data or information processing; they inherently advocate an engineering approach to the process of developing a KBS. The central theme in this approach is the conceptual modelling of the system in the analysis and design stages of the development process. Many knowledge engineering (KE) methodologies have been developed with an emphasis on the use of models, for example CommonKADS [2], MIKE [4], Protégé [5], and KARL [4].

Traditional KE techniques were widely used to construct expert systems – systems built from the knowledge of one or more experts – essentially, a process of knowledge transfer [3]. This is the development process of the first generation of expert systems, in which the knowledge of the expert is directly transferred into the knowledge base in the form of rules. The disadvantage of this approach is that the knowledge of the expert is captured in the form of hard codes within the system with little understanding of how they are linked or connected with each other [2]. This creates a new problem if the knowledge base is to be updated as changes require substantial effort in reconstituting the coded rules in order to implement the needed changes.

KE is no longer simply a means of mining the knowledge from the expert's head [2]. It now encompasses *"methods and techniques for knowledge acquisition, modelling, representation and use of knowledge"* [2]. The shift towards the modelling approach has also enabled knowledge to be re-used in different areas of the same domain [3]. In the past, most knowledge systems had to be developed from scratch every time a new system was needed, and it could not interact with other systems in the organization. The paradigm shift towards a modelling strategy has resulted in reducing development costs [2].

3 Knowledge Modelling

Knowledge modelling is used in knowledge acquisition activities as a way of structuring projects, acquiring and validating knowledge and storing knowledge for future use [6]. Knowledge models are structured representations of knowledge. They use symbols to represent pieces of knowledge and their relationships. Knowledge models are as follows: (1) symbolic character-based languages – logic; (2) diagrammatic representations – networks and ladders; (3) tabular representations – matrices and frames and (4) structured text – hypertext. Most models are constructed from knowledge objects such as concepts, instances, processes (tasks, activities), attributes and values, rules and relations.

Knowledge representation is one of the fundamental topics in the area of artificial intelligence (which investigates representation techniques, tools and languages). Knowledge about the domain and the implementation independent reasoning-process of the KBS however is usually addressed through the use of ontologies and problem-solving methods. There are five prominent representation techniques widely used in developing KBSs; they are: attribute-value pairs, object-attribute-value triplets, semantic networks, frames and logic.

By analysing the knowledge objects and representation techniques described earlier in this section, it will be noticed that they have similar concepts to those adopted for object-oriented modelling. Examples of these concepts are: objects, attributes, class, subclass, relationship, instances and others. Though these concepts have different meanings in different techniques, in most cases they refer to a similar thing. This paves the way to consider using object-oriented techniques as the standard means of representing them.

3.1 Ontology and Problem-Solving Method

Ontologies and Problem-Solving Methods (PSMs) enable the construction of KBSs through reusable components across domains and tasks [7]. Systems developers in the KE community are currently trying to adopt component-based development by incorporating ontologies and PSMs in order to deploy KBSs faster.

Ontologies are used to represent domain knowledge in knowledge-based programs. This is achieved using formal declarative representations of the domain knowledge; that is sets of objects and their describable relationships [8]. In the context of knowledge modelling, ontology defines the content-specific knowledge representation elements such as domain-dependent classes, relations, functions and object constants [7]. Researchers in the area of conceptual modelling and knowledge modelling have started to realise the importance of ontology in developing domain models since the underlying principle of modelling is to achieve agreed representations in a unified manner for the domains in which they are investigating. The works of Gomez-Perez and Benjamins [7], Gruber [8] and Kende [9] demonstrate such efforts to use ontologies.

PSMs describe the reasoning-process (generic inference patterns) at an abstract level independent of the representation formalism (e.g. rules, frames etc.) [5], [7]. PSMs have influenced the leading knowledge-engineering frameworks such as Task Structures, Rôle-Limiting Methods, CommonKADS, Protégé, MIKE, Components of Expertise, EXCEPT, GDM and VITAL [7]. Most of these frameworks suggest that a PSM: decomposes the whole reasoning task into elementary inferences that are easy to understand, defines the types of knowledge that will be used by the inference steps to be completed, and defines the control mechanisms and flow of knowledge among the inferences.

3.2 Knowledge Modelling Techniques

The importance of knowledge modelling in developing KBSs has been discussed by Schreiber *et al* [2]. They argue that models are important for understanding the working mechanisms within a KBS; such mechanisms are: the tasks, methods, how knowledge is inferred, the domain knowledge and its schemas. Modelling contributes to the understanding of the source of knowledge, the inputs and outputs, the flow of knowledge and the identification of other variables such as the impact that management action has on the organizational knowledge. Using conceptual modelling, systems development can be faster and more efficient through the re-use of existing models for different areas of the same domain. Therefore, understanding and selecting the modelling technique that is appropriate for different domains of knowledge will ensure the success of the KBS being designed.

Amongst the many techniques used to model knowledge, the most common are CommonKADS, Protégé 2000, the Unified Modeling Language (UML), and Multi-perspective modelling.

CommonKADS has become the *de facto* standard for knowledge modelling and is used extensively in European research projects. It supports structured KE techniques, provides tools for corporate knowledge management and includes methods that perform a detailed analysis of knowledge intensive tasks and processes. A suite of models is at the core of the CommonKADS methodology [2]. The suite supports the modelling of the organization, the tasks that are performed, the agents that are responsible for carrying out the tasks, the knowledge itself, the means by which that knowledge is communicated, and the design of the knowledge management system. Common-KADS incorporates an object-oriented development process and uses UML notations such as class diagrams, use-case diagrams, activity diagrams and state diagrams. CommonKADS also has its own graphical notations for task decomposition, inference structures and domain schema generation [2].

It has become a trend for system developers and researchers in KE to adopt object oriented modelling in developing conceptual models for knowledge systems [10] [11] [12]. A careful analysis of the literature shows that they have all been influenced by CommonKADS – an approach that is highly favoured, since it encourages the use of object-oriented development and the notations from UML.

Protégé was developed for domain specific applications [5] at Stanford Medical Informatics. Protégé 2000 is defined as *"an extensible, platform-independent environment for creating and editing ontologies and knowledge bases"* [13]. The Protégé 2000 knowledge modelling environment is a frame-based ontology editing tool with knowledge acquisition tools that are widely used for domain modelling.

The Unified Modeling Language (UML) together with the Object Constraint Language (OCL) is the *d-facto* standard for object modelling in software engineering as defined by the Object Management Group (OMG). UML is a general-purpose modelling language that covers a wide spectrum of different application domains. UML is incorporated in other mainstream techniques such as CommonKADS and Multi-perspective modelling for knowledge modelling purposes. Multi-perspective modelling enables a number of techniques to be used together, each technique being the most appropriate for modelling that particular aspect of knowledge [14]. It has its roots in software engineering (multiple-view technique).

3.3 Current Trends

Although KBSs are developed using knowledge engineering techniques, the modelling aspects of it are largely dependent on software engineering modelling languages. Most of the modelling techniques adopted, use a mix of notations derived from different modelling languages. The object-oriented paradigm has influenced systems development activities in software engineering and this trend has also been reflected in knowledge engineering methodologies such as CommonKADS [2], MOKA [12] and KBS developments in general [10], [15] and [16]. However, the main adopters of UML for knowledge modelling are CommonKADS [2] and MOKA [12]. The MOKA Modelling Language (MML) is an extension of UML that represents engineering product design knowledge at a user level for deployment in knowledge-based engineering applications. It provides default meta-models for the product and design process so as to manage engineering knowledge. However, it is an informal extension to UML and does not fulfill the OMG's requirements for an extension mechanism; these are presented in section 5.

Object oriented methods are gaining in popularity because of their expressiveness, flexibility and ease-of-use. One of UML's important features is that it is an extensible language brought about by the application of profiles. This makes UML one of the favoured techniques for knowledge modelling, for both the methodological aspect of KBS development and its standardisation. Thus, extensions to UML, can be formally introduced using UML Profiles for knowledge modelling.

4   Need for UML Extension

The major problem with knowledge modelling is that there is no standard technique available to model the knowledge for developing a knowledge-based system. Most of the techniques used by the researchers in the field of knowledge engineering are adapted from the software engineering community. The techniques used in knowledge modelling are project based using a mix of notations such as UML, IDEF, SADT, OMT, Multi-perspective Modelling and so on. Examples mentioned earlier are the CommonKADS methodology and Multi-perspective Modelling. Having recognised the importance of standardising knowledge modelling, OMG have started to work on the process of production rule representation [17] and knowledge-based engineering services for engineering design [18]. Benefits of having a standardised approach are: better tool support for designing the conceptual models, a large user base that is familiar with the language, and training is made easier by having many related publications focused on the standard. Furthermore, with a standards body monitoring evolving use, the standard remains live and relevant to industry.

Knowledge system projects are extremely specialised, requiring the team members to have knowledge of both the problem domain and the development tools. As a result the team members are highly skilled individuals, and this poses a great problem to the overall project if they should leave the team early in the development or maintenance period [19]. Having a standard modelling notation would help overcome such problems as new team members could quickly comprehend the design of the system.

Another important factor to consider is that many system analysis and design courses these days are teaching object-oriented modelling techniques as a tool for systems modelling and development. The main influence is the growing importance of object-oriented programming languages like Java in systems development. Because of the formal training received and the adoption of object-oriented programming by this generation of system analyst, most will have the knowledge of UML and use it for modelling purposes.

In addition to this, enterprise systems these days are an integration of software tools built on different platforms with the ability to communicate with each other. Most of these systems especially the new ones are built on platforms that support object-oriented languages, model driven architectures, object-based modelling etc. Knowledge-based systems are no longer stand-alone systems, but are part of the enterprise group of systems. As there is no standard way of modelling knowledge systems using knowledge engineering techniques, there is a need to extend those that have been standardised in software engineering. This promotes the use of a common modelling language, so that the vision of integration, reusability and interoperability within an enterprise's system will be achieved. It is proposed to model knowledge using an extension to UML.

UML is widely adopted as the object oriented way for systems development and has been deployed in other domains such as real-time systems, hypermedia design, embedded systems and ontology modelling. There are arguments that UML semantics are not well defined [20][21] compared to formal methods and these are being addressed by the OMG in developing UML version 2.0. This new version will have enhanced meta-model concepts and improved semantics. Developing UML Profiles for knowledge modelling will enable KBS developers to use UML in a formal and systematic manner. This can be achieved through the means of developing UML profiles with precisely defined notations, semantics and syntax which together enable this extension to be formally integrated into the existing profiles of UML (and adheres to the profiles requirements proposed by OMG [22]).

The UML is a general-purpose modelling language that covers a wide range of different application domains. While this feature might be adequate for modelling in a broader area, some domain-specific concepts and techniques need a more specialised refinement to the existing construct of the language [22]. This is achievable through the usage of the extension mechanism provided by UML known as a profile.

5   Profile Extension Mechanism

The OMG [23] has defined two mechanisms for extending the UML: profiles and metamodel extensions both of which are known (confusingly) as profiles.

Profiles are sometimes referred to as the "lightweight" extension mechanism of UML [22]. It contains a predefined set of Stereotypes, TaggedValues, Constraints, and notation icons that collectively specialize and tailor the UML for a specific domain or process. The main construct in the profile is the stereotype that is purely an extension mechanism. In the model, it is marked as <<stereotypes>> and has the same structure (attributes, associations, operations) defined by the metamodel that describes it. However, the usage of stereotypes is restricted. The semantics and the structure cannot be changed, and the introduction of new elements to the metamodel are not permitted [24]. The "heavyweight" extension mechanism to UML known as the metamodel extension is defined through the Meta-Object Facility (MOF) specification [25] which involves the process of defining a new metamodel. Using this extension, new metaclasses and metaconstructors can be added to the UML metamodel. This extension is a more flexible approach as new concepts may be represented at the metamodel level. So, profile based extensions must comply with the standard semantics of the UML model, but no such restriction is imposed on the MOF based extensions which can define a completely new metamodel.

UML Profile for Enterprise Application Integration (EAI), UML Profiles for CORBA, UML Profile for Enterprise Distributed Object Computing (EDOC), UML Testing Profile, and UML Profile for Schedulability, Performance and Time are some of the formal profiles developed by OMG.

6 UML Knowledge Modelling Profile

The scope of the profile described below is adapted from [26]. The aim of the UML Knowledge Modelling Profile is to define a language for designing, visualizing, specifying, analyzing, constructing and documenting the artifacts of knowledge-based systems. It is a knowledge modelling language that can be used with all major object technologies and applied to knowledge-based systems in various application domains and task types. The UML profile is based on the UML 2.0 specifications and is defined by using the profile extension approach of UML. It is being designed with the following principles in mind: UML integration - as a real UML based profile, the knowledge modelling profile is based on the metamodel provided in the UML superstructure and follows the principles of UML profiles as defined in UML 2.0.

6.1 Profile Design – XMF Approach

The XMF (eXecutable Meta-modelling Language) is an object-oriented meta-modelling language, and is an extension to existing standards for meta-models such as MOF, OCL and QVT, which are also defined by OMG. XMF exploits the features of these standards and adds a new dimension that allows them to be executable using an associated XMF software tool. The most comprehensive use of these standards are seen in the UML in which its meta-models are described using MOF. Details of XMF can be found in [27]. The XMF approach to profile creation can be divided into three steps: the derivation of an abstract syntax model, a description of the semantics, and a presentation of the profile's concrete syntax. XMF supports stereotypes and tagged values, but in a way that is significantly more controllable and powerful. XMF enables "meta profiles" to be constructed, in which stereotyped elements are true instances of specialised concepts.

Abstract Syntax
The abstract syntax model describes the concepts in the profile and their associations. It defines the rules that determine its validity. The processes involved in creating the abstract syntax model are:

- Identifying the concepts including the related rules. Reusing an existing BNF definition of the profile domain is an alternative at this stage.
- Modelling concepts – this involves the process of creating an abstract syntax model using the identified concepts.
- Defining the well-formed-ness rules of the profile in OCL – this will help in ruling out illegal models.
- Defining the operation and the queries related to the profile.
- Validating and testing the profile using an object diagram and relevant tools.

Semantics
The semantics describe the meanings of concepts within the profile in terms of behaviour, static properties or how it may be translated into another language. The semantics are a core part of the profile's meta-model and replace formal (mathematical) methods that are often difficult to comprehend by the majority of users and with which it would be difficult to describe the interrelationships within the meta-model. In XMF there are four types:

- Translational – concepts in one language are translated into the concepts of another language, both of which have precise semantics.
- Denotational – modelling the mapping to semantic domain concepts.
- Operational – modelling the operational behaviour of language concepts.
- Extensional – extending the semantics of existing language concepts.

Concrete Syntax
The concrete syntax is a means of presenting the abstract syntax to end users of the profile, using either textual or diagrammatic forms.

- The textual form of the profile is modelled using the Extended Backus-Naur Form (EBNF).
- The diagrammatic form involves synchronised mapping between the modelling elements and the diagram elements (boxes, lines and shapes). This is a new technique introduced into the meta-model by XMF.

The profile is designed based on the XMF specifications and is defined using the meta-class sub-classing approach of the XMF core meta-model, XCore. This paper only concentrates on the creation of the abstract syntax model of the profile. It excludes the processes of defining operations, queries and tool validation for the profile, as these discussions are more appropriate when executing the models and this is not the primary motivation of this paper.

6.2 Identification of Concepts

The discussion in this section mainly refers to the CommonKADS methodology for KBS development [2]. Tasks are the main categorisation of action that need to be performed by the KBS; typically this refers to the "what we want the system to do". Each task type will have their own terminology, task methods, inputs, outputs, inference mechanism being used, and the type of knowledge used; this is presented in [2]. Current studies on extending UML to model knowledge only concentrates on certain task types such as product design in MOKA [12] and UML-based product configuration design [10]. There are no specific studies being conducted in creating a generic profile that can be used for different task types; research now underway at York is focusing on this work. The following important knowledge modelling concepts have been identified from the literature [2] and are itemised in Table 1.

The authors believe that the level of abstraction is appropriate, and it naturally fits a KBS design, which is based on the PSM and ontology discussed earlier. Of course trying to maintain an overall picture of a complex system, including the interactions between its parts, will remain difficult for a human to perform. A re-engineering of the CommonKADS based system is also possible using the concepts from this profile.

6.3 Abstract Syntax Model

The abstract syntax of the knowledge modelling language has been derived using the modelling concepts shown in Table 1. The CommonKADS language has been adopted for specifying knowledge models that are defined in the BNF notation [2]. That BNF description has been translated into a UML model. In its current form it is a model of the abstract syntax of a knowledge modelling language, becoming a complete model of the language: a meta-model. Due to the size, and repetitive nature of the concepts described using BNF, and the complexity of the model, it has been condensed to show only the important features of modelling knowledge concepts.

Table 1. Main Knowledge Modelling Concepts

Modelling Concept	Description
Concept (class)	Class that represents the category of things
Inference	The lowest level of functional decomposition consisting of primitive reasoning steps
Inference Method	Method for implementing the inference
Transfer Function	Transfers information between the reasoning agent and external entities (system, user)
Task	Defines the reasoning function
Task Method	Describes the realization of the task through subfunction decomposition
Static Knowledge Role	Specifies the collection of domain knowledge that is used to make the inference
Dynamic Knowledge Role	Run-time inputs and outputs of inferences
Rule Type	Categorization and specification of knowledge
Rule	Expressions that involve an attribute value of a concept
Knowledge Base	Collection of data stores that contains instances of domain knowledge types

The Domain Concept package within the Knowledge Modelling package describes the concept constructs of the profile that are related to knowledge elements. This package is shown in Fig.1.

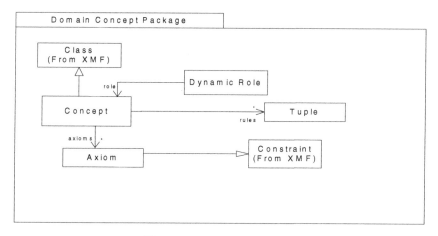

Fig. 1. Domain Concept Package

The Knowledge Base package of the profile describes the modelling of a knowledge base that represents instances of knowledge elements (instances of rule type) within the domain concepts. These instances are important as they contain the actual knowledge on which the KBS reasoning process is based. Knowledge elements within the knowledge base are accessed by an inference through a static role. This package is shown in Figure 2.

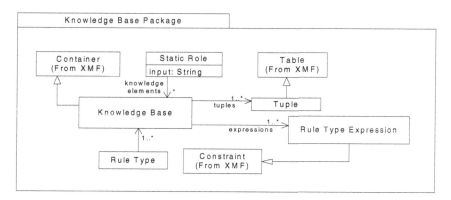

Fig. 2. Knowledge Base Package

The Inference package of the profile describes the inference, inference method, task, task method, transfer function and both the static and dynamic knowledge roles. The inference package plays a pivotal role in designing the KBS as it defines the inference structure of the system, the type of knowledge used in the reasoning process and the task associated with the execution of the inference. An important point to note here is that the KBS is designed independently of the target implementation platform and inference engines, overcoming the difficulties of reusing implementation specific designs. This package is shown in Fig.3.

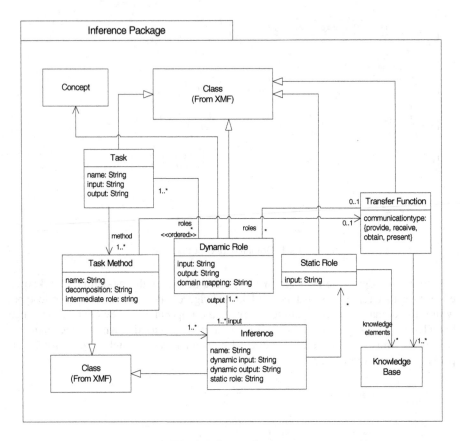

Fig. 3. Inference Package

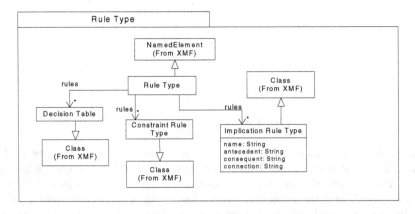

Fig. 4. Rule Type Package

The Rule Type package (shown in Fig. 4) within the profile describes the modelling of rules. There are three types of rule: constraint rule, implication rule and decision table. A decision table is an addition to the used set of rule types. It is introduced here because certain rules are best expressed in the form of a decision table. This paper concentrates on rule-based KBSs; Case-Based Reasoning (CBR), fuzzy-based logic, neural network systems are not considered here.

6.4 Model Extension

The knowledge modelling profile concept extends the existing meta-models of XMF by defining the profile's abstract syntax. There are five places where the profile can be viewed as an extension to XMF and these are: Class, Container, Table, Named Element and Constraints, all of which are central to the Core XMF meta-model.

The knowledge modelling class concept is viewed as a special class that is a subclass of the XMF Class. This enables the concept to inherit all the features of a class and allows it to define additional constraints such as "concepts do not have any operations or methods". The implication rule type, decision table and constraint rule type, are also examples of this. The inference package of the profile (which has the task, task method, inference, dynamic role, static role, and the transfer function concepts) can be viewed as a subclass of an XMF Class. This allows operations related to objects to be expressed, such as an execute inference call from the task method, the execution of the inference process and the access to knowledge in the knowledge base through the static role and at the same time allows the inference package elements to specify attributes.

Constraint class is a subclass of the XMF meta-model that incorporates profile concepts such as axioms and rule type expressions. All these concepts need the ability to express constraints and this class allows for this. Knowledge base is a subclass of the Container class of XMF. It has a 'content' slot that is a table. This is a natural choice for a subclass as the knowledge base is actually a collection of tables grouped together in order to store rule type instances. The table class of XMF is extended to incorporate the profile's concepts of tuple.

7 Conclusion and Future Work

Managing knowledge through knowledge-based systems is an important part of an enterprise's knowledge management initiative. Knowledge-based systems have evolved from being stand-alone machines to being part of the enterprise's group of systems. The process of constructing a KBS is similar to that required by other software systems, with conceptual modelling playing an important role in the development process. Software engineering has adopted UML as a standard for modelling, but the field of knowledge engineering is still searching for the right technique. UML can be adopted for knowledge modelling by exploiting the profile extension mechanism defined by OMG. This paper has described the process of creating such an extension by basing the design of the knowledge modelling profile on that of the XMF framework. This is a novel approach in profile design as the XMF approach is an extension to existing standards for meta-modelling such as MOF, OCL and QVT, which are defined by OMG. The creation of a profile is important as it allows a KBS to be designed using an object-oriented approach.

Developing a profile involves many steps as listed in Section 6 of this paper. The future work in this area involves the specification of the profile's well-formed-ness rules, semantics and construction of the concrete syntax model. Both the latter activities involve the use of the XMF tool, which is in its final stage of development. The profile will be validated using this tool and it is hoped to make the profile accessible to all UML and MOF compliant tools. The profile's ability to model the requirements of KBSs has only been tested on a few simple case studies. Testing the profile in a number of real-world situations would be beneficial, it would identify any limitations and assist in the refinement of the profile. Together these case studies should provide a wide range of applications in order to validate the generic nature of the profile.

Acknowledgement. The authors gratefully acknowledge the provision of a fellowship from Universiti Utara Malaysia that has enabled this research to take place, and are grateful to Xactium for early access to XMF. Details of XMF can be found at http://albini.xactium.com.

References

1. Speel, P., Schreiber, A. Th., van Joolingen, W., and Beijer, G.: *Conceptual Models for Knowledge-Based Systems*, in *Encyclopedia of Computer Science and Technology*. 2001, Marcel Dekker Inc, New York.
2. Schreiber, G., Akkermans, H., Anjewierden, A., de Hoog, R., Shadbolt, N., de Velde, W.V. and Wielinga, B.: *Knowledge Engineering and Management: The CommonKADS Methodology*. 1999, Massachusetts: MIT Press.
3. Studer, R., Benjamins, R.V., and Fensel, D.: *Knowledge Engineering: Principles and Methods*. Data & Knowledge Engineering, 1998. **25**: p. 161-197.
4. Angele, J., Fensel, D., Landes, D., Studer, R.: *Developing Knowledge-Based Systems with MIKE*. J of Automated Software Engineering, 1998. **5**(4): p. 389-418.
5. Grosso, W.E., Eriksson, H., Fergerson, R.W., Gennari, S., Tu, S., Musen, M.A.: *Knowledge Modelling at the Millennium (The Design and Evolution of Protege 2000)*. 1999, Stanford Medical Institute.
6. Milton, N.: *Types of Knowledge Models*. 2002. Accessed at http://www.epistemics.co.uk/Notes/90-0-0.htm
7. Gomez-Perez, A., Benjamins,V.R.: *Overview of Knowledge Sharing and Reuse Components: Ontologies and Problem-Solving Methods*. in *IJCAI-99 Workshop on Ontologies and Problem-Solving Methods (KRR5)*. 1999. Stockholm, Sweden.
8. Gruber, T.R.: *Toward principles for the design of ontologies used for knowledge sharing*. 1993, Report KSL-93-04, Stanford University.
9. Kende, R.: *Knowledge Modelling in Support of Knowledge Management*. Lecture Notes in Artificial Intelligence, 2001. **2070**: p. 107-112.
10. Felfernig, A., Friedrich, G.E., Jannach, D.: *Generating product configuration knowledge bases from precise domain extended UML models*. in *12 th International Conference on Software Engineering and Knowledge Engineering (SEKE'00)*. 2000. Chicago, USA.

11. Manjarres, A., Pickin, S., Mira, J.: *Knowledge model reuse: therapy decision through specialisation of a generic decision model.* Expert Systems with Applications, 2002. **23**(2): p. 113-135.
12. Stokes, M., *Managing Engineering Knowledge: MOKA - Methodology for Knowledge Based Engineering Applications.* 2001, London, UK: Professional Engineering and Publishing Limited.
13. Protege,: *Protege Frequently Asked Question.* 2002. Accessed at http://protégé.stanford.edu/faq.html
14. Kingston, J. and A. Macintosh, *Knowledge management through multi-perspective modelling: representing and distributing organizational memory.* Knowledge-Based Systems, 2000. **13**: p. 121-131.
15. Chung, L., Subramaniam, N.: *Adaptable architecture generation for embedded systems.* Journal of Systems and Software, 2003. **17**(3): p. 271-295.
16. Kalogeropoulos, D.A., Carson, E.R., Colinson, P.O.: *Towards Knowledge-Based Systems in Clinical Practice: Development of an integrated Clinical Information and Knowledge management Support System.* Computer Methods and Programs in Biomedicine, 2003. **72**: p. 65-80.
17. OMG: *Production Rule Representation- Request for Proposal.* 2003
18. OMG: *KBE Services for Engineering Design- Request for Proposal.* 2004
19. Gill, G.T. *Early Expert Systems: Where Are They Now?.* MIS Quarterly, 19, 51-81.
20. Kobryn, C.: *A Standardization Odyssey.* Communications of the ACM, 1999. **42**(10): p. 29-37.
21. Steimann, F., Kuhne, T.: *A Radical Reduction of UML's Core Semantics.* Lecture Notes in Computer Science, 2002. **2460**: p. 34-48.
22. OMG: *Requirements for UML Profile.* 1999.
23. OMG: *Unified Modeling Language specification (version 1.4).* 2001.
24. Perez-Martinez, J.E.: *Heavyweight extensions to the UML metamodel to describe the C3 architectural style.* ACM SIGSOFT Notes, 2003. **28**(3).
25. OMG: *MOF Specification version 1.4.* 2002.
26. OMG: *UML 2.0 Testing Profile specification.* 2003.
27. Clark, T., Evans, A., Sammut, P., Willians, J.: *Metamodelling for Model-Driven Development (draft): To be published.* 2005

Author Index

Lecture Notes in Computer Science

For information about Vols. 1–3522

please contact your bookseller or Springer

Vol. 3572: C. De Felice, A. Restivo (Eds.), Developments in Language Theory. XI, 409 pages. 2005.

Vol. 3571: L. Godo (Ed.), Symbolic and Quantitative Approaches to Reasoning with Uncertainty. XVI, 1028 pages. 2005. (Subseries LNAI).

Vol. 3570: A. S. Patrick, M. Yung (Eds.), Financial Cryptography and Data Security. XII, 376 pages. 2005.

Vol. 3569: F. Bacchus, T. Walsh (Eds.), Theory and Applications of Satisfiability Testing. XII, 492 pages. 2005.

Vol. 3568: W.-K. Leow, M.S. Lew, T.-S. Chua, W.-Y. Ma, L. Chaisorn, E.M. Bakker (Eds.), Image and Video Retrieval. XVII, 672 pages. 2005.

Vol. 3567: M. Jackson, D. Nelson, S. Stirk (Eds.), Database: Enterprise, Skills and Innovation. XII, 185 pages. 2005.

Vol. 3566: J.-P. Banâtre, P. Fradet, J.-L. Giavitto, O. Michel (Eds.), Unconventional Programming Paradigms. XI, 367 pages. 2005.

Vol. 3565: G.E. Christensen, M. Sonka (Eds.), Information Processing in Medical Imaging. XXI, 777 pages. 2005.

Vol. 3564: N. Eisinger, J. Małuszyński (Eds.), Reasoning Web. IX, 319 pages. 2005.

Vol. 3562: J. Mira, J.R. Álvarez (Eds.), Artificial Intelligence and Knowledge Engineering Applications: A Bioinspired Approach, Part II. XXIV, 636 pages. 2005.

Vol. 3561: J. Mira, J.R. Álvarez (Eds.), Mechanisms, Symbols, and Models Underlying Cognition, Part I. XXIV, 532 pages. 2005.

Vol. 3560: V.K. Prasanna, S. Iyengar, P.G. Spirakis, M. Welsh (Eds.), Distributed Computing in Sensor Systems. XV, 423 pages. 2005.

Vol. 3559: P. Auer, R. Meir (Eds.), Learning Theory. XI, 692 pages. 2005. (Subseries LNAI).

Vol. 3558: V. Torra, Y. Narukawa, S. Miyamoto (Eds.), Modeling Decisions for Artificial Intelligence. XII, 470 pages. 2005. (Subseries LNAI).

Vol. 3557: H. Gilbert, H. Handschuh (Eds.), Fast Software Encryption. XI, 443 pages. 2005.

Vol. 3556: H. Baumeister, M. Marchesi, M. Holcombe (Eds.), Extreme Programming and Agile Processes in Software Engineering. XIV, 332 pages. 2005.

Vol. 3555: T. Vardanega, A.J. Wellings (Eds.), Reliable Software Technology – Ada-Europe 2005. XV, 273 pages. 2005.

Vol. 3554: A. Dey, B. Kokinov, D. Leake, R. Turner (Eds.), Modeling and Using Context. XIV, 572 pages. 2005. (Subseries LNAI).

Vol. 3553: T.D. Hämäläinen, A.D. Pimentel, J. Takala, S. Vassiliadis (Eds.), Embedded Computer Systems: Architectures, Modeling, and Simulation. XV, 476 pages. 2005.

Vol. 3552: H. de Meer, N. Bhatti (Eds.), Quality of Service – IWQoS 2005. XVIII, 400 pages. 2005.

Vol. 3551: T. Härder, W. Lehner (Eds.), Data Management in a Connected World. XIX, 371 pages. 2005.

Vol. 3548: K. Julisch, C. Kruegel (Eds.), Intrusion and Malware Detection and Vulnerability Assessment. X, 241 pages. 2005.

Vol. 3547: F. Bomarius, S. Komi-Sirviö (Eds.), Product Focused Software Process Improvement. XIII, 588 pages. 2005.

Vol. 3546: T. Kanade, A. Jain, N.K. Ratha (Eds.), Audio- and Video-Based Biometric Person Authentication. XX, 1134 pages. 2005.

Vol. 3544: T. Higashino (Ed.), Principles of Distributed Systems. XII, 460 pages. 2005.

Vol. 3543: L. Kutvonen, N. Alonistioti (Eds.), Distributed Applications and Interoperable Systems. XI, 235 pages. 2005.

Vol. 3542: H.H. Hoos, D.G. Mitchell (Eds.), Theory and Applications of Satisfiability Testing. XIII, 393 pages. 2005.

Vol. 3541: N.C. Oza, R. Polikar, J. Kittler, F. Roli (Eds.), Multiple Classifier Systems. XII, 430 pages. 2005.

Vol. 3540: H. Kalviainen, J. Parkkinen, A. Kaarna (Eds.), Image Analysis. XXII, 1270 pages. 2005.

Vol. 3539: K. Morik, J.-F. Boulicaut, A. Siebes (Eds.), Local Pattern Detection. XI, 233 pages. 2005. (Subseries LNAI).

Vol. 3538: L. Ardissono, P. Brna, A. Mitrovic (Eds.), User Modeling 2005. XVI, 533 pages. 2005. (Subseries LNAI).

Vol. 3537: A. Apostolico, M. Crochemore, K. Park (Eds.), Combinatorial Pattern Matching. XI, 444 pages. 2005.

Vol. 3536: G. Ciardo, P. Darondeau (Eds.), Applications and Theory of Petri Nets 2005. XI, 470 pages. 2005.

Vol. 3535: M. Steffen, G. Zavattaro (Eds.), Formal Methods for Open Object-Based Distributed Systems. X, 323 pages. 2005.

Vol. 3534: S. Spaccapietra, E. Zimányi (Eds.), Journal on Data Semantics III. XI, 213 pages. 2005.

Vol. 3533: M. Ali, F. Esposito (Eds.), Innovations in Applied Artificial Intelligence. XX, 858 pages. 2005. (Subseries LNAI).

Vol. 3532: A. Gómez-Pérez, J. Euzenat (Eds.), The Semantic Web: Research and Applications. XV, 728 pages. 2005.

Vol. 3531: J. Ioannidis, A. Keromytis, M. Yung (Eds.), Applied Cryptography and Network Security. XI, 530 pages. 2005.

Vol. 3530: A. Prinz, R. Reed, J. Reed (Eds.), SDL 2005: Model Driven. XI, 361 pages. 2005.

Vol. 3528: P.S. Szczepaniak, J. Kacprzyk, A. Niewiadomski (Eds.), Advances in Web Intelligence. XVII, 513 pages. 2005. (Subseries LNAI).

Vol. 3527: R. Morrison, F. Oquendo (Eds.), Software Architecture. XII, 263 pages. 2005.

Vol. 3526: S. B. Cooper, B. Löwe, L. Torenvliet (Eds.), New Computational Paradigms. XVII, 574 pages. 2005.

Vol. 3525: A.E. Abdallah, C.B. Jones, J.W. Sanders (Eds.), Communicating Sequential Processes. XIV, 321 pages. 2005.

Vol. 3524: R. Barták, M. Milano (Eds.), Integration of AI and OR Techniques in Constraint Programming for Combinatorial Optimization Problems. XI, 320 pages. 2005.

Vol. 3523: J.S. Marques, N. Pérez de la Blanca, P. Pina (Eds.), Pattern Recognition and Image Analysis, Part II. XXVI, 733 pages. 2005.